Eating Disorders and Cultures in Transition

Eating disorders, once viewed as exclusive to specific class and ethnic boundaries in western culture, are now spreading worldwide. This groundbreaking volume puts to rest the notion that eating disorders are simply appearance-based concerns.

Eating Disorders and Cultures in Transition is written by an international group of authors to address the recent emergence of eating disorders in various areas of the world including countries in South America, Asia, Africa and Eastern Europe. It offers an in depth analysis of the existing socio-cultural model arguing for the need to extend both our theoretical understanding and clinical work to account properly for this global phenomenon. Eating disorders are seen as reflecting sweeping changes in the social and political status of women in the majority of societies that are now undergoing rapid cultural transition.

This multidisciplinary, multinational volume reflects wide-ranging, intellectually stimulating and frequently provocative viewpoints. It promises to be of great interest to medical and mental health professionals, public policy experts and all those watching for the processes of cultural transformation and their impact on mental health.

Mervat Nasser is Senior Lecturer in Psychiatry at Leicester University, UK and Consultant Psychiatrist for the South Lincolnshire Health Trust, UK. She is the author of *Culture and Weight Consciousness*.

Melanie A. Katzman is Assistant Professor of Psychology, Weill Medical College, Cornell University, New York, USA, and Honorary Senior Lecturer in Psychology, University of London, and Consultant Psychologist, Eating Disorders Unit, Institute of Psychiatry, London. This is her fifth book on eating disorders.

Richard A. Gordon is Professor of Psychology at Bard College in Annandale-on-Hudson, New York and a practising clinical psychologist in Red Hook, New York. He is author of *Eating Disorders: Anatomy of a Social Epidemic (2nd edition)*.

Eating Disorders and Cultures in Transition

Edited by
Mervat Nasser
Melanie A. Katzman
Richard A. Gordon

First published 2001 by Brunner-Routledge
27 Church Road, Hove, East Sussex BN3 2FA

Simultaneously published in the USA and Canada
by Taylor & Francis Inc
29 West 35th Street, New York, N.Y. 10001

Brunner-Routledge is an imprint of the Taylor & Francis Group

© 2001 Editorial matter and selection, Mervat Nasser, Melanie A. Katzman
and Richard A. Gordon; individual chapters, the contributors.

Typeset in Times by Keystroke, Jacaranda Lodge, Wolverhampton
Printed and bound in Great Britain by T J International, Padstow

Cover designed by Jim Wilkie

British Library Cataloguing in Publication Data
A catalogue record for this book is available from the British Library

Library of Congress Cataloging in Publication Data

ISBN 0–415–22860–3 (pbk)
ISBN 0–415–22859–X (hbk)

To the memory of my father who allowed me to challenge accepted views.
Mervat Nasser

To the memory of my sister Karen E. Katzman who blazed paths, challenged borders and conquered terrain never thought open to women anywhere.
Melanie A. Katzman

To my mother, Fanny Beale Gordon, who showed me how to write and work with other writers.
To my parents-in-law, Larry and Goldie Hill, who helped me develop a global consciousness.
Richard A. Gordon

Contents

Notes on contributors

Beatrice Bauer, Head Of Diadasco, Verona, Italy, and University of Milan Breconi Business School, Milan, Italy.

Katarzyna Bisaga, MD, Associate Professor Department of Child Psychiatry, Columbia University, NY, and New York State Psychiatric Institute New York, NY, USA.

Cynthia M. Bulik, PhD, Associate Professor of Psychiatry, Virginia Institute for Psychiatric and Behavioral Genetics, Virginia Commonwealth University, VA, USA.

Ana Catina, PhD, Research Fellow, Centre for Psychotherapy Research, Stuttgart, Germany.

Vincenzo Di Nicola, Professor of psychiatry, University of Montreal, Chief, Child Psychiatry Service, Maisonneuve-Rosemont Hospital, Montreal, Canada.

Ivan Eisler, PhD, Senior Lecturer in Clinical Psychology, Institute of Psychiatry, University of London, London, UK..

Horacio Fabrega Jr, Professor of Psychiatry and Anthropology, University of Pittsburgh, Department of Psychiatry and Anthropology, Pittsburgh, PA, USA.

Richard A. Gordon, Professor of Psychology, Bard College, Annandale-on-Hudson, New York, USA.

Phillipe Gorwood, MD, PhD, Psychiatrist, Hospital Louis Mourier (AP-HP), Colombes, Paris VII, France.

Noah E. Gotbaum, Senior Vice President and Head of European Corporate Development, Level 3 Communications, Inc., London, UK.

Sneja Gunew, Professor of English and Women Studies, University of British Columbia, Vancouver, BC, Canada.

Jhon Hein, MD, Research Staff, Clinic for Child and Adolescent Psychiatry and Psychotherapy, Charité Hospital, Humboldt University of Berlin, Schumannstraße 20/21, D–10098, Berlin, Germany.

Oltea Joja, PhD, Clinical Psychologist & Research Fellow, Institute of Endocrinology, Bucharest, Romania.

Melanie A. Katzman, Assistant Professor of Psychology, Weill Medical College, Cornell University, New York, USA, and Honorary Senior Lecturer in Psychology, University of London, and Consultant Psychologist, Eating Disorders Unit, Institute of Psychiatry, London.

Sing Lee, Director, Hong Kong Eating Disorders Center, Faculty of Medicine, The Chinese University of Hong Kong, Hong Kong, PRC, and Visiting Lecturer, Department of Social Medicine, Harvard Medical School, MA, USA.

Daniel le Grange, Director, Eating Disorders Program, Assistant Professor of Psychiatry, The University of Chicago, IL, USA.

Roland Littlewood, Professor of Anthropology and Psychiatry, Royal Free and UCL Medical School, Department of Psychiatry and Behavioural Sciences, London, UK.

Arlene Elowe MacLeod, Political Science Department, Bates College, Lewiston, Maine 04240, USA.

Oscar L. Meehan, MRCPsych, Psychiatrist, Cordoba, Argentina, South America.

David Bardwell Mumford, Reader in Cross-Cultural Psychiatry, Division of Psychiatry, University of Bristol, UK.

Mervat Nasser, Consultant Psychiatrist and Senior Lecturer, University of Leicester, UK.

Klaus Neumärker, MD, Chairman and Professor, Clinic for Child and Adolescent Psychiatry and Psychotherapy, Charité Hospital, Humboldt University of Berlin, Schumannstraße 20/21, D–10098, Berlin, Germany.

Bob Palmer, Senior Lecturer/Consultant Psychiatrist, Leicester University, Section of Social and Epidemiological Psychiatry, Brandon Mental Health Unit, Leicester General Hospital, LE5 PPW, UK.

Julie Park, PhD, Senior Lecturer in Anthropology, The University of Auckland, New Zealand.

Niva Piran, Professor, Department of Adult Education and Counseling Psychology, OISE/University of Toronto, Toronto, Canada.

Günther Rathner, Assistant Professor, Department of Paediatrics, Eating Disorders Unit, University of Innsbruck, Innsbruck, Austria.

Giovanni Ruggiero, Psychiatric Department "Guardia II", Ospedale Maggiore di Milano, IRCCS, University of Milan, Italy and "Studi Cognitivi" Psychotherapy and Research Centre, Milano, Italy.

Finn Skårderud, Psychiatrist and Film Critic, Institute of Psychiatry, University of Oslo, Norway.

Leslie Swartz, Professor of Psychology, Department of Psychology, University of Stellenbosch, Private Bag XI, Matieland 7602, Republic of South Africa.

Chris Paul Szabo, Senior Lecturer, Department of Psychiatry, Faculty of Health Sciences, University of Witwaterstrand, Johannesburg, Republic of South Africa.

Cynthia King Vance, MBA, Economist and Management Consultant, New York, NY, USA.

Penny Van Esterik, Professor of Anthropology at York University, Toronto, Canada

Preface

In *'The Unbearable Lightness of Being'*, Tereza is staring at herself in the mirror. She wonders what would happen if her nose were to grow a millimeter longer each day. How much time would it take for her face to become unrecognizeable? And if her face no longer looked like Tereza, would Tereza still be Tereza? Where does the self begin and end? You see: not wonder at the immeasurable infinity of the soul; rather, wonder at the uncertain nature of the self and of its identity.

> Milan Kundera *(1988, p. 28) The art of the novel* (trans. by L Asher).
> New York: Harper & Row

Why, after so many books on eating disorders have been published, do we think anyone would care to read another? Well, because we think this one is different. It is the product of an evolving and increasingly sophisticated quest to understand the cultural forces inherent in aberrant eating and we believe this is the first book that provides such immediate and intimate access to a variety of international issues relating to the phenomenon of body and weight dissatisfaction.

Who are we and why should you trust us to be the tour guides on this intellectual journey? Mervat Nasser, an Egyptian known for her work on culture and eating disorders, and Melanie A. Katzman, an American who had been working on the marriage of transcultural and feminist ideas, met in Padua, Italy. Given that they were both living and working in England (or at least most of the time) they agreed to keep their conversations going, which resulted in, among other things, a joint publication on how sociocultural approaches could impact and inform efforts to prevent eating disorders. Leaving from different intellectual and national terminals they had arrived at the same port – cultural analyses of eating disorders were challenged to explain why women, why now and why seemingly everywhere you look? The late twentieth century perspectives were not only culture bound, they were also discipline bound and fell short of explaining the complex contributions of economic and political forces on individual bodily expressions of distress.

Back in America, where you might have thought at least the two New Yorkers would have met earlier, Richard A. Gordon was busy completing the second edition of his book, *Eating Disorders: Anatomy of a Social Epidemic*. Richard Gordon and Mervat Nasser had recognised their shared interests in this subject when they met at an international conference in Swansea, Wales, in 1984 and had been intermittently in touch regarding their common interests in the field since that time. Melanie Katzman and Richard Gordon had also worked together on sociocultural issues in food and weight disturbance.

But, as these things go, it was not until the 1998 international conference on eating disorders in New York that the three of us met to share not only similar notions about the gaps in the field, but many common meals – a critical ritual in the study of eating disorders! At that time, each one of us was already in the middle of muddling through the morass of interdisciplinary explanations for what appeared to be a universal expression of distress in bodily terms, when the idea of this book was formed and captured our thoughts and now hopefully your imagination.

The aim of this book is to highlight some of the limitations in our current sociocultural understanding of eating disorders, which tend to focus on one culture and one sex and construe eating disorders almost exclusively in terms of weight. We thought, perhaps, that one way to overcome such limitations was to invite contributions from different researchers around the world and ask them to share their inevitably unique insights.

Perhaps the most obvious first step was to organise an edited volume with a spokesperson from each region to document the presentation and prevalence of eating disturbances in his or her respective areas. But that was not what we wanted. We feared replicating the same fat obsession of the typical cross-cultural study in our discipline, one which measures women's bodies and attitudes and not their social opportunities, joys and despairs. We did not want to rely heavily on quantification – we needed to contextualise and re-conceptualise. Besides, the quality of epidemiological work carried out in different countries has been inconsistent – research designs have often been faulty and the validity of Western measures in non-Western settings has been questioned. Few two-stage survey and interview studies have been completed and sampling has often been inadequate.

We already knew the kind of deductions we are able to make from these studies. We had the knowledge that eating disorders do exist in other countries and cultures and are no longer exclusive to the West, as previously thought. The fact that their prevalence rates could vary slightly from one country to the next was not necessarily of great consequence. What seemed more significant was the meaning attached to such problems in different cultural settings and whether other forms exist that mimic the phenomenon and could arguably be seen as possible cultural equivalents of what is defined in the West as anorexia or bulimia. As a result we looked thematically at several countries and decided to ask our authors to build upon existing data to answer the following specific questions . . .

1 Does the emergence of eating disorders outside of the United States and Western Europe invalidate the traditional notions of eating disorders as culture-bound syndromes? Are eating disorders genuinely rising in non-Western societies and perhaps falling or levelling off in the West?

2 Does the recent emergence of eating disorders among black South African women reflect a transition in their definition of identity?

3 Does self-starvation in China carry a different meaning that would call into question Western conceptualisations of the diagnostic requirements for anorexia nervosa?

4 What are the implications of recent genetic research for cultural interpretations of eating disorders?

5 Is the marketing of thinness in post-communist societies an inevitable commodity of free market capitalism with predictable consequences?

6 Does the fall of communism in Eastern Europe and the associated reduction in social support make women more vulnerable to eating disorders?

7 Is it possible that in one country, in this case Italy, internal cultural struggles could mirror those experienced in many nations globally?

8 Does the psychobiography of a nation such as Argentina reveal that the pursuit of thinness could possibly have 'weighty' political and economic meaning?

9 Do women use forms of body control other than disordered eating at times of cultural transition, for example the 'voluntary veiling' of young women of Egypt?

While answering these questions might have been enough of a challenge, we knew before we started that our current research formulae and typical mental health mindset might prevent us from assessing and creating new models for understanding, treating and preventing eating disorders. We wanted to stimulate cross-fertilisation and safeguard against the usual seductions – talking of *Westernisation*, where the old dichotomous approach to culture is maintained (that is West versus East), or *acculturation*, even though we know that the dominant or host culture is continually changing as we speak, or *modernisation*, which could potentially undermine the non-biomedical perspectives.

So we decided to formulate a kind of debate where each chapter is challenged by two commentators, one from a clinical discipline and the other from a diverse field such as sociology, economics, or political, gender and culture studies. While we sought experts in eating disorders for the chapters and the majority of the clinical commentary, this was not a 'requirement' for the non-clinical commentaries. We strove for diversity of perspectives, nationalities and expertise.

Within this framework, the objective of the book is meant to be critical, that is, its purpose is to examine and challenge the assumptions currently held within the field of culture and eating psychopathology. It is our hope that, whilst not prescribing future development of the discipline, the book could perhaps play a significant role in shaping it.

We are pleased to bring together voices of different nationalities. It is our intention to incorporate reference material that would not otherwise be available to the exclusively English speaking reader. To this end many of our authors translated their local resources. Our cast of contributors and commentators represent various disciplines and countries and reflect interesting hybrids. For example, among our authors are an Asian English professor living in Canada, who was born in Germany and part of whose education was in Australia, or a psychologist and business consultant born to a Hungarian father and Austrian mother in Germany and now working in Italy, and an American businessman living in England and working in the Eastern European business world.

National backgrounds represented by authors and commentators include the United States, Canada, Panama, the United Kingdom, Austria, Belgium, the Netherlands, Germany, Romania, Italy, the Czech Republic, Australia, China, Egypt, India, Israel, South Africa, France, Bulgaria and Norway.

In each chapter you will find that we first pose the debate question, and then offer the main article, which is followed by the two commentaries. The authors of the chapters did not see the comments before we went to press and therefore were not in a position to alter their views. We wanted to leave the next step in the dialogue up to you, the reader.

Chapter I

In the first chapter, **Richard Gordon** offers an overview on the transformation of the status of eating disorders from that of 'culture-bound syndrome' to global phenomenon. Gordon documents the countries and regions in which eating disorders have appeared, and suggests that a particular set of cultural factors unify the very disparate countries in which they have arisen. He concludes his chapter with some intriguing recent evidence that suggests that, just as eating disorders have been on the rise in areas of the world outside of Western Europe and the United States, they may now be declining in the West, at least in the United States.

His argument is questioned by **Bob Palmer**, a well-known authority in the field of epidemiological research on eating disorders. Palmer questions the meaning of prevalence data, particularly whether what may appear to be an eating disorder to a Western or Western-trained observer could in fact be something else when examined in local contexts.

Anthropologist **Penny Van Esterik** believes that the essay opens up the possibility of a greater dialogue between scholars of different disciplines, particularly psychiatry and anthropology, with a view toward better understanding of this perceived global problem.

Chapter 2

The emergence of eating disorders among black South African women is dealt with in the second chapter, jointly written by **Christopher Szabo** and **Daniel le Grange**. They put forward the questions why South Africa and why black women and why eating psychopathology? They discuss the kinds of pressures that are now facing black women in a rapidly changing South Africa and refute the possibility that the phenomenon can simply be reductively or exclusively explained in terms of Westernising forces. As a result, this chapter ushers in the debate on eating disorders and identity, an issue that is central to the whole volume.

They are challenged nonetheless by **Leslie Swartz**, an authority on cultural and mental health issues in South Africa. Swartz queries the importance of focusing on eating disorders in a new South Africa which is riddled with violence and AIDS, issues that perhaps should take precedence over any other health concern. However, the second commentator, **Finn Skårderud**, seems to be in general agreement with the chapter's premise. He is a Norwegian psychiatrist and cultural critic who sees that the psychological conflicts underpinning eating disorders may be a result and a window to the tensions of establishing a local and national identity.

Chapter 3

In the third chapter **Sing Lee** criticises the excessive reliance on 'fat phobia' as a diagnostic criterion for anorexia to make the point that modern Western biomedical models have created (in the Diagnostic and Statistical Manuals of the American Psychiatric Association) a constricted and self-confirming set of explanations for 'disease'. In the field of eating disorders in particular, people who do not relate the expected 'fat terminology' for their difficulties are construed as dishonest deniers. Yet, perhaps, the series of exceptions or atypical cases that are found in Asian as well as in Western clinics call for a revisiting of just what it means to refuse food and what may ultimately be the underlying social causes of anorexia nervosa

Roland Littlewood discusses not only the cultural politics of food refusal in South Asian societies but the efficacy of eating disorders as a means of enhancing a sense of personal agency. Towards this end he compares eating disorders to involuntary spirit possession and dissociative states. He concludes that the heightened sense of agency yielded by eating disorders is reduced medically to a distorted perception. In terms of practical instrumentality this makes the final consequences of eating disorders seem poor while those of possession states relatively good.

In the second commentary, **Horacio Fabrega** provides an instant primer on cross-cultural psychiatry. Drawing from Lee's data, he offers not only a cross-cultural but an evolutionary perspective on psychiatric disorders.

Chapter 4

In the fourth chapter, **Cynthia Bulik**, one of the first experts to deal with the issue of eating disorders among immigrants in the USA and recently a major investigator into the role of genetics in eating disorders, suggests that 'twins studies' could lead us to the inescapable conclusion that genetic factors play a central role in the aetiology of eating disorders.

In her discussion of the chapter, **Julie Park**, an anthropologist from Auckland, New Zealand, points to some of the cultural and experiential nuances that may be overlooked from the standpoint of twins research or quantitatively oriented studies and concludes that the study of the environment is as intricate if not even more complex than the human genome.

The second commentary is by **Phillipe Gorwood**, a geneticist from France, who challenges the notion that a voluntary behaviour can have a genetic basis and alerts us to the social responsibility that follows if we believe it does.

Chapter 5

In the fifth chapter, **Günther Rathner** takes us from the arena of genes to political economy. Rathner predicts that Eastern Europeans will not only become more engaged in commercialism but that their bodies themselves will become more comodified as capitalism rises in the region. As a result he anticipates that eating disorders as well as plastic surgery will proliferate accordingly.

In his commentary, **Noah Gotbaum** begins by describing himself as an American capitalist charged with instigating turmoil in Eastern Europe and denounces Rathner's assault on market philosophy by questioning the unique psychological impact of transitional economies compared to previous Stalinist dictates. He nonetheless acknowledges the potential effects of the changing economy on mental health, even if he is dubious that such is the case with eating disorders given that their epidemiology under communist regimes was never adequately ascertained or documented.

Katarzyna Bisaga, the second commentator of this chapter, is a Polish psychiatrist who is currently practising in the United States. Bisaga is in a strong position to comment here, given her specialist experience of eating disorders in Poland. While she appears to be in essential agreement with Rathner's argument, she challenges him on the use of a unitary concept such as 'Eastern Block', urging the need to examine aspects of cultural diversity within 'Eastern Europe'.

Chapter 6

The issue of market economy is discussed further in the sixth chapter, jointly written by two Romanian women, **Ana Catina**, who is currently a practising psychotherapist in Germany, and **Oltea Joja**, a psychologist in Bucharest. The debate here is focused on the position of women in post-communist Europe. The economic changes of the 1990s are seen as having undermined the provisions given to women under the old socialist/collectivist regimes. Catina and Joja argue that these changes have increased women's confusion over gender roles and rendered them more at risk for developing eating disorders. Hence this chapter attempts to integrate feminist and socio-economic themes.

The first commentator **Ivan Eisler**, who is a clinical psychologist in the UK, explains his lack of sympathy with their argument on the basis of being a male from former Czechoslovakia who spent most of his adult and working life in the UK. He raises once more the issue of taking Eastern and Central Europe as one homogenous entity, urging the need to balance uncertainties and opportunities that any cultural transition engenders. He also questions the possibility of exploring the position of women in these societies in isolation from that of the men.

Cynthia King Vance, a management consultant recently returned to America after living for eight years in London, is the second commentator who challenges the argument in this chapter for glorifying communist practices. While she supports the notion that working women under socialist regimes may have experienced an increased sense of efficiency and social usefulness, it is her argument that this was done in response to social mandates, not pure personal choice. She introduces economic models to expand the debate and urges us to remember the efficacy of socialist 'communication' programmes when considering prevention efforts.

Chapter 7

In chapter 7, **Giovani Ruggiero** addresses what he argues is a special case, the 'two Italies'. In the field of culture and eating psychopathology, research has tended to make comparisons between two countries or different ethnicities. However, in this essay, Ruggiero talks more of inter-cultural differences exemplified by the cultural division within Italy itself. The argument here is more concerned with the emergence of two cultures within one state due to differences in economic structure and level of development between the south and north of Italy.

One of the commentators on this essay is Professor **Klaus Neumärker**, who pioneered this inter-cultural exploration when he assessed the issue of eating disorders morbidity in East and West Berlin before and after the fall of the Berlin Wall. The commentary is jointly written with his assistant **Jhon Hein** and seems to take the same view expressed by Ruggiero in his essay, emphasising the sociocultural differences that may lie within the fabric of one society.

The second commentator is **Beatrice Bauer**, a psychologist and a management consultant in Verona. She brings forward the dimension of '*Bellezza*', that is the Italian obsession with 'beauty', and how the 'visual' is so integral to the Italian self-image. She argues that the preoccupation with aesthetics in Italy is just as important as a gateway to power as particular family dynamics.

Chapter 8

In this chapter, **Oscar Meehan**, who has just returned to Argentina to set up eating disorders clinics after training in England for seven years, joins **Melanie A. Katzman** in an effort to integrate economic, political, historical and psychological data to create a psychobiography of the Argentinean nation. Katzman's theory that eating disorders are best understood not by a discourse around food, weight and diet but rather discussions of transition, dislocation and oppression serves as an organising schema for this chapter. The vulnerabilities of Southern American women to eating problems and the possible path to reversing them are the focus of this anthropometric contribution.

The first comment is by Professor **Niva Piran**, an expert in education and eating disorders prevention. She examines the multiple levels of social prejudice inherent in Argentina and encourages us to consider the untold stories of bodily violation and their contributions to individual and socio-economic self-esteem. She also highlights the importance of recognising the relationship of professionals (either academics or clinicians) to the political context in which they work. She introduces the method 'participatory action project', which proved successful in a Canadian ballet school to effect behaviour change through culture change not simply information exchange.

The chapter is also commented on by Professor **Sneja Gunew**, an Indian woman who works as a professor of English and Women's Studies in Canada and is a self-described postcolonial feminist. She questions the different impact of Argentina's cultural forces on men and women and the impact of decoding diet and health discourses on social norms. Professor Gnew draws on literary references to illustrate ways in which appearance regulations could lead to dehumanisation of both the viewer and the viewed.

Chapter 9

In the final chapter **Mervat Nasser** and **Vincenzo Di Nicola**, both psychiatrists with a long-standing interest in placing eating morbidity in a cultural context, engage in a dialogue that deepens the book's exploration of the impact of cultural transition on the definition of self and identity. They try to weave into their discussion themes raised in the previous chapters. Nasser introduces the notion of 'veiling', which began in Egypt but has now been taken up in increasing numbers by many young Moslem women around the world. She sees in it a new form of body regulation reactive to forces of cultural change and argues that it is, as is the case of anorexia nervosa, a quest for self-definition in relation to the needs of others. Di Nicola raises doubts and debates Nasser's conclusions. He offers additions and digressions from his own work on self-mutilation, which has several manifestations in common with the anorexic phenomenon and invites a similar kind of cultural reading.

The first commentator on this chapter is **Arlene MacLeod**, a political scientist from the United States and the author of *Accommodating Protest: The New Veiling* *in Egypt*. Nasser acknowledges this book as instrumental in helping her to draw comparative analysis of both anorexia and the veil. In her discussion, MacLeod supports Nasser's argument that both situations could possibly be expressions of body politics and therefore regarded as problem-solving tactics in the face of stressful, transitional cultural forces.

David Mumford, a reader in cross-cultural psychiatry and known for his research on eating disorders among Asian women in Britain, provides the second commentary. He argues that the chapter could be seen as highly speculative and questions the validity of using the term 'equivalent' in the absence of operational criteria to support the notion of equivalence between various forms of body regulation, be it social or political and the more familiar clinical forms of disordered eating.

In writing this book we laid bare the best work in our field to members of other disciplines and learned that what may seem to be such obvious truths to members of the mental health professions are barely supported, let alone understood, by other disciplines. We saw our blind spots, we learned new vocabulary. The divide between what science wants to know in order to act and what would convince a business-oriented professional became clearer.

At best we managed to demonstrate that eating disorders mark cultural changes that must be read and responded to; at worst we offered ways to dismiss concerns about a growing global problem on the grounds that there is really no hard evidence to indicate that this is the case.

If we succeeded in stimulating new combinations of research and discussion across national and academic lines we will be happy. However, if you throw your hands up in frustration, then we have at least communicated just how hard it is to understand the role of society in shaping psychiatric distress!

Acknowledgements

To all the contributors and commentators who made this book possible, we thank you for expressing yourselves in many different cultural, written, and disciplinary languages.

To our families; Ragai Shaban, Russell, Wyndam and Harper Makowsky and Patti Hill Gordon, we thank you for providing the space and support for each of us to do "just one more book".

Chapter 1

Eating disorders East and West: A culture-bound syndrome unbound

Richard A. Gordon
Professor of Psychology, Bard College,
Annandale-on-Hudson, New York

Debate question
Eating disorders appear to be on the increase in developing countries,
as is evident from case reports and research data. What are the likely
mechanisms for this phenomenon? While these disorders are rising in
prevalence around the globe, is it possible that their incidence could be
leveling off or even declining in the West?

The sociocultural panorama

Since the early 1980s, when papers on cultural influences on eating disorders began to appear in the literature, it has been evident to many observers that eating disorders are unique among psychiatric disorders in the degree to which social and cultural factors influence their epidemiology, development and perhaps their etiology (Barlow and Durand, 1999). Hilde Bruch (1978) was one of the first to implicate cultural factors in the increasing incidence of eating disorders, citing both the fashionable emphasis on slenderness as well as the conflicting demands on contemporary young women that created severe identity confusion. The incidence of eating disorders appeared to increase sharply in the United States, the United Kingdom and many Western European countries beginning in the mid- to late 1960s and then in accelerating fashion into the 1970s and through the late 1980s (Willi and Grossman, 1982; Lucas *et al.*, 1991, 1999; Eagles *et al.*, 1995). This was remarkable for anorexia nervosa, which had been identified as a medical syndrome since the 1870s in Europe and the United States but had been considered a relatively obscure, almost exotic, condition over the first 100 years of its medical history (Bruch, 1973). The situation was even more startling for bulimia nervosa, which had been virtually unknown prior to the 1970s until its description by Boskind-Lodahl (1976) and Russell (1979). By the 1980s, however, it was widely agreed that bulimia nervosa was considerably more common than anorexia nervosa (Pope *et al.*, 1984).

The rise of eating disorders in the United States and Western Europe has been described as a modern epidemic (although not without controversy – see Williams and King, 1987, and Fombonne, 1995) and has coincided with a number of sweeping changes in Western societies in the second half of the 20th century (Sours, 1980). Among these are the rise of a consumer economy, which places an enormous emphasis on the achievement of personal satisfaction at the expense of more collective goals, an increasingly fragmented family that seems beset on all sides by forces such as increasing conflicts in intergenerational relationships and upheavals in sex roles that have introduced great strain and confusion into the developmental experiences of adolescents. Some of these cultural trends seem to play a direct role in the rise of eating disorders. More specifically, because eating disorders affect mainly females and revolve around issues of identity and body image, it is not surprising that observers have linked the rise of eating disorders in the West with the crisis of female identity and the forces impinging on women that followed the cultural upheavals of the 1960s (Gordon, 2000).

Because eating disorders revolve centrally around the issues of body image and weight control, it is important to focus specifically on these factors. Seminal research by Garner and his colleagues (1980) and later by Wiseman et al., (1992) confirmed that idealized representations of the female form in the wider culture have became increasingly thin and relatively less curvaceous in shape from 1960 until the late 1980s. By all accounts, it appears that these trends have continued relentlessly throughout the 1990s. Whether such media images play a causal role in eating disorders or whether they merely reflect the standards of the wider culture is a matter of some controversy (Becker and Hamburg, 1996), but there seems little doubt that there has been an increasingly stringent expectation for thinness in women. Given the centrality of drive for thinness and body image preoccupation in the psychopathology of eating disorders, it seems implausible that the relationship between the increasing demand for thinness in the wider culture and the rise of eating disorders would be accidental. It is likely, however, that only those individuals who are vulnerable to these pressures, such as those with pre-existing depression or anxiety, low self-esteem in childhood, a history of weight preoccupation, and perhaps genetic predispositions will respond to these cultural demands with the symptoms of an eating disorder (Fairburn et al., 1997; see Bulik, chapter 4 of this volume).

A related factor is the sharply accelerating increases in overweight in the Western countries, particularly within the last two decades in the 20th century. In the United States, in particular, the percentage of individuals whose weight exceeded levels that are considered medically healthy increased from 25% in 1980 to 32% in 1990 and accelerated even further into the 1990s (Kuczmarski et al., 1994; Mokad et al., 1999). The trends are in evidence, albeit to a lesser degree, in most countries in Western Europe (Seidell and Flegal, 1997). Despite the apparent dramatic increases in weight in the general population, overweight and obesity continue to be highly stigmatized, particularly for women (Hebl and Heatherton, 1998). As a result, an acute tension has arisen between the drive for thinness, on the one hand, and the forces that have led to increases in weight in the general population, on the other. This contradiction is centrally related to the increase in eating disorders. Eating disorders such as anorexia nervosa and bulimia nervosa could be viewed from one perspective as pathologies of dieting, and their increasing prevalence in Western countries has risen in step with the pervasiveness of dieting. A number of research studies have clearly indicated that dieting is a particularly powerful antecedent of eating disorders, especially of bulimia nervosa (Polivy and Herman, 1985; Hsu, 1997).

The fact that eating disorders occur overwhelmingly in women, however, cannot be fully comprehended without addressing the critical transitions in female identity that have characterized the late twentieth century in industrialized or rapidly industrializing societies. As women have moved in increasing numbers into the spheres of education and work around the globe, expectations for achievement and performance have sometimes conflicted sharply with insistent demands for traditional postures of dependency and submissiveness as well as a renewed cult of physical appearance that has been fed by corporate forces (Wolf, 1991). The result of these contradictory pressures has been for many an enhanced sense of personal uncertainty and self-doubt, along with an increased sense of powerlessness (Gordon, 2000). The paradoxical character of this increased identity confusion in the face of enhanced opportunity is captured in the title of a book by Silverstein and Perlick (1995), *The Cost of Competence*. These authors have suggested that the thin ideal so touted in traditional sociocultural accounts of eating disorders can be understood as a body ideal that de-emphasizes traditional 'feminine' curvaceousness, in a society still riddled with sexist stereotypes that associate curvaceousness with low female intelligence.

In fact, it could be argued that the contradictions and transitions in female identity represent the most profound basis of eating disorders throughout history and across cultures (Bemporad, 1996; Katzman and Lee, 1997). This may account for the fact that eating disorders, as they have emerged in the newly industrialized areas of the world, do not necessarily express themselves as body image preoccupations, but rather may draw on a variety of cultural vocabularies to express some common underlying psychosocial conflicts. The fact that female identity issues are at the core of eating disorders will be evident in many of the essays in the present volume.

The global rise of eating disorders: Discussing the evidence

The apparent uniqueness of eating disorders to Western societies strongly suggested that these syndromes are culture-bound (Prince, 1983, 1985). This issue was discussed by Gordon (1989, 2000), who countered the traditional constructs of culture-bound syndromes with the notion of an ethnic disorder. The latter could better embrace the broad array of cultural forces that are shared by a large number of societies, rather than a particular geographic locale. Nasser (1997) posited that the meaning-centered approach to understanding culture may have emphasized cultural differences at the expense of similarities. She argued, based on a review of published research from around the globe, that eating disorders may no longer be unique to Western societies.

Prince (1985) had suggested that as the reach of Western cultural norms became more influential around the world, as initially illustrated in the case of Japan, that eating disorders would become more common in areas that had previously been considered immune to them. This appears to have been precisely the case since 1990. Table 1.1 shows the countries that have reported eating disorders in the literature. It is apparent that the almost all those countries that had reported eating disorders prior to 1990 were European or North American, with the exception of Japan and Chile. Countries reporting after 1990 include Hong Kong and mainland China, South Korea, Singapore, South Africa, Nigeria, Mexico, Argentina and India.

It needs to be pointed out that our knowledge of eating disorders in the areas in which they have recently emerged is based almost entirely on case histories, and in some instances there have yet to be relevant publications in the scientific literature. There are virtually no formal epidemiological studies that document these trends. It is also possible that eating disorders may have existed in at least some of these areas prior to the 1990s, but were either unidentified as such or diagnosed and treated by local healers. We have no evidence that this is the

Table 1.1 Countries reporting eating disorders

Argentina*	Mexico*
Australia+	The Netherlands
Belgium	New Zealand+
Brazil*	Nigeria
Canada	Norway
Chile	Poland
China*	Portugal*
Czech Republic	Singapore*
Denmark+	South Africa (blacks)*
Egypt	South Africa (whites)+
France	South Korea*
Germany	former Soviet Union
Hong Kong*	Sweden+
Hungary	Switzerland+
India*	Turkey*
Iran	United Arab Emirates*
Israel+	United Kingdom+
Italy	United States+
Japan	

+ Formal epidemiological studies carried out
* First reports since 1990

case, and yet the possibility cannot be completely discounted either. Psychiatric services in many of these areas have been sparse and not accessible to much of the population. Nevertheless, it is unlikely, given the cultural logic of eating disorders, that the appearance of these disorders in highly urbanized areas within the 1990s is merely an artifact of observation.

For the remainder of this chapter, I will briefly review some of the major geographical areas in which eating disorders appear to be newly emerging, and will preview some of the issues that will be discussed in greater depth throughout this volume. My scope is not meant to be comprehensive. For example, I will not discuss here the apparent increase in eating disorders in European countries such as Spain or Italy, which appears to have intensified during the 1990s (for a discussion of the situation in Italy, see Ruggiero, chapter 7, this volume). Nor will I discuss here the phenomenon of post-communist Eastern Europe and the clash of the values of market economies and the historical transition for women in a post-communist world (see Rathner, chapter 5, this volume, and Catina and Joja, chapter 6, this volume).

1 Southern and Southeastern Asia

Outside Europe and the United States, there is only one country in which eating disorders have been as well known in the second half of the 20th century as in the West, and that is Japan. In a symposium on eating disorders held in Germany in the 1960s, Ishikawa (1965) suggested that the incidence of anorexia nervosa had been increasing since the Second World War. He attributed the increase to changes in traditional family structure in the post-war period. During the 1980s a survey of a large number of medical facilities all over the country showed that the number of patients in treatment for anorexia nervosa doubled between 1976 and 1981 (Suematsu et al., 1985). Even from 1980 to 1981 alone, the total number of patients in treatment jumped from 1080 to 1312. A later survey found that between 3500 and 4500 patients were estimated to have been treated in hospitals in Japan in 1985, whereas in 1992 the number was estimated to be a slightly larger 4500 to 4600 (Kuboki et al., 1996). In the latter study, the prevalence among females between the ages of 13 and 29 was estimated to be 25.7–30.7 per 100 000 population, a figure that is substantial but somewhat lower than comparable US estimates (Lucas et al., 1991). The increasing incidence of eating disorders was confirmed in a study of patients who sought treatment at an outpatient clinic at a University Hospital in the Yamagata Prefecture in Northern Japan, an area of approximately 1200 000 inhabitants about 350 miles north of Tokyo (Nadaoka et al., 1996). Over the period 1978–1992, the number of patients with anorexia nervosa increased sharply with even greater increases in the number of patients with bulimia nervosa.

These temporal patterns are closely parallel to the incidence patterns of anorexia nervosa in the United States and Western Europe. While the reasons for the perhaps singular incidence of eating disorders in Japan vis-à-vis other Asian nations are not clear, one possible explanation would follow from the fact that Japan could probably be characterized as the most economically developed society in Southern Asia after the Second World War. From a cultural standpoint, many of the same tensions that have exploded in the advanced industrial societies of the United States and Europe have been in evidence in Japan. These would include an increased emphasis on individualism that conflicts with traditional collective values, a conflicting female role associated with altered societal expectations, and the ever-expanding impact of consumerism and media (White, 1993; Skov and Moeran, 1995). In contemporary Japan, images of thinness are glorified in the media and Japanese teenagers are extraordinarily weight conscious, despite the low levels of obesity in the society. There is considerable tension regarding gender roles and the status of women in Japan, with female aspirations for greater parity with men conflicting sharply with powerful traditions of male dominance. While it is important to recognize the unique characteristics of Japanese society and not to attribute simplistically the emergence of eating disorders to 'Westernization', it can at least be hypothesized that the impact of such forces are extremely pervasive. It should be pointed out, however, that Japan has extensive psychiatric facilities and many psychiatric workers who have adopted many of the concepts of American and European psychiatry. This would inevitably lead to a more ready recognition of such syndromes as anorexia nervosa. While such factors should not be discounted, it is however unlikely that such a sharp increase in disordered eating could be totally attributed to them.

Reports about eating disorders in other Asian countries began to emerge after 1990. The first of these was contained in a series of papers by Sing Lee, a Hong-Kong based psychiatrist (Lee, 1991; Lee et al., 1993). Lee was not sure as to whether these cases, which had occurred during the 1980s, represented an increase in the prevalence of the condition or perhaps a greater awareness of the syndrome by Western-trained psychiatrists. In any case, he noted a number of ways in which patients from Hong Kong differed from their Western counterparts. First, most were from the lower socio-economic levels of society. Second, patients often interpreted their inability to eat in terms of gastric distress (for example, symptoms of 'bloating') rather than a fear of fatness. Third, and perhaps most important, over half of these patients did not suffer from body image distortion and most did not voice body image concerns. Lee suggests that these patients resemble more those seen by physicians and psychiatrists in England and France in the late 19th century, for whom body image distortion was also not a prominent symptom. He proposed that these observations suggest that current Western diagnostic criteria for anorexia nervosa are ethnocentric, and that they should be revised accordingly (see Lee, chapter 3, this volume).

While the relative lack of body image concerns among anorexic patients in Hong Kong is intriguing, it is important to note that by the mid- to late 1990s, weight consciousness was becoming pervasive among high school students and college students in Hong Kong (Lee and Lee, 1996). This trend is in direct contradiction to the traditional value that the Chinese place on plumpness as a sign of health, and yet it is compatible with the increased influence of consumerist norms in a relatively affluent Hong Kong. It is possible that the lack of evident body image distortion found in those patients may represent an unwillingness to admit to such a culturally dissonant idea.

During the period from 1988 to 1997, Lee reported treating 68 patients with anorexia nervosa and 25 with bulimia nervosa, with the majority of these patients being seen after 1995. Thus, whereas eating disorders were extremely rare in Hong Kong as recently as the 1980s, it may well be that the finding of an intense degree of weight preoccupation that students are now evidencing will soon give rise to an increase in the prevalence of eating disorders to levels comparable to those in Europe and the United States.

Little information is available on the prevalence of clinical eating disorders on mainland China. One survey in the early 1990s of 509 first-year medical college students at universities in Shanghai and Chongqing indicated that slighly more than 1% suffered from bulimia nervosa (Chun et al., 1992). Such results suggest that bulimia was less common on the Chinese mainland than among American college populations, in which prevalence estimates from the 1980s typically ranged from 2 to 4%. However, the 1% figure may be more in line with more recent prevalence estimates from Western countries, which tend to be somewhat lower than those from the 1980s (Hoeken et al., 1998). It is notable that 78% of the females in the Chinese study admitted to a fear of gaining weight or becoming fat (Chun et al., 1992). This finding is consistent with a later study indicating the emergence of widespread dieting among Chinese adolescents (Huon et al., 1999). Again, such behavior was unheard of in traditional Chinese society and probably reflects the impact of consumerist norms of thinness as well as a growing problem of obesity among Chinese youth. The latter may well be due to the greater availability of Western-style high-fat, high-calorie foods in the Chinese diet, as well as an increased degree of sedentariness in the Chinese urban population.

Given the variation of Chinese society with respect to degree of socio-economic development, one might well expect the impact of these forces to differ by geographic locale. In support of this notion, one study (Lee and Lee, 1999) compared the degree of distorted eating attitudes among high school students towards food and dieting in Hong Kong, an international financial center with high per capita income, Shenzhen, a rapidly developing city of over 3 million people that seems to capture the social and cultural impact of market economies in contemporary China, and rural Hunan province, an area of relatively low per capita income and minimal exposure to Western influences such as television and fashion magazines. Interestingly, while the actual body-mass index (a measure of weight relative to height) was lowest for students in Hong Kong, 74% wanted to weigh less. The students in rural Hunan, on the other hand, showed the reverse trend, that is, the highest body-mass index of the three groups and the lowest drive to lose weight. This is a unique study, the results of which reflect the varying impact of degrees of economic development and exposure to the consumer culture on weight consciousness within the same society. While it does not yield information about clinical eating disorders per se, since the results were based on a questionnaire about eating attitudes, the findings suggest that with increasing degrees of economic modernization and accompanying changes in food practices, weight consciousness, and ambivalence about the changing female role, eating disorders may well emerge as a problem for an increasing number of Chinese youth.

Based on journalistic accounts (Efron, 1997), there is also some indication that eating disorders have become common in South Korea, where the forces of industrialization, urbanization, consumerism and democratization have produced an enormously rapid cultural transition. The emergence of eating disorders in South Korea is particularly remarkable, given traditional attitudes towards plumpness as a requirement for marriage, attitudes which held sway as recently as the 1970s. Koreans point to dramatic changes in attitudes towards food over a generation or two. Following the Second World War, the common question 'have you eaten?' was a reflection of pervasive food shortages; to respond in the affirmative to the question was a sign of status and well being. Now, some surveys have shown that 90% of high school girls, the vast majority of whom are of normal weight, feel that they are overweight. Fashion standards have become particularly stringent, with dresses often being offered in only one size, the equivalent of an American size 4. The only survey of eating disorders, conducted among college students in 1990, found a prevalence rate of anorexia of 0.7% and bulimia nervosa of 0.8% (Efron, 1997). These rates, while lower than those of American or European samples, may well be rapidly increasing at the end of the 1990s. One psychiatrist, Kim Joon Ki, had only seen one patient prior to 1991, during which he spent a year studying eating disorders. In a 1997, he had seen over 200 patients, about half of whom were anorexic and half of whom were bulimic, in a 2½ year period since he opened a private eating disorder clinic. Surveys of eating attitudes in student populations in South Korea have found high degrees of weight preoccupation and eating disorder symptoms, comparable to or greater than those found in Western samples (Lee et al., 1998).

In Singapore, a relatively affluent and technologically advanced society, the death of a 21-year old, 70-pound student from anorexia nervosa at the National University in 1996 gained a tremendous amount of attention in the national press (Efron, 1997). In an upscale shopping area in Singapore, a message on a T-shirt seems to capture the conflicted female consciousness about weight:

> *'I've got to get into that dress. It's easy. Don't eat . . . I'm hungry. Can't eat breakfast. But I ought to . . . I like breakfast. I like that dress . . . Still too big for that dress. Hmm. Life can be cruel'*

A survey of secondary school student attitudes in Singapore in the 1990s showed the same pervasive body image dissatisfaction and other disturbed eating attitudes as were found in Hong Kong, with scores in some cases exceeding those of students in the United States (Pok and Tian, 1994). Yet, the authors of this survey point out that despite the dramatically increased weight consciousness, the prevalence of anorexia nervosa in Singapore still remains quite low. This they attribute to such factors as the inherently smaller body-mass index of Singaporean women, the lack of pervasive obesity in the culture, the typical cohesiveness of the family, and ready availability of a culturally normative healthy diet should one want to lose weight. Despite these protective factors, the authors suggest that given the high degree of body image consciousness and associated vulnerabilities of young women in Singapore, the prevalence of eating disorders is likely to increase.

The noted Indian epidemiologist Shridhar Sharma remarked on the absence of any reports of anorexia nervosa in the Indian psychiatric literature up until the early 1980s. This situation has changed, however, with published accounts of eating disorders appearing in the1990s (Khandewal *et al.*, 1995; Bhugra *et al.*, 2000). To date, the number of cases that have been published are small, and we have as yet nothing in the way of epidemiological studies. Interestingly, the few cases that have been published emphasize a lack of body image concerns and fear of obesity in Indian patients, which is analogous to the situation that Sing Lee has described in Hong Kong (Khandewal *et al.*, 1995). And yet recent studies suggest that the 'eating distress syndrome', a pattern of preoccupation with body image and overweight without the severe symptoms of anorexia nervosa (drastic weight loss) or bulimia nervosa (binge eating and purging), may be emerging in significant numbers of Indian students (Srinivasan *et al.*, 1995; Srinivasan *et al.*, 1998). The authors of these studies suggest that as norms of thinness become more insistent throughout Indian culture, eating disorder as now conceptualized in the Western countries may emerge in large numbers in the future.

The very existence of eating disorders in India is frequently met with disbelief by Western audiences, given the familiar imagery of economic deprivation in India that still pervades Western views of Indian society. Despite the continued existence of both urban and rural poverty, it needs to be emphasized that the India of the early 21st century is a rapidly developing country, with a very large and burgeoning educated and professional class. Like China in this regard, India is enormously diverse in its economic development, ranging from urban areas such as Delhi and Bangalore, which are characterized by rapid industrial development and the emergence of a high technology economy, to rural village areas still living in the traditional cultural style of the past. Finally, the transitional situation for women in India cannot be overlooked, with new professional, public and work roles conflicting sharply with traditional limitations (Mitter, 1991).

2 Africa

Traditional ideal body image among Africans has always tended towards a large, full form. Hortense Powdermaker (1960), in an early review of cross-cultural attitudes towards obesity and fatness, offered numerous examples from various African locales in which fatness in the female was particularly celebrated. She cited one popular song in the Copperbelt of the former Northern Rhodesia that reflected typical attitudes:

'Hullo, Mama, the beautiful one, let us go to town; you will be very fat, you girl, if you stay with me.'

In African religious and cultural symbolism, fatness in the female is closely tied with fertility; hence the once widely practiced ritual of fattening, which was applied to pubescent girls in order to make them marriageable. Studies carried out in the 1980s and 1990s show that both Kenyans and Ugandans continue to prefer a greater degree of fullness in the female form in Westerners (Furnham and Alibhai, 1983; Furnham and Baguma, 1994). Nevertheless, there is some indication that these traditional aesthetics may be changing. For example, in an article entitled 'Africans look for beauty in Western mirror' in the *Christian Science Monitor* (Dec. 1999), Corina Schuler described the current views of black women in South Africa in Thandi Ntshihoeoe words: *'It's embarrassing to be a fat African mama now . . . we are more aware since we got democracy, we want to be healthy, independent women who look good'* (personal communication, Le Grange, 2000).

Some isolated case reports of eating disorders in African women appeared in the 1980s (Buchan and Gregory, 1984; Nwaefuma, 1981; Famuyiwa, 1988), as well as one study that indicated that symptoms such as self-induced vomiting were not uncommon among Nigerian students (Oyewumi and Kazarian, 1992). More recently, a number of case reports of eating disorders in black South Africans have emerged in the 1990s (Szabo *et al.*, 1995) and surveys of university students show levels of weight concern and eating disorder symptoms at least equal to that of the white population (Le Grange *et al.*, 1998). It is plausible that the unique historical and cultural situation in South Africa is linked with the rise of eating disorders in that country (see Szabo and Le Grange, chapter 2, this volume).

3 Latin America

In traditional South American societies, with the exception of perhaps very small elite groups who have been exposed to European and North American influences, the existence of eating disorders has probably been quite low. The celebration of the voluptous figure in young women has probably been the most typical ideal body image. However, in recent years there have been changes, at least in certain locales.

The first country to report eating disorders in Latin America was Chile, in the form of a description of 30 cases of anorexia nervosa that appeared in a Chilean journal in 1982 (Pumarino and Vivanco, 1982). The authors of this report note the pervasiveness of the relentless drive for thinness in their patients, and in most respects the disorder was indistinguishable from that described in the American and European literature. In a previous publication, Pumarino had observed a notable increase in the incidence of the condition in Chile throughout the decade prior to the publication of the study (that is, the 1970s). Such an increase coincided precisely with an increase in the incidence of the condition in the United States and Western Europe. During the 1970s, Chile had gone through a momentous political change, with the overthrow of the Allende regime in 1973 and the rise of the military regime of Pinochet. Under the influence of American policies, Chile rapidly developed into an advanced capitalist economy. One can only speculate about the connection between these events and the rise of eating disorders, but at minimum it would be surprising if the radical commercialization of culture that took hold during the 1970s did not have an impact.

More recently, in the 1990s, eating disorders have emerged as a significant problem in urban areas of Mexico, particularly Mexico City. This appears to be a relatively recent phenomenon (Barriguete, 1998), and the main group that appears to be affected is university students. One must understand in this context that Mexico is undergoing extremely rapid change as a society, as a result of increased industrialization, urbanization, and the cultural transformations that are associated with these changes. It is not surprising therefore that the typical Western phenomenon of eating disorders is beginning to emerge. One only needs to look casually at magazine racks in Mexico to see Spanish editions of such stalwarts of the culture of thinness as *Mademoiselle* or *Harper's Bazaar*. Fashion magazines that are primarily published in Spanish, such as *Vanidades*, are replete with articles about weight control and shape conditioning. It is also the case that in Mexico there is a growing awareness of a significant problem with obesity and the high fat and carbohydrate content of the traditional diet. This is particularly true in the upwardly mobile social groups.

During the 1990s, there have been reports of what has been referred to as an 'epidemic of eating disorders' in Argentina, particularly in Buenos Aires. While the true extent of the phenomenon has not been documented by epidemiological studies, professional interest in the treatment and prevention of eating disorders in Argentina has been intense. The rise of eating disorders in Argentina may be associated with the confluence of a number of cultural factors, such as a particularly powerful aesthetic of beauty and weight control (Dupuertis, 1998) as well as certain ambiguities and conflicting cross-currents regarding the sense of national identity and that of female identity in particular (see Meehan and Katzman, chapter 8, this volume).

Conclusion

The remarkable emergence of eating disorders in areas that were once thought to be culturally incompatible with them will be discussed from a number of vantage points throughout this volume. However, one theme that seems to unite these disparate geographic and cultural regions is that they are either highly developed economies (such as Hong Kong and Singapore) or they are witnessing rapid market changes and their associated impact on the status of women. The impact of a global consumer culture, with powerful mandates for the cultivation of a certain type of body ideal, appears to play a significant role. Equally important, however, are the contradictory pressures that emerge when women begin to have access on a mass level to education and a role in public life, and struggles about sexual equality come to the foreground. This may be especially problematic in societies in which the transition to a new female role is especially sudden and conflicts sharply with traditional forces that demand deference to one's family and submissiveness to men. Finally a much neglected factor in discussions of eating disorders is the impact of new patterns of food consumption and production, as well as new styles of eating, both of which conflict sharply with traditional food practices and ways of relating to food. The introduction of a modern Western-style diet, with high calorie and fat density, coupled with increasing degrees of sedentariness of contemporary work and lifestyles, is a major factor in a growing international problem of obesity, one which clashes with both new aesthetic ideals but also a heightened consciousness of the medical risks of obesity.

With the rise of eating disorders in developing countries, it is perhaps ironic that the incidence of these conditions may be leveling off or even declining in the West, or at least the United States. An important study by Heatherton and his colleagues, for example, found the degree of weight dissatisfaction, intensity of dieting, and eating disorder symptoms had actually declined among students at Harvard College between 1982 and 1992 (Heatherton *et al.*, 1995). We were able to replicate these findings at two liberal arts colleges in New York State (Gordon and Neal, 1998). These studies are too preliminary and population-specific to be conclusive, but they are congruent with other findings in other research conducted in the late 1980s (Pyle *et al.*, 1991). If in fact this trend holds up in future research, one could speculate that just as sociocultural factors are responsible for the rise of eating disorders, they could also account for their possible decline. What might such factors be? First, the high degree of familiarity with eating disorders through widespread public discussion of them in the press, entertainment media, and educational settings may have led young women to be more cautious about undertaking starvation dieting regimes or other dangerous weight control practices, however much thinness may still be desired. Heatherton (1995) suggested that in the 1990s, owing to such diverse factors as knowledge about the risks of extreme dieting and negative connotations associated with extreme thinness, eating disorders have become stigmatized, somewhat in contrast to their glamorization in the late 1970s and early 1980s. Finally, perhaps after years of influence of feminist thinking within college settings and the impact of a very vocal anti-dieting movement, many women have adopted a posture of rejection when it comes to an excessive focus on weight and dieting. From the public health standpoint, such a development can only be seen as salutary.

References

Barlow DH, Durand VM (1999). *Abnormal Psychology* (Second Edition). Pacific Grove, CA: Brooks Cole.

Barriguete A (1998). Personal communication.

Becker AE, Hamburg P (1996). Culture, the media and eating disorders. *Harvard Review of Psychiatry*, **4**, 163–7.

Bemporad JR (1996). Self-starvation through the ages: Reflections on the pre-history of anorexia nervosa. *International Journal of Eating Disorders*, **19**, 217–37.

Bhugra D, Bhio K, Gupta, KD (2000). Bulimic disorders and sociocentric values in north India. *Social Psychiatry and Psychiatric Epidemiology*, **35**, 86–93.

Boskind-Lodahl M (1976). Cinderella's stepsisters: A feminist perspective on anorexia nervosa and bulimia: Signs. *Journal of Women in Culture and Society*, **2**, 342–56.

Bruch H (1973). *Eating Disorders: Obesity, Anorexia Nervosa and the Person Within*. New York: Basic Books.

Bruch H (1979). *The Golden Cage: The Enigma of Anorexia Nervosa*. New York: Basic Books.

Buchan T, Gregory LD (1984). Anorexia nervosa in a black Zimbabwean. *British Journal of Psychiatry*, **145**, 326–30.

Chun ZF, Mitchell JE, Li K, *et al.*, (1992). The prevalence of anorexia nervosa and bulimia nervosa among Freshman medical college students in China. *International Journal of Eating Disorders*, **12**, 209–14.

Dupuertis DG (1998). Personal communication.

Eagles JM, Johnston MI, Hunter D, Lobban M, Millar HR (1995). Increasing incidence of anorexia nervosa in the female population of Northeast Scotland. *American Journal of Psychiatry*, **152**, 1266–71.

Efron S (1997). Eating disorders go global. *Los Angeles Times*, October 18.

Fairburn CG, Welch SL, Doll HA, Davies BA, O'Conner ME (1997). Risk factors for bulimia nervosa: A community-based case-control study. *Archives of General Psychiatry*, **54**, 509–17.

Famuyiwa OO (1988). Incidence of anorexia nervosa in two Nigerians. *Acta Psychiatrica Scandinavica*, **78**, 550–4.

Fombonne E (1995). Anorexia nervosa: No evidence of an increase. *British Journal of Psychiatry*, **166**, 462–71.

Furnham A, Alibhai N (1983). Cross-cultural differences in the perception of female body shapes. *Psychological Medicine*, **13**, 829–37.

Furnham A, Baguma P (1994). Cross-cultural differences in the evaluation of male and female body shapes. *International Journal of Eating Disorders*, **15**, 81–90.

Garner D, Garfinkel PE, Schwartz D, Thompson M (1980). Cultural expectations of thinness in women. *Psychological Reports*, **47**, 483–91.

Gordon RA (1989). A sociocultural interpretation of the current epidemic of eating disorders. In Blinder BJ, Chaiting BF, Goldstein R. *The Eating Disorders*, PMA Publishing. Great Week, New York.

Gordon RA (2000). *Eating Disorders: Anatomy of a Social Epidemic* (second edition). Oxford: Blackwell.

Gordon RA, Neal N (1998). *Is the prevalence of eating disorders declining among college students? A partial replication*. Presented at Eighth New York International Conference on Eating Disorders, New York, NY.

Heatherton TF, Nichols P, Mahamedi F, Keel P (1995). Body weight, dieting and eating disorders symptoms among college students, 1982–1992. *American Journal of Psychiatry*, **152**, 1623–29.

Hebl MR, Heatherton TF (1998). The stigma of obesity in women: The difference is Black and White. *Personality and Social Psychology Bulletin*, **24**, 417–26.

Hoeken D van, Lucas AR, Hoek HW. Epidemiology. Chapter 4 (pp. 97–126); in Hoek

HW, Treasure JL, Katzman MA (1998). *Neurobiology in the Treatment of Eating Disorders*. London: Wiley.

Hsu LKG (1997). Can dieting cause an eating disorder? *Psychological Medicine*, **27**, 509–13.

Huon GF, Walton CJ, Lim J, Zheng R (1999). Dieting among adolescent girls in Bejing. *Eating Disorders: Journal of Treatment and Prevention*, **7**, 271–8.

Ishikawa K (1965). Ueber die Eltern von anorexia-nervosa-Kranken. In Meyer JE, Feldmann H. (eds). *Anorexia Nervosa*. Stuttgart: Verlag.

Katzman MA, Lee S (1997). Beyond body image: The integration of feminist and transcultural theories in the understanding of self-starvation. *International Journal of Eating Disorders*, **27**, 317–27.

Khandewal SK, Sharan P, Saxena S (1995). Eating disorders: An Indian perspective. *International Journal of Social Psychiatry*, **41**, 132–46.

Kuboki T, Nomura S, Ide M, Suematsu H, Araki S (1996). Epidemiological data on anorexia nervosa in Japan. *Psychiatry Research*, **16**, 11–16.

Kuczmarski RJ, Flegal KM, Campbell SM, Johnson CL (1994). Increasing prevalence of overweight among US adults: The national health and nutrition examination surveys, 1960 to 1991. *Journal of American Medical Association*, **272**, 205–11.

Lee S (1991). Anorexia nervosa in Hong Kong: A Chinese perspective. *Psychological Medicine*, **21**, 703–11.

Lee S, Ho TP, Hsu LKG (1993). Fat phobic and non-fat phobic anorexia nervosa: A comparative study of 70 Chinese patients in Hong Kong. *Psychological Medicine*, **23**, 999–1017.

Lee AM, Lee S (1996). Disordered eating and its psychosocial correlates among Chinese adolescent females in Hong Kong. *International Journal of Eating Disorders*, **20**, 177–84.

Lee S, Lee AM (1999). Disordered eating in three communities in China: A comparative study of high school students in Hong Kong, Shenzhen, and rural Hunan. *International Journal of Eating Disorders*, **27**, 312–16.

Lee YH, Rhee MK, Park SH, *et al.*, (1998). Epidemiology of eating disordered symptoms in the Korean general population using a Korean version of the Eating Attitudes Test. *Eating and Weight Disorders*, **3**, 153–61.

Le Grange D, Telch CF, Tibbs J (1998). Eating attitudes and behaviors in 1,435 South African Caucasian and Non-Caucasian college students. *American Journal of Psychiatry*, **155**, 250–4.

Lucas AR, Beard CM, O'Fallon WM, Kurland LT (1991). 50-year trends in the incidence of anorexia nervosa in Rochester, Minn: A population-based study. *American Journal of Psychiatry*, **148**, 917–22.

Lucas AR, Crowson CS, O'Fallon WM, Melton LJ (1999). The ups and downs of anorexia nervosa. *International Journal of Eating Disorders*, **26**, 397–405.

Mitter SS (1991). *Dharma's Daughters: Contemporary Indian Women and Hindu Culture*. New Brunswick, New Jersey: Rutgers University Press.

Mokad AH, Serdula MK, Dietz WH, Bowman BA, Marks JS, Koplan JP (1999). The spread of the obesity epidemic in the United States, 1991–1998. *Journal of the American Medical Association*, **282**, 1519–22.

Nadaoka T, Oiji A, Takahashi S, Morioka Y, Kashiwakura M, Totsuka S (1996) An epidemiological study of eating disorders in a northern area of Japan. *Acta Psychiatrica Scandinavica*, **93**, 305–10.

Nasser M (1997). *Culture and Weight Consciousness*. London: Routledge.

Nwaefuna A (1981). Anorexia nervosa in a developing country. *British Journal of Psychiatry*, **138**, 270.

Oyewumi LK, Kazarian SS (1992). Abnormal eating attitudes among a group of Nigerian youths: I Bulimic behavior. *East African Medical Journal*, 663–6.

Pok LP, Tian CS (1994). Susceptibility of Singapore Chinese schoolgirls to anorexia nervosa – Part I (psychological factors). *Singapore Medical Journal*, **35**, 481–5.

Polivy J, Herman CP (1985). Dieting and binging: A causal analysis. *American Psychologist*, **40**, 193–201.

Pope HG, Phillips KA, Olivardia R (2000). *The Adonis Complex: The Secret Crisis of Male Body Obsession*. New York: The Free Press.

Pope HG, Hudson JI, Yurgelun-Todd D (1984). Prevalence of anorexia nervosa and bulimia in three student populations. *International Journal of Eating Disorders*, **3**, 45–51.

Powdermaker H (1960). An anthropological approach to the problem of obesity. *Bulletin of the New York Academy of Sciences*, **36**, 286–95.

Prince R (1983). Is anorexia nervosa a culture-bound syndrome? *Transcultural Psychiatric Research Review*, **20**, 299–301.

Prince R (1985). The concept of culture-bound syndromes: Anorexia nervosa and brain fag. *Social Science and Medicine*, **21**, 197–203.

Pumarino H, Vivanco N (1982). Anorexia nervosa: medical and psychiatric characteristics of 30 patients. *Revista Medica de Chile*, **110**, 1081–92.

Pyle RL, Neuman PA, Halvorson PA, Mitchell JE (1991). An ongoing cross-sectional study of the prevalence of eating disorders in freshman college students. *International Journal of Eating Disorders*, **10**, 667–78.

Russell GFM (1979). Bulimia nervosa: An ominous variant of anorexia nervosa. *Psychological Medicine*, **9**, 429–48.

Seidell JC, Flegal KM (1997). Assessing obesity: Classification and epidemiology. *British Medical Journal*, **53**, 238–52.

Silverstein B, Perlick D (1995). *The Cost of Competence: Why Inequality Causes Depression, Eating Disorders and Illness in Women*. Oxford: Oxford University Press.

Skov L (1995). *Women, Media and Consumption in Japan*. St. Johns: Honolulu University of Hawaii Press.

Sours JA (1980). *Starving to Death in a Sea of Objects*. New York: Jason Aronson.

Srinivasan TN, Suresh TR, Vasantha J (1998). Emergence of eating disorders in India. Study of eating distress syndrome and development of a screening questionnaire. *International Journal of Social Psychiatry*, **44**, 189–98.

Srinivasan TN, Suresh TR, Jayaram V, Fernandez MP (1995). Eating disorders in India. *Indian Journal of Psychiatry*, **37**, 26–50.

Suematsu H, Ishikawa H, Kuboki T, Ito T (1985a). Statistical studies on anorexia nervosa in Japan: Detailed clinical data on 1,011 patients. *Psychotherapy and Psychosomatics*, **43**, 96–103.

Szabo C, Berk M, Tiou E, Allwood CW (1995). Eating disorders in black South African females: a series of cases. *South African Medical Journal*, **85**, 588–90.

White M (1993). *The Material Child: Coming of Age in Japan and America*. New York: The Free Press.

Willi J, Grossman S (1982). Epidemiology of anorexia nervosa in a defined region of Switzerland. *American Journal of Psychiatry*, **140**, 564–8.

Williams P, King M (1987). The "epidemic" of anorexia nervosa: Another medical myth? *The Lancet*, 205–7.

Wiseman CV, Gray JJ, Mosimann JE, Ahrens AH (1992). Cultural expectations of thinness in women: An update. *International Journal of Eating Disorders*, **11**, 84–9.

Wolf N (1991). *The Beauty Myth: How Images of Beauty Are Used Against Women*. New York: Dutton.

Commentary 1

Robert Palmer,
Consultant Psychiatrist, Leicester University, UK

Nosology is about defining disorders. Epidemiology is about counting cases. Both are surprisingly slippery fish. In an ideal world, reliable conclusions would follow clarity in definition and accuracy in counting. But the world is not ideal. The eating disorders swim in muddy waters and our tackle is not wonderful. When, to our disappointment, our keep net remains poorly stocked, we are all tempted to tell fishermen's tales.

We really know little enough about the prevalence of defined eating disorders in the Western world (van Hoeken *et al.*, 1998). We know less still – next to nothing – about such disorders in the rest of the world. Of course, there are some reports and observations but few allow valid conclusions about rates (Nasser, 1997). Positive findings – catching some fish – mean that limited conclusions can be drawn; that there are eating disorders in the population studied. However, negative findings from studies with limited power or a lack of reports of cases in clinical practice may not mean that eating disorders do not exist. And if they subsequently become more evident that may not mean that there has been a true change in frequency. It may be the waters or the tackle or just our luck that have changed rather than the number of fish. At best we can make educated guesses.

Richard Gordon makes some interesting guesses. And once one starts guessing it makes sense to elaborate conjectures about possible aetiological factors which may influence the frequency of disorder in different societies. However, the observations against which these conjectures should be tested are rarely available and perhaps their chief function should be to inform how we should seek to make such observations in future. With a bit of luck, hypothesis testing might come to replace haphazard fishing trips. Hypotheses are guesses that are worth testing out.

Study of the issues postulated as relevant to the aetiology of eating disorders is of interest in its own right as is shown by the cited work of Lee and Lee in the contrasting Chinese communities. However, eating attitudes are not eating disorders; at best they are proxies for disorder and when used in that way there is a real danger of question begging. Substantial – and unfortunately that means expensive – epidemiological studies are still required if findings are to be shown to be truly relevant to clinical disorder. After all, it would be fascinating if there were populations with high levels of attitudinal proxies but low levels of actual disorder and vice versa. If we rely too much on easy proxies of disorder, we could remain unaware of such situations. The more difficult it is to study rates in a country or culture the more tempting it is to make do with such proxies. (In this respect the past is also another country and a remarkably fascinating but inaccessible one.) The same argument applies to other supposed risk factors.

And, of course, there may be more than one kind of fish. Overlap notwithstanding, there do seem to be good grounds for thinking about anorexia nervosa and bulimia nervosa separately. Likewise, binge eating disorder or something like it seems to be a useful nosological entity. There may be different speculations to be made about anorexia nervosa, which seems the more stable over place and time, and bulimia nervosa, which seems to be the "new" and more variable upstart (Palmer, 1998). Again the temptation is to use proxies or to lump all eating disorders together in a way which may obscure more than it reveals.

Furthermore, our cherished and defined disorders must be viewed against a background in which at least a substantial minority of disorder presenting to services even in the 'West' is of a kind which does not exactly fit our diagnostic categories. 'EDNOS' (Eating disorders not otherwise specified) is often the commonest eating disorder. We cannot be too satisfied with classificatory systems which leave out many of the fish which we catch even in our local pools. Studying different populations may stimulate, if not demand, that we look carefully at our conceptual tackle as we go fishing. Again, Lee's observations of Chinese anorexia nervosa 'cases' without weight concern are of great interest but if we use our present classification we should not be calling them anorexia nervosa. Or perhaps we should be revising what we mean by the term (Palmer, 1993). Or better still, trying both.

But then upon what safe ground do we stand and how do we decide what counts as a fish and what not? And in epidemiological terms, what do we count? There is a tension between this need to count and define and the need to be open to the culturally relative nature of concepts of disorder, including our own cherished canon. We feel that we should be sensitive but yearn for a less shifting world. Anthropologists may feel at home in such wobbly and relativistic territory but some of us feel queasy without at least some concepts onto which we can hang with a measure of trust. Perhaps we should dissect and pare down our categories and describe separately more limited items such as aspects of weight, eating behaviour, eating restraint and its various motivations, the urge to eat and so on. Might these be more cross-culturally reliable? Armed with observations of these more basic issues we could see how they vary and hang together. There may indeed be rather basic types out there which are widespread or even nearly universal. However, they may not be defined by the features which just happen to be most prominent in our local and familiar cases. And remember that even many of our local cases are 'atypical'.

What is most evident may not be most important and what is most important may not be most evident. Dolphins are not fishes, even though they look like fishes. Fishes are not mammals, even though they look like dolphins. We are not that good at fishing. We are not that good at describing and categorising what we catch. Chatting about what we think we know is part of the joy of the exercise. But acknowledging what we do not know is necessary. However, there is no need for such acknowledgement to make us downhearted. Or to stop us doing more fishing.

References

Nasser M (1997). *Culture and Weight Consciousness*, London: Routledge.

Palmer RL (1993). Weight concern should not be a necessary criterion for the eating disorders: A polemic. *International Journal of Eating Disorders*, **14**, 459–65.

Palmer RL (1998). Culture, constitution, motivation and the mysterious rise of bulimia nervosa. *European Eating Disorders Review*, **6**, 81–4.

van Hoeken D, Lucas AR, Hoek HW (1998). Epidemiology, in Hoek HW, Treasure JL, Katzman MA (editors), *Neurobiology in the Treatment of Eating Disorders*, New York: Wiley.

Commentary 2

Penny Van Esterik
Professor of Anthropology, York University, Toronto, Canada

Anthropologists and psychologists are fellow travellers on a road to explain and hopefully one day eradicate eating disorders. The way forward has been cleared by psychologists, therapists, sociologists, historians and clinicians, not by anthropologists. In fact, there is at present no adequate anthropological approach to eating disorders, although anthropology has much to contribute to understanding and explaining the processes that underlie eating disorders.

Gordon's chapter reviews the available literature that confirms the impression of a growing epidemic of eating disorders in the West. The author provides examples of eating disorders in places where they have not previously been reported. He acknowledges, however, that in the past there may not have been a cultural vocabulary for talking about eating disorders. With the publication of this book, that vocabulary now exists. That raises the interesting question of how cultural vocabularies and clinical vocabularies will mutually influence one another.

There is much in this chapter that would be supported by anthropologists. That the Diagnostic and Statistical Manual of Disorders (DSM: American Psychiatric Association) is ethnocentric and based on biomedical explanatary models is an assumption widely shared among medical anthropologists. They would also agree with the points raised concerning somaticization of eating disorders in Hong Kong. Differences in class and ethnicity are areas of mutual concern. And we certainly share the assumption that the body is a culturally constructed category, a point of great importance for understanding body image cross-culturally.

It is also not surprising that anthropologists would challenge many of the arguments developed here. For example, opposing the West and the rest does not sit well, given the trans-national movement of ideas and people under conditions of globalization. Nor does conflating modernization with Westernization. In the case of Japan, economic and technological change did not result in the adoption of the cultural patterns of Westerners, particularly with regard to food. This is made very clear in recent ethnographic studies of the expansion of McDonald's restaurants into Japan and throughout Asia, where the fast food eating experience has very different meanings. In Japan, McDonald's popular teriyaki burgers are considered snacks that compete with *obento* (lunch boxes) and stand-up noodle stands (Watson, 1997).

Anthropologists might also call for a more nuanced approach to hunger – one that considers both objective and subjective experiences in different contexts. For example, hunger results from religious fasting for purity, penance, power or other spiritual goals, fasting as a means of political protest, as well as the deliberate refusal of food as personal protest in the form of anorexia or bulimia. What is the relation between these practices, and hunger resulting from poverty and food insecurity?

Medical anthropologists no longer make much use of the concept of culture-bound syndromes to refer to locally-specific disorders not easily assigned to Western categories of disease, arguing that the label may reinforce and essentialize differences, and result in dismissing the complaints of women, refugees, First Nations patients, or marginalized groups. A focus on static categorization may also obscure how meanings are linked to larger social and political contexts, and how diseases and disorders may be a form of resistance.

Psychologists and clinical practitioners are not permitted the speculative and interpretive distance of an anthropologist. They must intervene to prevent harm to specific individuals with particular eating disorders. Without the obligation to intervene, anthropologists can explore more multi-causal explanatory models.

I have always wanted to write a manual on 'The Care and Feeding of Anthropologists' for colleagues in other disciplines who would like to work with anthropologists but don't know how to go beyond expecting them to deliver 'cultural factors' and provide anecdotes of the 'exotic other' from a little further off the beaten track. That interdisciplinary work is often difficult with anthropologists is usually the fault of stubborn independent anthropologists. Nevertheless, for those eating disorder specialists or mental health professionals who would like to cross into the world of anthropology, expect that a different set of questions would be asked. To begin with, anthropologists would look at eating disorders from a holistic comparative perspective, placing them in the context of food systems, gender systems and kinship systems.

The literature on eating disorders appears to have a lot to say about the oppression of women, the tyranny of slenderness and the role of the mass media, but very little to say about people's relation to food itself, its textures, smells, tastes; what was eaten, how it was eaten, what was rejected. Anthropologists can help fill this gap by drawing more attention to food praxis, the practical mastery of food practices. By limiting attention to consumption (or non-consumption), without examination of other temporal phases in the food system such as production, processing, storage, preparation, distribution and disposal, we lose the opportunity to ask questions about the relation between women's work with food and their rejection of it. I would want to know more about cuisine and the system of meals; at what level does food rejection take place? individual food items? complex dishes? whole meals? Are everyday meals rejected, but do the special meals that punctuate food cycles – weddings, birthdays, religious celebrations – encourage binging? The excess and indulgence of some meals contrasts with the ascetic rejection of others. Fasting and feasting are at the heart of most religious traditions. Perhaps the prescriptions and proscriptions associated with ritual meal cycles kept eating tightly rule-governed. The loss or rejection of this ritual logic governing food consumption leaves many young people without a sense of discipline, a meaningful etiquette of eating together. Food refusal signifies denial of social relationships, denial of sociability. How does this fit with the decline in commensality (food sharing) in many urban settings? How is food hoarding or food refusal related to changes in commensality?

These questions about the food system could be combined with gender analysis to examine the relation between women and food in different societies. Gender writ larger than body image would include more feminist analysis of power relations (cf. Counihan, 1999).

To anthropologists, these questions about the meaning of food, gender and commensality could not be answered from surveys or clinical interviews. They require long-term participant observation and ethnographic methods to provide more cultural and historical context. For example, in Korea, 'have you eaten' was interpreted as a response to pervasive food shortages; the same greeting in Thailand reflects the Thais' intense interest in food and often preceeds an invitation to eat together. An anthropologist with deep insights into Thai Buddhism used his knowledge of asceticism to raise new questions when his own daughter became anorexic: 'To heal anorexics and help others, we need to study the niches they've fled. That's where culture-wide gender and media oppression explanations err' (O'Connor, 2000, p. 8). A great deal of ethnographic research on these niches is done; the question is how to use it for applied interdisciplinary research on the subject of eating disorders.

It is my hope that anthropologists can contribute to the discussion of eating disorders not by providing more exotic examples of food refusal, but by helping to examine eating disorders in their broadest possible context. In the 1930s and 1940s, Audrey Richards in England and Margaret Mead in the United States both called for closer interdisciplinary work between anthropologists and nutritionists (cf. Counihan and Van Esterik, 1997). To tackle problems like eating disorders, interdisciplinary research between anthropologists and psychologists is now necessary. Take us on board and we will help bridge the gap between macro level explanations for eating disorders such as globalization, individualization or gender oppression, and individual pathologies, and perhaps suggest some of the mechanisms linking the two. We must leave clinical treatment to the psychologists and therapists, but might well be able to contribute to the work of developing preventive strategies, including culturally meaningful indicators to predict the early signs of eating disorders. Fellow travellers, we have a long road ahead.

References

Counihan C (1999). *The Anthropology of Food and Body*. New York: Routledge.
Counihan C, Van Esterik P (1997). *Food and Culture: A Reader*. New York: Routledge.

O'Connor R. (2000). Is anorexia a post-modern asceticism? *Anthropology News*, February.

Watson J (1997). *Golden Arches East: McDonald's in East Asia*. Stanford: Stanford University Press.

Chapter 2

Eating disorders and the politics of identity: The South African experience

Christopher Paul Szabo
Associate Professor, Department of Psychiatry, University of the Witwaterstrand, Johannesburg, Republic of South Africa

Daniel le Grange
Assistant Professor of Psychiatry, The University of Chicago, Chicago, USA

Debate question
This essay explores the possible impact of recent political events on the development of a new identity among black South Africans. Political emancipation in the absence of economic emancipation could contribute to a confused identity . Individuals may be aspiring to material progress which is informed by Westernization, while at the same time attempts are made to reinvigorate past political struggles that are influenced by romantic pride. These aspects of shifting identity, particularly on women, may explain the recently reported increase in the prevalence of eating disorders in South Africa.

Eating disorders: Crossing the colour barrier

Eating disorders are considered rare on the African continent. A handful of case histories in black Africans have been reported over the years (Nwaefuna, 1981; Buchan and Gregory, 1984; Famuyiwa, 1988), all from either Zimbabwe or Nigeria, and at least two of these had major exposure to Western European culture via schooling in England and assimilation of their parents. Generally speaking, the notion that has pervaded eating disorders research is that problems such as anorexia and bulimia are more or less confined to white Europeans or Americans. The reasons for this are postulated to be largely cultural (Swartz, 1985; Dolan, 1991). In the Western world, women are exposed to a particularly stringent thin body ideal that presses them to engage in weight control practices (Garner *et al.*, 1980). Furthermore, self-doubt associated with identity conflicts and role choices in

Western women are believed to be widespread, and there is evidence that these anxieties are the driving force of the thin body ideal (Silverstein and Perlick, 1995; Gordon, 2000).

The notion of ethnicity as a protective factor has been dispelled in recent case reports and community studies among different ethnic groups and cultural affiliations from around the world (for example, Dolan et al., 1990; Choudry and Mumford, 1992; Lee et al., 1992; Nasser 1997). Also the validity of such conceptualization in the South African context is currently being questioned (Swartz, 1998). Numerous cases of anorexia nervosa began to emerge in the late 1990s, and studies of eating disorders among black students in South Africa now suggest that disordered eating attitudes could be as high as, or indeed higher in some respects than, they are in whites.

South Africa provides an important window on the emergence of eating disorders. With the major political transition from the apartheid government to political democracy and the asendancy of majority rule in the mid-1990s, the country has been the center of a very dramatic political and cultural transition. In particular, the change has been momentous for the black population, who have experienced not only new political freedoms but also dramatic challenges to their own sense of cultural and personal identity. In this chapter, we will explore the rise of eating disorders among blacks in South Africa, the possible connection of this phenomenon to political and social changes, and in particular the relationship of the emergence of eating disorders to a drastically altered self-conception among black South African females.

Eating disorders in South Africa

Eating disorders have been well-documented in Caucasian women in South Africa since the 1970s (Beumont et al., 1976; Norris, 1979). However, there were no reports of cases among black patients until Szabo and his colleagues reported on three cases of anorexia nervosa, bulimic subtype (Szabo et al., 1995). Significantly, all three had either received or were currently receiving higher education, and one in particular had begun to drastically restrict her food intake in preparation for exams. From a clinical standpoint, the cases were not remarkably different from the typical presentations of these disorders among Western patients, and two included typical fear of fatness. Features of comorbid depression and anxiety were present.

In addition to the identification of clinical cases, community based multi-racial surveys have been conducted to investigate abnormal eating attitudes in adolescent females (Szabo and Hollands, 1997) and young adults (Le Grange et al., 1998; Wassenaar et al., 2000). These studies have shown that significant levels of abnormal eating attitudes and behaviors are evident in females of all ethnic groups in South Africa, that is, black, Caucasian, mixed-race, and Asian (from the Indian sub-continent). In particular, one of the studies (Le Grange et al., 1998) suggests pronounced disturbed eating attitudes among black college students. Black female students scored significantly higher than whites on questionnaires that measure both anorexic and bulimic behaviours. Moreover, a comparable percentage of black and white female students scored within the clinical range on these scales.

While the data are still rather limited, clearcut clinical cases of anorexia nervosa and bulimia nervosa have been identified in the South African black community within the past five years (Szabo, 1999). Studies indicate that attitudes and symptoms characteristic of bulimia nervosa are quite prevalent among black college and secondary school students, suggesting that it is highly likely that clinical eating disorders will become a growing problem in the near future. The remainder of this chapter will be devoted to some interpretations of these developments from a sociocultural standpoint. First, however, some caveats must be raised regarding the detection of problems such as eating disorders and information must be provided about South African racial politics, including the politics of the health-care system.

Is the increase real or a matter of changing perceptions?

The association of eating disorders with white, upper-class Euro/American culture is a powerful one. It persists in the minds of health professionals and the public, despite recent evidence that supports a more uniform social-class distribution for eating disorders (Gard and Freeman, 1996) and the substantial prevalence of eating disorders in American minority groups (Crago et al., 1996). In fact, a number of observers have argued that eating disorders are underdiagnosed in Western minority groups, particularly because of the powerful class-bound assumptions of health-care providers (Thompson, 1994).

Such considerations may apply with particular force in South Africa, because of the legacy of apartheid and the marginalization of health care, and particularly aspects of psychiatric care for the black population. Such rigidly institutionalized racism may have led to the dismissal of the presence of eating disorders among blacks prior to the democratization of the country. To put it more bluntly, most clinicians may have thought of eating disorders as an exclusively 'white problem' and therefore may not have expected to see them in black patients. A related problem has to do with the utilization of the Western health-care system by blacks. Traditional healing practices still abound in South Africa, and it is quite possible that patients who suffer from self-starvation, psychogenic weight loss, or even psychogenic vomiting may have been treated by traditional healers and therefore escaped detection by the establishment medical system.

This is one of those epidemiological conundrums that is very difficult to unravel. It is likely, however, that both types of factors may be operating. That is to say, despite the very real possibility that eating disorders may have existed in blacks prior to the demise of apartheid, it is also highly likely that their increase in the present social environment is a real one. The reasons for this might have to do with the profoundly altered sociocultural environment post-apartheid, and the particular changes that have occurred in the status of South African women.

The wider context: Sociopolitical changes in South Africa

The policy of apartheid in South Africa came about mainly through the ascent to power of an all-white nationalist government in a watershed election after the Second World War. This 1948 election marked the beginning of the apartheid years, where a policy of racial segregation, some 15 years in the making, was implemented (Harrison, 1987). This policy was the cornerstone of the white nationalist government's agenda and it persisted into the 1990s. Apartheid not only sought to create a racially divided society but was used to actively promote and exploit the diversity which existed between different African language and ethnic groups. This was done primarily in the form of separate 'homelands' for each ethnic group, situated outside the so-called 'white' South Africa, but still remaining under white control.

The extent to which the politics of apartheid were influential in the presentation of eating disorders in South Africa is crucial in this discussion. The apartheid policies served to enforce the separation of peoples based on racial classification as well as to actively discriminate against those of colour. This discrimination took various forms and ranged from the limitation of the right of abode to specified areas (as well as the restriction of the right to property ownership), as well as access to education and health resources. With specific reference to health resources, each racial group, as determined by the government, was allocated separate facilities located in their respective area of residence. Several international task forces highlighted the inequalities in medical care during the apartheid years. The American Association for the Advancement of Science's (AAAS) April 1989 medical mission inquiry in South Africa concluded, *'more government funds were allocated to hospitals for whites than to hospitals that treat blacks (i.e. mixed race, African and Asian). In addition, black hospitals are generally overcrowded and white hospitals are underutilized'* (Nightingale et al., 1990, p. 6).

The findings of this inquiry highlighted inequalities that had been documented in an earlier report by a committee of the American Psychiatric Association (APA), which had specifically investigated psychiatric facilities in South Africa. The APA reported that *'Medical and psychiatric care for blacks was grossly inferior to that for whites'* (APA Committee, 1979). This resulted in significant inequalities in terms of health care to the degree that some disorders were regarded as the 'domain' of one racial group as opposed to the other. In this context, eating disorders were perceived as first world 'elitist' illnesses that were not expected to be found in non-Caucasian communities, a virtual caricature and exaggeration of the characteristic attitudes towards these conditions. As a result, no one can be certain of the extent of eating disorders psychopathology during the apartheid years.

Following the release from jail of the leader of the main liberation movement in South Africa, Nelson Mandela, the policies of segregation were abandoned and the first multi-racial elections took place in 1994. This marked the beginning of a new political era in South Africa in which a racially all-encompassing and non-discriminatory dispensation was established. Today, a very different political philosophy is shaping the social landscape and the popular phrase is 'transformation'. South Africa, now a country in transition, is rapidly eroding previous ethnic barriers. Racial integration of schools, affirmative action in the workplace, and African migration to urban areas on a massive scale are only some of the relevant consequences. Besides changes within the country, external sociopolitical attitudes towards South Africa have also changed. From being a pariah state, South Africa's reputation has been restored to that of an acceptable member of the international community. Cultural exchange is now commonplace and is actively promoted. The country has been rehabilitated into a constitutional democracy and has restored its place as part of the global community of nations.

A parallel process of national healing in the form of the Truth and Reconciliation Commission was set in motion (Swartz, 1998). This commission was mandated to investigate the abuses of the past, perpetrated in the struggle to maintain as well as oppose the apartheid system. For this to happen, it was believed that past atrocities had to become known for healing to take place. Those who were found guilty of apartheid atrocities and confessed were pardoned by the state in order to promote the process of reconciliation. The euphoria and optimism of the initial process of sociopolitical transformation is now giving way to the harsh realities of turning a fractured country into a unified nation. South Africans are faced with the heavy burden of creating a new national identity. For the purposes of this essay we will turn our attention to a specific sub-group of this changing society. The question that begs exploration here is how these events of significant social and political magnitude may have affected black South African women, specifically in terms of gender roles, and subsequently the development of disordered eating.

Women's roles, shapes, and expectations in the 'new' South Africa

It is our contention that the evolving emancipation of women in South Africa against the background of a struggle between seemingly opposing identities, could explain, at least in part, why eating disorders have developed in this part of the world. If the central dynamic of an eating disorder is an identity struggle, then this struggle could be defined as a desire to become more *'Western'* while at the same time embracing a new found pride in being African, that is, to take pride in one's African culture, psychology, and literature. Howe (1998) describes such pride in one's African heritage as 'Afrocentrism' as opposed to Eurocentrism. Loss of an African identity or striving to rekindle a past African identity while pursuing achievement defined in Western terms may create considerable internal psychological turmoil. As Nasser (1997) puts it, the conflict over gender roles may no longer be an exclusive predicament of Western women. Eating disorders may therefore be one way in which this search for identity in black South African women is expressed.

Over and above this struggle, we may also add the challenge that Ifekwunigwe (1999) refers to as 'the dynamic construction of identities in a globalizing world'. As part of these struggles, we suggest that a previously narrowly defined role prescription for black females is making way for one that creates room for greater choice and opportunity. It is in the way in which this challenge is addressed, at least in some individuals, that eating disorder pathology may become more evident.

Black South African women have in recent years experienced a period of significant emancipation. This is well illustrated by the listing of an all black female company on the Johannesburg Stock Exchange [*WIPHOLD, Financial Sector*]. The directors of this company (black women) reflect an image that is congruent with women in Western industrialized corporate environments. The physical appearance of these executives is vividly captured in a mid-1990s advertising campaign for a leading black-orientated clothing chain [*Sales House*]. The campaign was entitled 'Power Dressing' and featured black individuals from various parts of Africa (North, East, West, Central, and South) dressed for battle. In each instance the dress was predictably tribal, with facial and body paint, beads and reeds. However, for South Africa, which was last in the sequence, *power dressing* was depicted through clearly Western, business executive, urban, sophisticated clothing worn by a male and female model. The black female model was in fact not South African, but American. The message was implicit but clear: *power dressing* in South Africa takes on a different form, a form that is different from the rest of Africa, which in turn is depicted as tribal and 'primitive'. In this instance, as certainly in others, the advertising industry was promoting the standard to which black women in South Africa should aspire. The advertisement was about more than a specific type of clothing or a particular clothing store. Instead, it was a seductive 'Western' image that reflected sociopolitical empowerment in South Africa achieved through the cultivation of a certain style. However, the issue of Western style of power dressing still coincided with traditional dressing as a symbol of ethnic pride. The struggle to balance these contradictory messages about the ideal woman may be at the center of the confused or muddled identities that many black South African women may be experiencing.

In subsequent years, empowerment has taken the form of business creation and has helped propel black women to the forefront of corporate contemporary South African society. Moreover, with a significant increase in numbers of female politicians (of all ethnic groups), both in terms of members of parliament as well as cabinet ministers, women are now occupying positions of authority and responsibility within most para-state organizations. This is in stark contrast to the height of the apartheid era when the legendary Helen Suzman was the only female member in an all-white parliament – she occupied a lone opposition seat for most of the 1970s (Harrison, 1987).

Another relevant question to examine concerns the new perception of one's body against a traditional backdrop. A recent press article entitled 'New spin on empowerment' (Philp, 1999), provides an insightful perspective. Philp's article describes the passage of a black woman from domestic servant to fitness enthusiast and spinning instructor. This woman's emancipation takes place against the background of an almost exclusively white health club in an affluent suburb in the city of Johannesburg. In response to the notion that fat is a status symbol in African culture she succinctly says, ' . . . *rubbish* . . . '. The newly emancipated black woman goes on to add that any such notion is most likely ' . . . *a chauvinist thing* . . . '. This latter sentiment appears to have particular validity for our argument. Cloete (1951) [cited by Cassidy, 1991] clearly spells out the 'glorification' of fatness that is evident among many black South African males: *'Be fat above all things. To be fat himself, to have a fat wife, to have fat children and fat cattle'*. This desire for excess is understood within the context of the association between fat, abundance, and wealth. It would appear that, at least for this fitness instructor, such associations are predominantly male (and sexist) perceptions, not necessarily shared by many black women in the present-day South Africa. For some women in South Africa, such as the fitness instructor for instance, wealth and success is associated with something other than indulgence. In fact, restraint, discipline, and self-control seem more suitable ways to demonstrate achievement. Anecdotally, the increasing numbers of black women in South Africa who join health clubs or embark on a course of dieting best illustrate this quest for accomplishment.

It is therefore less than surprising that eating disorders are increasing in the general population. Moreover, it is clinically evident that women at local clinics experience this conflict of identity. Training of health-care providers in post-apartheid South Africa has become much more sensitive to these cultural issues. However, convincing governmental health departments as well as clinicians that eating disorders are not the prerogative of the Western industrialized world might be a much harder task.

It is impossible to discuss eating disorders without highlighting the process of urbanization in South Africa that is prompting social change and identity as its basis and has an impact specifically on black females. With the abolition of apartheid, South Africa's black rural population has in large part become more urbanized. Census data from 1996 reveal that 55.4% of the population is urbanized (Central Statistical Service, 1997), although the extent of urbanization varies considerably between the nine provinces of the country. This is illustrated by figures for the two most populated provinces that account for approximately 40% of the population. In Gauteng province nearly everyone is an urban dweller (96.4%), whereas less than half the population of KwaZulu-Natal province reside in urban areas (43.5%). With increased urbanization comes a re-negotiation of the balance between rural and urban values. For instance, attempting suicide in traditional black South African society was considered taboo. In the last decade though the rate among black females has increased dramatically (Jackman, 1998). The impact of social and political change therefore seems not to be limited to the emergence of eating disorders. Despite the apparent trend toward embracing more Westernized or urban values and lifestyles, young urban women were more likely than young men to endorse traditional rural values. Interestingly, one of the cited rural values was lack of materialism (Van der Reis and Mabaso, 1995).

The extent to which there is significant conflict in terms of value systems (rural versus urban) within the emerging generation of black urban dwellers is unclear. However, we are reminded by Back (1996) that *'urban cultures are highly promiscuous in their endeavor constantly to remake and invent traditions in the present'* (p. 8). What does seem to emerge in urban South Africa though is a desire to break with past repressive practices against women, while simultaneously wrestling to identify with new found value systems that might facilitate these changes. Trying to identify these value systems may be complicated by the speed of urbanization/modernization on the one hand, and the degree to which South Africans are prepared for these changes on the other. The attraction towards the Western value system is now conflicted with a new 'liberating' trend towards Africanization, a yearning for romanticized traditional rural values. The task of assimiliating these conflicting values could indeed affect black women more acutely than any other group.

Conclusion

Which is culture bound, *eating disorders* or the *theorists* (Steiger 1993)? The South African experience may help us in this regard. At a superficial level the emergence of eating disorders in black South African women has been viewed as a by-product of 'Westernization'. The balance of evidence suggests, however, that the situation is far more complex. Urbanization, as opposed to mere proximity to white communities or to Western culture, is a critical factor, as well as the overall political transformation that took place in South Africa and resulted in a radical revision of gender roles for black women in the South African society. Thus, the shift from being disempowered to being empowered has been especially dramatic and sudden for black women in South Africa. However, empowerment has its own pressures and expectations. The potential negative consequences of these expectations could be the force behind the emergence of eating disorders (Silverstein and Perlick, 1995). Eating disorders are perhaps one of several psychosocial disturbances that may serve as a pointer to the impact the sociopolitical changes are now having on the black community. What is needed is a 'cultural understanding' of the phenomenon to enable us to orchestrate better therapeutic approaches and effectively deal with the challenges that face mental health providers in South Africa today (Swartz, 1998).

References

American Psychiatric Association Committee (1979). Report of the Committee to visit South Africa. *American Journal of Psychiatry*, **136**, 1498–506.

Back L (1996). *New Ethnicities and Urban Culture. Racisms and Multiculture in Young Lives*. London: UCL Press.

Beumont PJV, George GCW, Smart DE (1976). "Dieters" and "vomiters" and "purgers" in anorexia nervosa. *Psychological Medicine*, **6**, 617–22.

Buchan T, Gregory LD (1984). Anorexia Nervosa in a Black Zimbabwean. *British Journal of Psychiatry*, **145**, 326–30.

Choudry IY, Mumford DB (1992). A pilot study of eating disorders in Mirpur (Pakistan) using an Urdu version of the Eating Attitude Test. *International Journal of Eating Disorders*, **11**, 243–51.

Cassidy CM (1991). The Good Body: When Big is Better. *Medical Anthropology*, **13**, 181–213.

Central Statistical Service (South Africa) (1997). *Census '96. Fast Facts No. 8.*

Crago M, Shisslak CM, Estes LS (1996). Eating disturbances among American minority groups: A review. *International Journal of Eating Disorders*, **19**, 239–48.

Dolan B (1991). Cross-Cultural Aspects of Anorexia Nervosa and Bulimia: A Review. *International Journal of Eating Disorders*, **10**, 67–78.

Dolan B, Lacey H, Evans C (1990). Eating behaviors and attitudes to weight and shape in British women from three ethnic groups. *British Journal of Psychiatry*, **157**, 523–8.

Famuyiwa OO (1988). Anorexia nervosa in two Nigerians. *Acta Psychiatrica Scandinavia*, **78**, 550–4.

Gard MC, Freeman CP (1996). The dismantling of a myth: A review of eating disorders and socioeconomic status. *International Journal of Eating Disorders*, **20**, 1–12.

Garner DM, Garfinkel, PE, Schwartz D, Thompson M (1980). Cultural expectations of thinness in women. *Psychological Reports*, **47**, 483–91.

Garner DM, Olmsted MP, Bohr Y, *et al.*, (1982). The Eating Attitudes Test: psychometric features and clinical correlates. *Psychological Medicine*, **12**, 871–8.

Gordon, RA (2000). *Eating Disorders: Anatomy of a Social Epidemic* (2nd ed.). Oxford: Blackwell.

Harrison D (1987). *The White Tribe of Africa. South Africa in Perspective.* Johannesburg: Southern Book Publishers.

Howe S (1998). Afrocentrism. *Mythical Pasts and Imagined Homes.* London: Verso.

Ifekwunigwe JO (1999). *Scattered Belongings. Cultural Paradoxes of "Race", Nation and Gender.* London: Routledge.

Jackman K (1998). Culture shock taking its toll. *Saturday Star*, December 12, p. 9.

Lee S, Hsu G, Wing Y (1992). Bulimia nervosa in Hong Kong Chinese patients. *British Journal of Psychiatry*, **161**, 545–51.

Le Grange D, Telch CF, Tibbs J (1998). Eating attitudes and behaviors in 1,435 South African Caucasian and non-Caucasian college students. *American Journal of Psychiatry*, **155**, 250–4.

Nasser M (1997). *Culture and Weight Consciousness.* London: Routledge.

Nightingale EO, Lawrence R, Spurlock J, *et al.*, (1990). *Apartheid Medicine. Health and Human Rights in South Africa.* Washington, DC: AAAS Publication.

Norris D (1979). Clinical Diagnostic Criteria for Primary Anorexia Nervosa. An Analysis of 54 Consecutive Admissions. *South African Medical Journal*, 987–93.

Nwaefuna A (1981). Anorexia nervosa in a developing country. *British Journal of Psychiatry*, **138**, 270–2.

Philp R (1999). New spin on empowerment. *Sunday Times Metro*, May 2, p. 8.

Silverstein B, Perlick D (1995). *The Cost of Competence: Why Inequality Causes Depression, Eating Disorders, and Illness in Women.* New York: Oxford University Press.

Steiger H (1993). Anorexia nervosa: is it the syndrome or the theorist that is culture- and gender bound? *Transcultural Psychiatric Research Review*, **30**, 347–58.

Swartz L (1985). Anorexia nervosa as a culture-bound syndrome. *Social Science and Medicine*, **20**, 725–30.

Swartz L (1998). *Culture and Mental Health: A Southern African View*. Cape Town: Oxford University Press.

Szabo CP, Berk M, Tiou E, Allwood (1995). Eating disorders in black South African females. A series of cases. *South African Medical Journal*, **85**, 588–90.

Szabo CP, Hollands C (1997). Abnormal eating attitudes in secondary-school girls in South Africa – a preliminary study. *South African Medical Journal*, **87**, 524–30.

Szabo CP (1999). Eating attitudes among black South Africans. *American Journal of Psychiatry*, **156**, 981–2.

Thompson A (1994). Expert committee on maternal and child health and family planning in the 1990s and beyond: Recent trends and advances [World Health Organization congress, Geneva, 7–13, December 1993]. *Midwifery*, *10*, 49–50.

Van der Reis AP, Mabaso LT (1995). *Aspirations, Values and Marketing Issues Among Black Youth in Gauteng, 1995*. Research Report No. 223. Pretoria: Bureau of Market Research, University of South Africa.

Wassenaar DR, Le Grange D, Winship J, Lachenicht L (2000). The prevalence of eating disorder pathology in a cross-ethnic population of female students in South Africa. *European Eating Disorders Review*, **8**, 225–36.

Commentary I

Leslie Swartz,
Professor of Psychology, Cape Town University,
Republic of South Africa

This interesting chapter by Szabo and Le Grange poses some important challenges for us. The authors show that previously we had no information on eating disorders in black South African women, but the assumption was that such disorders were rare. We now have some very limited information (a handful of surveys and a few case reports) and it is now thought that such disorders may be less rare. They provide a number of hypotheses as to why there is this perception of change.

For purposes of discussion it may be useful to separate out two issues. The first is the question of our perceptions of the changing prevalence and presentation of eating disorders, and the second is the substantive question of the cultural precursors and implications of the disorders themselves.

With regard to the first question – that of our perceptions – we simply do not have prevalence or incidence data for the past or for the present. The few recent surveys that have been done provide very compelling suggestive evidence that eating disordered pathology may be far more common amongst some black South African women than we thought (and possibly even more common than amongst whites). As far as I am aware, though, some basic epidemiological work has yet to be done. For example, I do not think we know whether self-report instruments of disordered eating have the same predictive value of disordered behaviour as has been found elsewhere in the world. We need research which in the South African context can link disorders themselves to the methods we use to detect such disorders in the community.

The authors argue that political considerations have affected how we have viewed eating disorders. I have no difficulty with this assertion – politics always affects our work. But they need to make a much more focused argument to show the specific ways in which eating disorders in particular may have been overlooked for political reasons, when other mental disorders were not. The debates in the literature on why for racist reasons depression was once thought to be rare amongst blacks may be useful here, as a template, but will not be sufficient to answer the specifics regarding eating disorders. At a banal level, is it possible that clinicians would find it hard to entertain the possibility that excessive thinness in an impoverished community could, in some cases, be evidence of psychopathology rather than the absence of available food?

The second challenge under this heading is to understand how current political imperatives may affect our current assessment of the situation. For example, the authors' arguments about increasing liberalization in a democratic South Africa and the wider choices open to black women tend to defocus firstly from the fact that rates of violence against South African women are stupendously high, and secondly from the fact that the gap between rich and poor has increased over the past five years. A very small number of black women have become wealthy but in general black women are if anything poorer and with very limited choices. South Africa has also become the HIV/AIDS capital of the world – conservative estimates calculate that by 2008 a million South Africans will die annually of AIDS, with women being more at risk than men. These factors tend to undercut arguments about the pervasive empowerment of black South African women.

The authors make the important point that indigenous healing systems may have seen, and may continue to see, cases of eating disorders which do not come to the attention of biomedicine. Interesting research remains to be done enquiring from indigenous healers whether they do see such cases.

The final issue regarding our perceptions relates to the question of risk for eating disorders. We now know that there are reported cases of black African women who suffer from eating disorders. This overturns the idea that such disorders are 'whites only' phenomena. But we need much more work on questions of risk for disorders and the kinds of risks which may be common or different in different social strata. This issue leads us to the substantive question of the cultural basis for eating disorders.

The second major question – that of the cultural precursors and implications of eating disorders amongst black South African women – is complex. In the history of thinking about eating disorders and culture there have been many glib but superficially appealing arguments put forward. Most notable amongst these is what may be termed the 'conspiracy theory' whereby eating disorders are seen as a conspiracy by male-dominated society against women. Equally appealing but equally superficial is the 'female weakness' argument, in which women are implicitly portrayed simply as more vulnerable than men to social influence and approbation. There are many other quick and easy formulations which come and go partly according to intellectual fashion.

Against this backdrop Szabo and Le Grange set themselves the task of beginning to explain why it may be the case (given all the caveats they mention) that black South African women are at higher risk for eating disorders than they once were. They turn to concepts such as Westernisation, modernisation, Africanisation, urbanisation and globalisation as competing contenders to explain the apparent phenomenon. All these terms are extremely complex, politically loaded, and the subject of enormous debate in the social sciences in South Africa and elsewhere. The authors in their short chapter demonstrate what for me is one of the key difficulties with clinicians' trying to make sense of complex and contested social theory. Like many other commentators, they reduce complex concepts to simple definitions, and they tend to reify historical debates into easily usable entities which lack subtlety. For example, to portray 'Africanisation' as 'the process of taking pride in one's African heritage and in an African culture' is to trivialise a highly contested concept which attracts fierce debate amongst Africanists of a range of political persuasions and ideologies. This difficulty with the chapter is not unique to the work of the authors; it is endemic to much clinical work on culture and mental health.

The social sciences in South Africa have been particularly strong in critiquing glib use of concepts such as 'culture', 'community', 'race', and so on (Boonzaier and Sharp, 1988), and I have no doubt that our thinking about the cultural issues surrounding eating disorders can be enriched by such contributions. Eve Bertelsen (1998), for example, has shown how profound ideological shifts in the ruling African National Congress from what she terms a 'quasi-socialist critique' (p. 221) to late capitalist free market policy have had an impact on black identities in this country. Her analysis shows how concepts such as African pride can be and have been commoditised within the context of advertising culture – the very culture about which there has been much debate in the eating disorders literature.

There are of course many other important social theorists internationally whose work has bearing on cultural questions around eating disorders. Unless clinicians who have an interest in culture engage with social theory in an informed way, the analyses we offer will continue to seem at best glib and superficial and at worst ill-informed and dangerously naïve. For our part, in addition, we have much to offer social theorists whose understanding of psychopathology (and eating disorders in particular) is often so infused by theoretical and ideological purism that we struggle to see our patients and our patients' struggles in their analyses.

References

Bertelsen E (1998). Ads and amnesia: black advertising in the new South Africa. In Nuttall S, Coetzee C. (Eds.), *Negotiating the past: The making of memory in South Africa*. Cape Town: Oxford University Press, pp. 221–41.

Boonzaier E, Sharp J (1988) (Eds.), *South African Keywords*. Cape Town: David Philip.

Commentary 2

Finn Skårderud
Psychiatrist and Researcher, University of Oslo, Norway

The contribution made by Christopher Paul Szabo and Daniel le Grange opens the discussion for the possibility that eating disorders are something more than a 'Western contagion'.

When examining the relations between culture, the individual and eating disorders, we need to move beyond the indolence that characterised previous discussions on this subject, the indolence of simplifying the issue of eating disorders as a morbid entity caused by the proliferation of slim aesthetic ideals through Western media and advertising.

The concrete body

What is the meaning of 'culture' in what has often been refered to as 'a culture-bound syndrome'? The authors link the incidence of eating disorders among black South African women to 'politics of identity'. This is an eminent starting point. The authors describe eating pathologies as reactions to a dramatically changing culture. And I believe that we must embark on our cultural analysis on this rather broad and unspecific level: that rapid social changes in themselves represent a cultural risk. I do find Mervat Nasser's concept of eating disorders as 'culture chaos syndromes' most helpful (Nasser, 1997). From this point of departure we can become more specific and reflect on how social changes are expressed in relation to the different arenas of identity formation, such as family, the relation-ship between the generations, gender, working life, media, diet, norms and ideals for self-realisation, health and aesthetics, and so forth.

A major characteristic of eating disorders is the degree of concrete communication. The concrete presence of the human body causes it to be used as a medium for symbolic messages. In their body-symbolism, eating disorders 'mime' both problems and solutions. Eating disordered behaviour communicates loss of control, not knowing oneself, being inadequate and the experience of chaos and boundlessness.

However, behaviour is also 'a solution'. One attempts to become someone else by recreating one's body. Or else one withdraws. The symptoms are in themselves delimiting – in relation to the others, to tomorrow, to the demands and expectations.

One withdraws, shields oneself, closes up, diminishes oneself, hardens oneself, anaesthetises oneself, intoxicates oneself or seeks oblivion. The anorectic isolates himself/herself in his/her own project. The bulimic enters into a more intimate relationship to food than to others.

The open body

Rapid social changes threaten the identity and obliterate the boundaries. The human being becomes more open, for better or worse. He or she is more open to change and to new possibilities, but also severed from contexts and routines and therefore more vulnerable. 'Identity' is about distinguishing between the inside and the outside, certainty and uncertainty. If the boundaries disappear, the hold on reality will also disappear.

Where boundaries do not exist, the body in the culture turns into a boundary definer, that is a tool of communication between one's self and others – in other words 'identity'. When confronted with increasing vagueness and fragmentation, there is an increased need for explicit and over-explicit signs. The body's concrete discourse is such that profound messages about ethics and psychology are transmitted via its surface.

Body ideals transmitted through the media have been central to the 'risk culture' that leads to bodily dissatisfaction and therefore eating disorders. But it is also relevant to ask about the impact of all of this on us and the extent to which we are obedient followers of such norms. Societies undergoing transformation face a real problem with the issue of control, change from being 'internally controlled' to being more 'externally controlled'. Controlling appetites/bodies may become in this context symbolic of self-control, efficiency and even moral strength.

The polysemic body

The body text is infinitely rich in its symbolism. The anorectic body may, therefore, be a symbol of both strength and weakness, that is, a platform for contradictory messages. The term used by the philosopher Paul Ricoeur for this type of symbolic ambiguity is polysemi (Ricoeur, 1981). The symbolic meaning of a certain kind of behaviour is dependent on its cultural context. Hence eating disorders should not have the same significance in South Africa as they have for instance in Norway!

The Western body?

What of the concept 'Westernisation'? It is true that the West is in a dominant position as far as economy, media and information are concerned. However, through linking global development to Western geography, we are in danger of becoming ethnocentrically myopic about the symbolic interplay between food, body, gender and the local culture. And, moreover, how in fact can we define what we mean by the 'cultural West'? For example, Buenos Aires is far more 'Western' than Bradford in England, where the majority of the population is of Muslim Asian descent. The 'West' can be found just as much in Nairobi's middle-class suburbia as it can in Melbourne. And Paris is today a major centre of 'African' culture, particularly North and West African music.

The global African body

Do Szabo and Le Grange create a somewhat unnecessary polarisation between 'Westernisation' and 'Africanisation'? Some may think it is paradoxical that black South African women are developing both eating pathologies and a heightened African identity. Why should this constitute a paradox? The conflict is there, but is it not precisely these conflicts which are at stake? We are currently living in the midst of the boundless tensions between the local and the global, which represents the new reality.

The authors give us good insight into the significant political and social changes that South Africa has undergone in the course of only a few years. The process of rapid modernisation is taking its toll on South Africa. The essence of modernity is to break with tradition and replace it with change and turnover. Unrest is thus a cultural premise and not merely an accidental circumstance, where the only 'stable condition' is the condition of instability.

Another trait of modernity is market economy, the global cultural melting pot which causes (almost) the whole world to be exposed to too much of the same!

Within these global changes cultures are more likely to adopt a more self-reflecting attitude – both as an individual and as a group – as regards where one comes from, where one wants to go and who one wishes to be. Setting boundaries around social identities becomes important when these are threatened by the integration of culture, technology, economy and power.

Ironically, it is natural that globalisation contributes to the search by many for their own local, national or ethnic identity. So, the more global the body becomes, the more African it will be!

References

Nasser M (1997). *Culture and Weight Consciousness*. London and New York: Routledge.
Ricoeur P (1981). *Hermeneutics and the Human Sciences*. Cambridge University Press.

Chapter 3

Fat phobia in anorexia nervosa: Whose obsession is it?

Sing Lee
Director, Hong Kong Eating Disorders Center,
The Chinese University of Hong Kong, Hong Kong,
PRC, and Lecturer, Department of Social Medicine,
Harvard Medical School, Harvard, MA, USA.

Debate question
The over-reliance on the biomedical discourse of fat phobia in the anorexic phenomenon discounts the manifold metaphorical meanings of voluntary self-starvation and the variable subjectivities of the anorexic experience in different cultural settings. The debate suggests that those working in this research field could be more obsessed with fat phobia than many starving patients!

> *'It isn't just weight and menses I lose, but my youth, friends, marriage opportunity, and everything else in life.'*
>
> A Chinese patient with 15 years of anorexia nervosa

Introduction

Until recently, anorexia nervosa was largely an obscure illness outside of the developed West. However, it is now becoming a common clinical problem among young females in Hong Kong and other high-income Asian societies such as Japan, Singapore, Taiwan, and the Republic of Korea. At the same time as economic liberalisation led to the deregulation of advertising, anorexia nervosa has also appeared in major cities in low-income Asian countries such as China, India, Malaysia, the Philippines, and Indonesia (Efron, 1997; Vaidyanathan *et al.*, 1998; Waterson, 2000). This new-found pathology, commonly associated with fat rejection, has ironically appeared among young Asian women who are constitutionally slim by Western standards.

Well-founded two-stage community epidemiological surveys of eating disorders are lacking in Asian societies, but what estimates are available appear alarming. For example, several community studies in Hong Kong have indicated that 3–10%

of young females suffer from disordered eating of a degree that warrants health concern. Moreover, the trend is for that to increase since the late 1990s and to affect ever younger subjects (Lee, 1993; Lee and Lee, 1996 and 2000). At the psychiatric out-patient clinic in Hong Kong where the author worked, the number of referrals of eating disorders increased from two per year ten years ago, to one per week in mid 2000. Patients were almost exclusively female. The situation in Singapore and Beijing is extraordinarily similar (Waterson, 2000). (The situation in Beijing, China, resembles this. The author knows of only one psychiatrist, Dr Darong Zhang, who has some degree of specialisation in treating anorexia nervosa. She saw about 80 patients with eating disorders in 1990–9.)

Societal modernisation with its gendered opportunities and constraints as well as media influence have been claimed to be responsible for the phenomenon. Mass media have repeatedly informed the public of rising trends of excessive weight control behaviour, cases of women who died from untreated eating disorders, and celebrities who recovered from anorexia nervosa. Whatever the culprit for this condition may be, the fact remains that a gradient of disordered eating is demonstrable across these Asian communities, attesting to the multifaceted outcomes of 'development' (Lee and Lee, 2000). The rising rate of eating disorders will predictably pose a public health challenge to Asian countries. In most of these countries, however, patients frequently have to detour round various practitioners before they receive some sort of psychological treatment. Specialised treatment facilities and support groups are barely available.

The Chinese term for anorexia nervosa (*yan shi zheng*) is now better understood by the general public in Hong Kong to refer to a condition of pathological food refusal initiated by fat rejection and other psychosocial determinants (Lee, 1997). But anorexic food refusal is not merely a problem of fat rejection. People's experiences around eating, food and body weight are influenced by diverse factors, and the anorexic condition is remarkably amenable to disparate exegeses (MacSween, 1993; Lee, 1995; Malson, 1998; Hepworth, 1999; Nasser and Katzman, 1999). Nevertheless, recent biomedical discourse has attributed anorexic subjects' food avoidance and emaciation solely to fat concern. As conceived by the DSM-IV (Diagnostic and Statistical Manual) (American Psychiatric Association, 1994), the essential clinical features of anorexia nervosa include: (i) refusal to maintain body weight at or above a minimally normal weight for age and height; (ii) intense fear of becoming fat, even though underweight, (iii) distorted experience of body weight and shape (for example, the individual feels globally fat or believes that certain parts of the body are too fat, even when obviously underweight); and (iv) amenorrhoea in females (or loss of libido in males). The second and the closely related third criteria, pertaining to the fear of fatness, have continued to be regarded as the 'core' psychopathology of anorexia nervosa (Fairburn and Cooper, 1993). Accordingly, it is expected that the legitimate reason given for non-eating by an anorectic subject is 'I don't want to be fat; I am already too fat.' Some authorities have ostensibly recommended that the resolution of such a 'fat phobia' or 'weight phobia' is a precondition to recovery (Bruch, 1962; Crisp, 1980).

Historical studies provide us with a unique opportunity to examine accounts of women with marked weight loss that followed self-starvation that are not viewed through lens of the DSM. Although subjective accounts of such anorexic subjects and hence the meanings of food refusal were typically lacking, these studies have concluded that 'miraculous maids' and 'fasting girls' who exhibited obdurate food denial could be traced back to as early as the 5th century. However, fat phobia, the raison d'être for extreme self-starvation in contemporary biomedical discourse, was absent (Brumberg, 1988; Bynum, 1988; Parry-Jones and Parry-Jones, 1994; Bemporad, 1996; Malson, 1998; Hepworth, 1999).

As anorexia nervosa was transformed from sainthood to patienthood, the early patients were accorded a diversity of visceral labels, such as 'apepsia hysterica' (Gull, 1874), 'bradypepsia', 'anorexia humoralis', 'anorexia atonica', 'gastrodynia', 'nervous dyspepsia', 'dyspeptic neurasthenia', 'dyspepsia uterina', 'neuralgia and hyperaesthesias of the stomach', or simply 'visceral neurosis' (Skrabanek, 1983; Shorter, 1987). Lasegue, in particular, made scrupulous description of anorexic patients' 'gastralgia' (that is, indefinite and painful gastric uneasiness after food intake), and the psychic origin of their food abstinence (Vandereycken and van Deth, 1990). Similarly, Louis-Victor Marce wrote that 'these patients arrive at a delirious conviction that they cannot or ought not to eat . . . all the intellectual energy centres round the functions of the stomach . . . these unhappy patients only regain some amount of energy in order to resist attempts at alimentation' (Silverman, 1989). J. M. Charcot too, thought that anorexia nervosa was a hysterical disorder of the stomach nerves (Shorter, 1987). In the Victorian era, these visceral complaints allowed young women to express feminine ideals and moral superiority much like fat phobia does nowadays for contemporary anorexics (Brumberg, 1988).

Even in between the two world wars, most anorexic patients in London, Toronto, Rome and Berlin were noted not to exhibit fat concern (Shorter, 1994). In an erudite review written as recently as 1958, Nemiah (1958) in the US made no allusion whatsoever to fat phobia, but attributed anorexic patients' psychogenic starvation to 'the wish not to eat', 'food phobia', 'aversion to food' or 'true loss of appetite' (p. 253), respectively. He also added that 'almost all of the patients are found to have a variety of other symptoms referable to the gastrointestinal tract' (p. 256).

In this essay, an attempt is made to assemble the growing evidence that an over-reliance on the biomedical discourse of fat phobia discounts the manifold metaphorical meanings of voluntary self-starvation and the variable subjectivities of anorexic individuals. It also discusses how non-fat phobic anorexic experience problematises the biomedical claim to universalism. By moving beyond a dichotomous debate over fat phobic versus non-fat phobic anorexia nervosa, it seeks to demonstrate that a critical analysis of the current biomedical paradigm can yield insights into the ontological status, clinical diagnosis, treatment and research on this intriguing condition.

The evolution of the fat phobic discourse in anorexia nervosa

Two influential authorities have contributed to the modern conceptualisation of anorexia nervosa as revolving around fat phobia. Hilde Bruch (1973) in the US discussed at length the distinction between primary and atypical anorexia nervosa (pp. 233–6). In the former group all patients exhibited 'relentless pursuit of thinness' and 'denial of even advanced cachexia as being too thin'. The latter represented a heterogeneous group of food refusers who actually complained about the weight loss but were unable to eat because of 'various symbolic misinterpretations of the eating function'. Bruch concentrated mainly on primary anorexia nervosa, perhaps for the sake of theoretical clarity. Her prolific work in this respect had great influence on the development of the concept of fat phobic anorexia nervosa and specifically on the diagnostic criteria of the DSM-III. However, Bruch's concept of 'relentless pursuit of thinness' did not refer to the increasingly common forms of fat phobic anorexia nervosa, as recognised in the DSM system. In fact, Bruch offered various explainations for the 'non-eating' behaviour among those anorexics (1973; p. 236).

> When the condition has existed for some time patients may be reluctant to give exact information or take delight in confusing 'the experts,' and patients with genuine anorexia will deny their 'denial of thinness.' I have observed this repeatedly when patients after many years of illness finally consent to one more consultation. They will describe in a submissive, pious-sounding voice how guilty they feel for having caused their family so much unhappiness. They say they know they are too thin and they want to regain their strength so that they can lead a normal life. They will promise that they will cooperate with whatever is necessary for them to get well. Within a few days, in particular if they gain a few pounds, the whole tone will change; they are concerned about weighing 'too much,' . . . and state outright 'I am happy looking like a skeleton.' A few patients with long-standing disease were shifted from one group to another when more detailed and exact information became available.

At a later date, Bruch (1985) concluded that since the 1980s, the nature of the anorexic illness has 'changed' and lost its former psychodynamic meanings.

In the UK, Arthur Crisp (1980) propounded the view that the essence of anorexia nervosa is the presence of an elicitable 'weight phobia'. This term was clinically derived from the theory of psychobiological regression. Unlike the phenomenologically based construct of fat phobia, it refers to anorectic patients' panicky avoidance of a normal body weight and the adult responsibilities it symbolises. Specifically, Crisp postulated a subpubertal threshold weight of 38–41 kg, near which patients exhibit defiance towards further weight gain in order not to reinstate the process of maturation. Accordingly, a patient who is symptomatically non-fat phobic but nonetheless demonstrates weight phobia during an extensive psychodynamic evaluation can qualify for the diagnosis of anorexia nervosa. Likewise, a mild anorectic subject who admits to fat phobia during a brief diagnostic interviewing but has no elicitable weight phobia may not be considered anorexic. Crisp has never indicated that the DSM notion of fear of fatness is the core psychopathology of anorexia nervosa, though he appears to have been taken by cursory readers to mean so.

The non-fat phobic discourse in anorexia nervosa: Empirical evidence

I Non-fat phobia: Non-Western studies

Fat phobia has increasingly been reported as absent among some anorexic patients in Asian societies (Suematsu et al., 1985; Vaidyanathan et al., 1998; Wang, 1999). In a large systematic clinical study, Lee and co-workers (1993) analysed 70 Chinese patients who were examined by experienced psychiatrists over a period of 12 years in Hong Kong. This study revealed that although these patients bore a compelling resemblance to Western anorexics, more than half (59%) of them did not exhibit fat phobia. (As Bruch (1973) also wrote, 'Patients with atypical anorexia nervosa and those with the genuine syndrome look deceptively alike' p. 236). Instead, they used epigastric bloating, lack of hunger, or simply 'don't know' as legitimating rationales for their food refusal. Unlike fat phobic patients, many of them actually complained about their thinness. Compared on a range of sociodemographic and clinical parameters, non-fat phobic anorexic patients differed significantly from their fat phobic counterparts only by being premorbidly slimmer and by exhibiting less bulimia. Because of its mostly retrospective nature, the study did not offer any data on the subjective account and contextual validity of non-fat phobic anorexia nervosa.

In an ethnographic study of two Chinese patients with chronic anorexia nervosa in Hong Kong, Lee (1995) showed that nowhere from clinical examination, psychometric assessment and home visits were fat phobia, the desire to pursue slimness for beautification, or the control over caloric intake relevant to their symptoms, illness narratives and social suffering.

The first patient was sensitised to loss during a lonesome childhood. In the patriarchal semi-rural context where she was brought up, having a timely marriage with a financially dependable man was every young woman's must in life. Yet, when she was at the marriageable age of 24, her boyfriend suddenly left for the UK without any explanation. The marked complaints of abdominal bloating and her staunch conviction that she could not eat were interpretable as somatopsychic symptoms that authenticated her chronic grief over a long-lost love. Her food denial conveyed sadness and relinquishment, not in the least fat phobia. The gruesome emaciation, self-neglect, social disconnection and unconquerable resistance toward treatment denoted a nearly extinguished interest in life itself. But the patient did not fulfil the diagnostic criteria for major depression. Lee (1995) argued that pleading abdominal discomfort was a more persuasive metaphor of distress than fat phobia in her local world.

The second patient's loss of interest in eating symbolised a loss of voice in a world perceived to be overwhelmingly oppressive. It echoed relational malaise, and permitted her to avoid and simultaneously resist a sexually abusive father at the dining table, the major spot Chinese family members obligatorily encountered one another. This was a profound act of communication by not communicating, and a non-confrontational style of expressing intrafamilial hostility that did not clash with Confucian values on demure female behaviour. Lee (1995) pointed out that at the age of 32, the patient's adoption of a permanently child-like body and outlook was expressive of a pseudo-power that both shielded and defeated her.

Apart from clinical and ethnographic accounts, support for the validity of non-fat phobic anorexia nervosa has come from psychometrically based studies. Using the Eating Disorders Inventory (EDI), Lee and co-workers (1998) showed that although the EDI profile of fat phobic patients was similar to that of Canadian patients with restrictive anorexia nervosa (Garner, 1991), the EDI profile of non-fat phobic patients was anomalous from a biomedical perspective. They displayed significantly more 'general psychopathology' than control subjects, but exhibited even less 'specific' or fat phobic psychopathology, as measured on the 'drive for thinness' subscale. The contrasting profiles of fat phobic and non-fat phobic patients furnished some empirical support for the clinical grouping of anorexia nervosa based on fat phobia in Chinese populations. Conversely, the lack of significant difference between the two groups, on other EDI subscales that measured 'general psychopathology' might indicate that they shared ontological similarities.

2 Non-fat Phobia: Western studies

Kleinman (1987) has cautioned that psychiatric researchers are predisposed to exaggerate what is universal in mental disorders according to the DSM paradigm and to de-emphasise what is culturally particular and often locally valid. Although anorexia nervosa without fat phobia can be 'excavated' from the English language literature, they are often marginalised as being 'misleading variants' (Vandereycken, 1993) or at best labelled as 'atypical' cases (Bruch, 1973; Mitchel et al., 1986). More often than not, their anomalously low scores on the EDI and other fat-centred psychometric instruments were simply dismissed as 'deceptive tendency' or 'denial of illness' (Lee et al., 1998).

But the condition has been reported from Europe (Faltus, 1986; Vandereycken, 1993), the UK (Fosson et al., 1987; Palmer, 1993; Russell, 1995), Canada (Steiger, 1995) and the US (Mitchel, et al., 1986; Banks, 1992; Yager & Davis, 1993; Strober et al., 1999). Experienced clinicians have also clearly affirmed its existence. For example, Steiger (1993) in Canada remarked that 'anyone who works with large numbers of anorectic sufferers knows that this disorder is not uniformly about a desire to be thin. Rather, the apparent pursuit of thinness or weight phobia seen in anorexia nervosa is often explicable in terms idiosyncratic to each case'. Recent research has affirmed that gastrointestinal disturbances among anorexic patients could have a biological basis and perpetuate the illness. For example, Robinson (1989) demonstrated that delayed gastric emptying produced 'fullness' signals and satiety that in turn sustained reinforced anorexic behaviour. Unsurprisingly, a British anorexic patient who went on a diet had this to say about her poor food intake, 'as you eat less and less your stomach actually shrinks and so eventually, if you're persistent enough, what you do eat makes you feel full, so you think, "Oh, I ought to eat less", and you just go on like that . . . when I went into hospital my stomach was about the size of a walnut' (MacSween, 1993, p. 92).

Palmer (1993) in the UK criticised the primacy given to weight concern in the biomedical understanding of anorexia nervosa and warned that this could lead to a premature closure of the inquiry into the nature of the eating disorders in general. In Eastern European countries, where the medical profession was apparently under less immediate influence from the DSM system, cases of non-fat phobic anorexia nervosa were reported. At an eating disorder unit in Czechoslovakia, aversion to food, refusal to eat, extreme emaciation, amenorrhoea and the absence of a primary disease, not fat phobia, were used for the diagnosis of anorexia nervosa (Faltus, 1986). In a study of 42 female anorexic patients in Warsaw, Poland, the condition was reported to be the result of 'weight reducing diets' in only half (52%) of the patients (Kasperlik-Zaluska et al., 1981).

Cases of non-fat phobic anorexia have recently been documented in the North American literature. Anthropologist Banks (1992) described two cases from religiously conservative backgrounds in the Twin Cities of Minnesota who exhibited typical clinical and psychodynamic features of anorexia nervosa, except for fat phobia. She challenged the assumption that secular ideals of slimness represent the exclusive hermeneutic context in which anorexia nervosa should occur in contemporary American society, proposing instead a model of religious asceticism. In this way she drew attention to the importance of taking the subjective meanings of the anorexic experience into account before embarking on therapy.

Non-fat phobic discourse: Implications for diagnosis, research and treatment

Cases of anorexia nervosa without fat phobia are generally regarded as 'atypical' according to the biomedical model. Three common explanations for the absence of fat phobia in those patients are 'denial' of their fat concern, somatised depression, or the fact that they are already premorbidly thin. In the latter explanation the urge to shed fat is not an issue for those patients. This is supported by the fact that about 15% of constitutionally slim young women in Hong Kong desired to gain rather than lose weight (Lee, 1996). But this cannot account for the variability of fat experience within the same patient. A further explanation is that non-fat phobic patients come from subcultures in which fat phobia is not an effective idiom of distress. Rather, non-fat phobic rationales for non-eating provide better excuses for food refusal in those patients' local worlds. This explanation may be partly true but does not seem compatible with the finding that some 75% of young females in Hong Kong do feel distressed about being fat even though they are slim (Lee and Lee, 2000).

The influence of the 'cultural fear of fatness' on the collective experience of subjects with disordered eating is hard to deny (Lee and Lee, 2000). Yet, on various occasions Western and non-Western clinicians admitted to seeing non-fat phobic patients among the overall anorexic populations in their clinical practice. This constituted a diagnostic problem for some Hong Kong psychiatrists where their diagnosis was often made on the basis of severe weight loss, food refusal and amenorrhoea. Among the reasons given for non-eating were a certain fear of fatness that was marginally present at the onset of the illness or the patients' dislike of a round face as a proxy for fat phobia!

Prince and Tcheng-Laroche (1987) argued that a slight broadening of one out of several criteria in the DSM axis-I designations may transcend local variations in the content of psychiatric disorders, and come close to an internationally useful disease classification. From this perspective, the DSM-IV diagnosis of anorexia nervosa can be made culture-flexible by broadening its criteria '2' and '3'. Instead of the mandatory requirement for 'fat phobia' in the face of obvious underweight, a polythetic criterion would read something like this: 'the low body weight is caused by a voluntary reduction of food intake which may variously be attributed to fear of fatness, abdominal bloating/pain, loss of appetite, no hunger, fear of food, distaste for food, or don't know.' The list of rationales is expandable but not endless, since the number of common initial rationales for food refusal may be limited (Lee et al., 2001). The increased cross-cultural applicability of the criterion may be indicated by the fact that all Chinese anorexic patients in Hong Kong, as well as some early onset and the non-fat phobic anorexic patients reported elsewhere in the world, satisfy them (Bryant-Waugh and Kaminski, 1993; Lee, 1995).

In a review of the epidemiology of eating disorders, Patton and Szmukler (1995) indicated that an over-reliance on fat phobia for diagnosis may result in a failure to recognise anorexia nervosa in broader cultural settings. The Study Group on Anorexia Nervosa (1995) has recommended that 'it is important to take a wide view and not to focus specifically on identifying cases defined on narrowly based Western criteria,' and that 'there is a need to develop appropriate local instruments in the first instance.'

Western community epidemiological surveys typically yielded a very low prevalence of anorexia nervosa (Hsu, 1990). One reason can be that all the existing screening instruments, such as the Eating Disorders Inventory, are based on the construct of fat phobia. For reasons discussed above, anorexic subjects might not endorse such items as 'I am terrified of gaining weight' (#16) and 'I am preoccupied with the desire to be thinner' (#32) when they are manifestly emaciated. As a result, some of them would be screened out as 'non-cases' in surveys. A possible means to enhance the sensitivity of the Eating Disorders Inventory, is to create an additional subscale that is grounded in the different idioms used by starving subjects to explain food denial. The subscale to be devised can plausibly be termed 'disordered alimentation'. It may contain such items as 'I feel bloated after eating a small amount of food', 'I do not feel hungry any more', 'I have lost my appetite', 'food has lost its attraction for me', or 'eating threatens me with the loss of self-control' (Lee *et al.*, 1998). This approach of incorporating complementary 'etic' (culture-universal) and 'emic' (culture-specific) items of eating attitudes into an item pool for validity and reliability analysis deserves more attention from researchers (Kleinman, 1987). Research in mainstream psychiatric epidemiology has already shown that small but culturally relevant changes in the stem questions of research instruments originally based on the DSM system can result in significant changes in the detected rates of non-psychotic mental disorders (Regier *et al.*, 1998). The obvious cultural basis of eating disorders notwithstanding, this approach to epidemiological work is yet to be explored in the field.

The last few decades have seen no clear breakthrough in the treatment of anorexia nervosa. Clinically, a pragmatic array of non-specific treatments such as nursing care, nutritional education, psychotherapy, social intervention and medications of uncertain efficacy, have been used for both fat phobic and non-fat phobic patients. Psychotherapy, generally considered the single most important form of treatment, does not rely on any distinctive theoretical approach. The 'core' psychopathology of fat phobia in particular, has ironically been said to be an unimportant clinical focus that needs not be directly confronted (Garner and Garfinkel, 1981). Other therapists have noted the difficulty of altering patients' fear of fatness, and would simply ask them to 'live with it' (Hsu, 1990, p. 146). Clearly, a monothetic diagnosis of anorexia nervosa based exclusively on fat phobia is inconsequential for the selection of psychotherapy, pharmacotherapy and perhaps prognostication. By delegitimising other rationales for non-eating, it may even bar patients' subjective expressions and hinder the understanding of their psychosocial problems.

Since fatness does not define the interaction between clinicians and non-fat phobic patients, the psychological treatment of these patients may shed light on the more fundamental problems that beset anorexic patients and women generally (Nasser and Katzman, 1999). According to Katzman and Lee (1997) and other feminist scholars, the portrait of the anorexic syndrome as an 'appearance disorder' incurred by young women lost in their world of fashion and calorie restricting is a belittling stereotype. This not only camouflages women's real worries but also misses the universal power of food refusal, as in proclaiming needs for self-control in social positions of relative powerlessness (for example, Lawrence, 1984).

From this instrumentalist perspective, food refusal is a means to an end, not merely the end result of fat phobia. What is needed in treatment then is a dialogue that transcends thin media ideals to honour personal control, relational satisfaction, and political position in the family and society at large (Katzman and Lee, 1997). It is perhaps not coincidental that these factors were identified in empirical studies that asked patients to name the variables critical to successful treatment (Peters and Fallon, 1994). Cultural factors also shape the treatment and recovery process as well as the criteria of what 'successful' outcomes are. For example, based on content analysis of family therapy sessions with five Chinese anorexic patients, Ma and co-workers (2000) identified five main themes of self-starvation in contemporary Hong Kong families that are relevant to treatment, namely, self-sacrifice for family well-being, filial piety over individuation, bridging of parental conflict, expression of love or control, and camouflage of family conflicts. They noted that some of these themes were socially constructed in the local Confucian culture.

Katzman and Lee (1997) further suggested that insensitivity to power issues of the provider as well as the recipient of care could account for the treatment resistance noted in medical settings in the US as well as Hong Kong. Indeed, reviews of patients' personal accounts of their psychiatric treatment experience often indicate substantial resistance because 'the solution is definitely not to take away the one and only one thing in her life she feels she has control over. It contradicts and defeats the entire purpose of what the anorexic needs to gain in recovery – positive coping skills to feel in charge of herself and her life' (Way, 1993, p. 76). Inasmuch as the anorexic body may be valued for its being proof of self-control, Katzman and Lee recommended substituting fat phobia with 'no control phobia' in understanding the nature of the syndrome. As noted by Bruch (1973), 'control' could be an issue for both primary and atypical anorexia nervosa during psychotherapy (p. 238). Since 'letting go' of the illusory control that anorexia furnishes to its sufferers often marks eventual recovery (Way, 1993, p. 83; Hornbacher, 1999), the application of a multidimensional theory of control and control therapy (Shapiro, 1998) to anorexia nervosa (be it fat phobic or non-fat phobic) is worth exploring.

From an anthropological perspective, a polythetic approach that accommodates disparate rationales for food refusal across cultural contexts and at different time points during a patient's illness trajectory is preferred. (A polythetic diagnostic system will be incorporated into the next edition of China's national system of classification of mental disorders [Lee, 1996].) This tends to promote subjective expressions, explorations of social meanings and the use of individualised therapeutics (Lee, 1995).

The importance of assuring anorexic patients that their particular afflictions make sense was demonstrated by the finding, based on interviews of recovered patients, that their feeling 'being understood' was one of the most important factors for recovery to occur (Hsu et al., 1992).

Conclusion

From a post-modern viewpoint, biomedicine has constructed anorexia nervosa discursively (Malson, 1998; Hepworth, 1999). Like other discourses, the diagnosis of fat phobic anorexia nervosa is a manner of social practice that forms its own object (Foucault, 1972). Stated differently, the DSM does not objectively 'describe' anorexia nervosa but constructs it in the specifically fat phobic fashion. Clinical and research work based on the DSM discourse then produces empirical facts that further authenticate the fat phobic discourse in this condition. The anthropologically salient question concerning the fat phobic discourse is why the current paradigm for conceptualising self-starvation is so 'fat obsessed' and yet so routinely applied. Given the plethoric ways of discoursing anorexia nervosa, why is there a seeming complacency with such a historically, cross-culturally and experientially encapsulated motif?

One of the reasons is that the DSM discourse has become an institutionalised form of truth used by clinicians, researchers, journal editors, pharmaceutical and insurance companies for dealing with psychiatric disorders. According to its epistemological mandates, a psychiatric disorder has a pathognomonic 'core' that is rooted in some universal and presumably biological changes. In the case of depression, for example, the DSM-IV prescribes that 'depressed mood' is its core symptom even though considerable evidence indicates that the condition is mediated principally by somatic experience in nearly all cultures (Kleinman, 1987; Simon et al., 1999). But there are powerful social, economic and global forces that reinforce the DSM construction of depression even in developing countries such as China where 'depression' was, until recently, an unfamiliar cultural category (Lee, 1999). When the same DSM epistemological approach is applied to anorexia nervosa, fat phobia becomes its 'core' symptom, whereas other more universally present features are marginalised as peripheral symptoms. This positivistic symptom configuration is held to be true in all cultures, and in all patients at every stage of illness. Patients who do not fit into this constructed (and constricted) template are conveniently discarded as unreal, atypical or simply dishonest deniers.

Although fat concern has become a collective experience in the modern world (be it Western or non-Western), anorexia nervosa is far from being a phenomenologically homogeneous condition. Kleinman (1999) discussed the dialectical relationships among cultural representation ('the collective patterns of meaning that inform art, theodicy, and other cultural forms'), collective experience ('the events and social processes that help to define the lives of whole generations of people'), and subjectivity ('the somato-moral dimension where the expression of illness typically occurs') in understanding everyday local experience and global social change. When this triangular model is applied to the subject of fat phobia, cultural representation in a market-driven consumerist society that denigrates 'fat as bad' reinforces the collective experience of fat loathing among young females in modern societies. But being also powerfully moulded by 'what is most at stake' in an individual's local moral world, subjective and intersubjective experience is composite, shifting and often ambivalent. Accordingly, anorexic patients' subjectivities and embodied states at different stages of illness do not always correspond to the cultural representations of fatness and appetitive control in the global superculture. Social, moral and biological factors in the local world remodel subjective experience, as a result of which patients' attributions for non-eating are more diverse and local than the global homogenising DSM discourse would have us believe. (The neglect of subjective diversity and motivational underpinnings in the DSM schema is true not only of eating disorders but also of other diagnostic categories. See Fabrega's commentary on this chapter.) The model suggests that fat phobic versus non-fat phobic (or typical versus atypical) anorexia nervosa is not a rigid dichotomy.

In the Kuhnian sense (Kuhn, 1970), enough 'anomalies' have accumulated to call for revision, not rejection, of the objectivist fat phobia paradigm. We are in urgent need of more facilitative interpretive frameworks that honour sufferers' multiple voices by treating lived meaning as equal to reductionistic categorisation.

References

American Psychiatric Association (1994). *Diagnostic and Statistical Manual of Mental Disorders* (4th edition) (DSM-IV). Washington, DC: APA.

Banks CG (1992). "Culture" in culture-bound syndromes: the case of anorexia nervosa. *Social Science and Medicine*, **34**, 867–84.

Bemporad JR (1996). Self-starvation through the ages: reflections on the pre-history of anorexia nervosa. *International Journal of Eating Disorders*, **19**, 217–37.

Bruch H (1962). Perceptual and conceptual disturbances in anorexia nervosa. *Psychological Medicine*, **14**, 187–94.

Bruch H (1973). *Eating Disorders: Obesity, Anorexia Nervosa, and the Person Within*. New York: Basic Books.

Bruch H (1985). Four decades of eating disorders. In: *Handbook of Psychotherapy for Anorexia Nervosa and Bulimia*, edited by Garner DM, Garfinkel PE, pp. 7–18. New York: Guilford Press.

Brumberg JJ (1988). *Fasting Girls: The Emergence of Anorexia Nervosa as a Modern Disease*. Cambridge, MA: Harvard University Press.

Bryant-Waugh R, Kaminski Z (1993). Eating disorders in children: an overview. In: *Childhood onset anorexia nervosa and related eating disorders*, edited by Lask B, Bryant-Waught R, chapter 2, pp. 17–29. Hove: LEA.

Bynum CW (1988). Holy anorexia in modern Portugal. *Culture, Medicine and Psychiatry*, **12**, 239–48.

Crisp AH (1980). *Anorexia Nervosa: Let me be*. London: Plenum Press.

Efron S (1997). Eating disorders go global. *Los Angeles Times*, October 18, A1.

Fairburn CG, Cooper PJ (1993). The Eating Disorder Examination. In: *Binge Eating: Nature, Assessment and Treatment*, edited by Fairburn CG, Wilson GT, chapter 15. New York: Guilford Press.

Faltus F (1986). Anorexia nervosa in Czechoslovakia. *International Journal of Eating Disorders*, **5**, 581–5.

Fosson A, Knibbs J, Bryant-Waugh R. *et al.*, (1987). Early onset anorexia nervosa. *Archives of Disease in Childhood*, **621**, 114–18.

Foucault M (1972). *The Archaeology of Knowledge and the Discourses on Language* (trans. A Sheridan). New York: Pantheon Books.

Garner DM (1991). *Eating Disorder Inventory-2: Professional Manual*. Florida: Psychological Assessment Resources, Inc.

Garner DM, Garfinkel PE (1981). Body image in anorexia nervosa: measurement, theory and clinical implications. *International Journal Psychiatric Medicine*, **11**, 263–84.

Gull WW (1874). Anorexia nervosa (apepsia hysterica, anorexia hysterica). *Transactions of Clinical Society (London)*, **7**, 22–8.

Hepworth J (1999). *The social construction of anorexia nervosa*. London: Sage.

Hornbacher M (1999). *Wasted – A memoir of anorexia and bulimia*. London: Flamingo.

Hsu LKG (1990). *Eating Disorders*. New York: Guilford Press.

Hsu LKG, Crisp AH, Callender JS (1992). Recovery in anorexia nervosa - the patient's perspective. *International Journal of Eating Disorders*, **11**, 341–50.

Kasperlik-Zaluska A, Migdalska B, Kazubska M, Wisniewska-Wozniak T (1981). Clinical, psychiatric and endocrinological correlations in 42 cases of anorexia nervosa. *Psychiatr. Pol.* **15**, 355–63.

Katzman M, Lee S (1997). Beyond body image: The integration of feminist and transcultural theories in the understanding of self starvation. *International Journal of Eating Disorders*, **22**, 385–94.

Kleinman AM (1987). Anthropology and psychiatry: the role of culture in cross-cultural research on illness. *British Journal of Psychiatry*, **151**, 447–54.

Kleinman A (1999). Experience and its moral codes: culture, human conditions and disorder. In Peterson GB ed: *The Tanner Lectures on Human Values*, Volume 20, pp. 355–420. Salt Lake City: University of Utah Press.

Kuhn TS (1970). The Structure of Scientific Revolutions (2nd edition). *International Encyclopedia of Unified Science*, vol. 2, no. 2, pp. 17–18. Chicago: University of Chicago Press.

Lawrence M (1984). *The anorexic experience*. London: Women's Press.

Lee AM, Lee S (1996). Disordered eating and its psychosocial correlates among Chinese adolescent females in Hong Kong. *International Journal of Eating Disorders*, **20**, 177–183.

Lee S (1993). How abnormal is the desire for slimness? A survey of eating attitudes and behaviours among Chinese undergraduates in Hong Kong. *Psychological Medicine*, **23**, 437–45.

Lee S (1995) Self-starvation in contexts: towards the culturally sensitive understanding of anorexia nervosa. *Social Science and Medicine*, **41**, 25–36.

Lee S (1996). Cultures in psychiatric nosology: the CCMD-2-R and international classification of mental disorders. *Culture, Medicine & Psychiatry*, **20**, 421–72.

Lee S (1997). How lay is lay: students' perceptions of anorexia nervosa in Hong Kong. *Social Science & Medicine*, **44**, 491–502.

Lee S (1999). Diagnosis postponed: shenjing shuairuo and the transformation of psychiatry in post-Mao China. *Culture, Medicine and Psychiatry*, **23**, 349–380.

Lee S, Ho TP, Hsu LKG (1993). Fat phobic and non-fat phobic anorexia nervosa – a comparative study of 70 Chinese patients in Hong Kong. *Psychological Medicine*, **23**, 999–1017.

Lee S, Lee AM, Leung T (1998). Cross-cultural validity of the eating disorder inventory: a study of Chinese patients with eating disorder in Hong Kong. *International Journal of Eating Disorders*, **23**, 177–88.

Lee S, Lee AM (2000). Disordered eating in three communities of China: a comparative study of female high school students in Hong Kong, Shenzhen, and rural Hunan. *International Journal of Eating Disorders*, **27**, 317–27.

Lee S, Lee AM, Ngai E, Lee DTS, Wing YK (2001). Rationales for food refusal among Chinese patients with anorexia nervosa in Hong Kong. *International Journal of Eating Disorders*, **29**, 224–229.

Ma JLC, Chow MYM, Lee S, Lai K (2000). *Family meaning of self-starvation in Hong Kong – themes discerned from family treatment.* Paper presented at the International Conference on Eating Disorders, New York, May 4–7.

MacSween M (1993). *Anorexic bodies: a feminist and sociological perspective on anorexia nervosa.* London: Routledge.

Malson H (1998). *The Thin Woman.* London: Routledge.

Michel J, Pyle R, Hatsukami D, Eckert E (1986). What a typical eating disorders? *Psychosomatics*, **27**, 21–28.

Nasser M, Katzman M (1999). Eating disorders: transcultural perspectives inform prevention. In: *Preventing Eating Disorders – A Handbook of Interventions and Special Challenges*, edited by Piran N, Levine MP, Steiner-Adair C. Philadelphia: Brunner/ Mazel.

Nemiah JC (1958). Anorexia nervosa: fact and theory. *American Journal of Digestive Disease*, **3**, 249–74.

Palmer RL (1993). Weight concern should not be a necessary criterion for the eating disorders: a polemic. *International Journal of Eating Disorders*, **14**, 459–65.

Parry-Jones WL, Parry-Jones B (1994). Implications of historical evidence for the classification of eating disorders. A dimension overlooked in DSM IIIR and ICD-10. *British Journal of Psychiatry*, **165**, 281–92.

Patton GC, Szmukler GI (1995). Epidemiology of eating disorders. In: *Epidemiological Psychiatry, Baillière's Clinical Psychiatry - International Practice and Research*, edited by Jablensky, p. 309. London: Baillière Tindall.

Peters L, Fallon P (1994). The journey of recovery: Dimensions of change. In *Feminist Perspectives on Eating Disorders*, edited by Fallon P, Katzman M, Wooley S. New York: Guilford Press.

Prince R, Tcheng-Laroche F (1987). Culture-bound syndromes and international disease classifications. *Culture, Medicine and Psychiatry*, **11**, 3–19.

Regier DA, Kaelber CT, Rae DS *et al.*, (1998). Limitations of diagnostic criteria and assessment instruments for mental disorders: Implications for research and policy. *Archives of General Psychiatry*, **55**, 109–115.

Robinson PH (1989). Perceptivity and paraceptivity during measurement of gastric emptying in anorexia and bulimia nervosa. *British Journal of Psychiatry*, **154**, 400–5.

Russell GFM (1995). Anorexia nervosa through time. In *Handbook of Eating Disorders – Theory, Treatment and Research*, edited by Szmukler G, Dare C, Treasure J, pp. 5–27. Chichester: Wiley.

Shapiro DH (1998). *Control Therapy – An Integrated Approach to Psychotherapy, Health, and Healing.* New York: Wiley.

Shorter E (1987). The first great increase in anorexia nervosa. *Journal of the Society Historical*, **21**, 69–96.

Shorter E (1994). Youth and psychosomatic illness. In: *From the Mind into the Body: The Cultural Origins of Psychosomatic Symptoms*, chapter 6, pp. 149–255. New York: The Free Press.

Silverman JA (1989). Louis-Victor Marce, 1828–1864: anorexia nervosa's forgotten man. *Psychological Medicine*, **19**, 833–5.

Simon GE, VonKorff M, Piccinelli M, Fullerton C, Ormel J (1999). An international study of the relation between somatic symptoms and depression. *The New England Journal of Medicine*, **341**, 1329–35.

Skrabanek P (1983). Notes towards the history of anorexia nervosa. *Janus*, **70**, 109–28.

Steiger H (1993). Anorexia nervosa: is it the syndrome or the theorist that is culture- and gender-bound? *Transcultural Psychiatric Research Review*, **30**, 347–58.

Steiger H (1995). Review. *Transcultural Psychiatric Research Review*, 64–9.

Strober M, Freeman R, Morrell W (1999). Atypical anorexia nervosa: separation from typical cases in course and outcome in a long-term prospective study. *International Journal of Eating Disorders*, **25**, 135–42.

Study Group on Anorexia Nervosa (1995). Anorexia nervosa: Directions for future research. *International Journal of Eating Disorders*, **17**, 235–41.

Suematsu H, Ishikawa H, Kuboki T, Ito T (1985). Statistical studies on anorexia nervosa in Japan: detailed clinical data on 1,011 patients. *Psychotherapy Psychosomatics*, **43**, 96–103.

Vaidyanathan G, Rodell JA, Cleminson ME *et al.*, (1998) *College-aged south-Asian females living in India report less body dissatisfaction than comparative Caucasian Americans, but endorse higher scores on nine other EDI-2 subscales.* Session on epidemiology and cross-cultural studies, The International Conference on Eating Disorders, New York, USA, April 24–26.

Vandereycken W (1993). Misleading variants in the clinical picture of anorexia nervosa. *European Eating Disorders Review*, **1**, 183–6.

Vandereycken W, van Deth R (1990). A tribute to Lasègue's description of anorexia nervosa (1873), with completion of its English translation. *British Journal of Psychiatry*, **157**, 902–8.

Waterson L (2000). Dying to be thin. *Reader's Digest*, May, 26–32.

Yager J, Davis C (1993). Letter to Sing Lee's review of 'Transcultural aspects of eating disorders'. *Transcultural Psychiatric Research Review*, **30**, 295–6.

Wang P (1999). A clinical analysis of 10 cases of anorexia nervosa. *Chinese Journal of Psychiatry*, **32**(1), 55 [in Chinese].

Way K (1993). *Anorexia nervosa and recovery: A hunger for meaning.* New York: Harrington Park Press.

Commentary I

Roland Littlewood
Professor of Anthropology and Psychiatry,
Royal Free and UCL Medical School, London, UK

As with any other social fact, one can interpret an illness as somehow characteristic of the particular society in which it is found. Such specificity has been a continuing problem for comparative studies in psychiatry. Can those patterns recognised by medicine as 'culture-bound syndromes' be fully explained through an under-standing of one particular society? Or should these patterns be subsumed under more universal categories? Or, more modestly, should they be placed in groups whose members merely demonstrate some family resemblances to each other? Can we argue both – local specification and superordinate category – when a 'behavioural syndrome appearing in widely differing cultures takes on local meaning so completely that it appears uniquely suited to articulate important dimensions of each local culture, as though it had sprung naturally from that environment' (Good and Good, 1992, p. 257).

Whether some general category adequately subsumes a characteristic local experience is fundamental for any human science. The case of medicine is complicated by its claim to demonstrate biological reality – so that individual illnesses can be identified as instances of some natural category that exists 'out there' independently of any local interests in which it appears embedded, our own included. The question recalls cultural psychiatry's debates, less as to whether tabu or stigmatisation are categories that transcend local particularities, than as to whether sexual avoidance of close kin by non-human primates is homologous to incest prohibition or whether it is merely analogous, primate sexual 'avoidance' than being an inappropriate extrapolation from our human concerns.

Most arguments about eating disorders, however, now recognise something 'cultural' as essential in their aetiology, whether body imagery or women's social and family experience (Lee, this volume). Support for women's 'fear of fatness' as the discrete cause in Western societies comes from a diversity of theoretical approaches (Littlewood, 1995). 'Fear of fatness' has accompanied economic and public health changes associated with industrialisation: improved nutrition and a general access to food beyond physiological requirements; the development of eating as a leisure activity, with a dislocation of palativeness from nutritiousness through the development of 'cuisine' and the commodification of cooked foods; lower mortality rates but reduced fertility; an increase of women in the labour market competing against men; with a theoretical but in practice not so accessible moral equality and perhaps identity with men; and thus a different 'fit' between social role, goals, class status, child bearing and body morphology, with a de-emphasis on women's subdominant maternal and domestic roles; and with a general discomfort with generational distinctions (Giddens, 1991); and even a possibly related shift in male sexual attraction to an androgynous and 'younger' female body, perhaps as a response to feminism (Littlewood and Lipsedge, 1987; Bordo, 1993).

In contrast, relative plumpness in women in non-industrial societies, while rarer, has been said to demonstrate health and prosperity (Polhemus, 1978; Furnham and Alibhai 1983; Brown and Konner, 1987; Lee *et al.*, 1992).

As Lee (this volume) notes, there is ample evidence of a cultural shift in European societies towards a preference for a thinner, 'slimmer' female body form but no agreement as to why this has occurred or whether it is fundamental to the aetiology of eating disorders. Let us start from the biological and political context. A number of general characteristics can be identified: absolute and relative wealth, industrialisation, urbanisation, literacy and formal education, commodification of cooked food with a disjunction between taste and nutrition, lower fertility and mortality rates, later age of marriage, the absence of prescriptive marriage patterns, the recent development of nationalism (an equation of the state with language, shared history and ethnic identity), and an immediate relationship with global capitalism and its contractual and entrepreneurial values. One overarching characteristic which has attracted some attention, given the emphasis on the role of autonomy and self-expression in eating disorders, has been what may be termed 'modernisation' (Deutsch, 1991).

'Modernisation' theorists argue that there has been a historical shift, driven by technological development, in social structure and patterns of marriage: away from personal status determined by kinship or other ascribed corporate membership to more contractual and individualised roles. This in turn leads to an earlier and more complete independence of children from their parents; to greater geographical and social mobility; to less ascription of identity through caste, kinship, or gender; together with literacy, tolerance, secularisation and cultural pluralism, and with greater value placed on self-determination, achievement motivation and future orientation. Modernisation also brings decontextualisation and differentiation out of a once enmeshed social domain of nutrition, comportment, sexuality, kinship, economics, politics and religion; with the internalisation of social constraints into the embodied self (see Morris, 1991; Hall and Jarvie, 1992; Turner, 1992; Bordo, 1993).

Eating disorders, however, now no longer appear so highly specific to women of European origin (Nasser, 1986; Mumford and Whitehouse, 1988; Dolan *et al.*, 1990; Bryant Waugh and Lask, 1991; Nasser, 1997; Gordon, Lee this volume).

When an identified clinical pattern bears a close relationship to cultural expectations, as has been argued for eating disorders, there are, as we have seen, problems of definition and comparison (Lee, this volume). Increasing convergence of psychopathology may be a convergence of the local meanings of the measures. Selection of cases will be biased through any local institutionalisation of food restriction such as licensed ascetism or extended fasting (Littlewood, 1990; Ritenbaugh et al., 1993; but see Bhadrinath, 1990). But there are no studies of the perception of 'normal' and 'abnormal' self-starvation by South Asian communities. In the same way it can be difficult to distinguish an eating disorder in the West from the normative expectations of body mass among dancers, or from such 'ritualised' patterns as periodic purging before examinations in American college sororities. The preferred methodology will be one which examines the contours of the pattern, not just in putative cases, but in a wider sample from the particular culture.

Recent studies do suggest no invariant cross-cultural association between ideals of personal morphology and symptomatology. For example, young adults in North India, thinner than Asian or white Britons, would ideally like to weigh more than they do, especially the men but also the women (Schmidt and Bakshi, 1993). Thus, attempting to lose weight, the major determinant of the development of eating disorders argued by clinicians for Western populations, is absent and yet their average scores on the BITE (which assesses bulimia) are not significantly lower. Indeed both Jaipur men and women have higher BITE scores than do European men in London. Thus bulimic perceptions and actions seem not uncommon in this Indian group but again they appear distinct from a specific concern with body fatness. By contrast, in Lahore, a city with a now established 'dieting culture' and with similar average body mass indices to British Asians, a concern with body fatness does correlate with the Eating Attitudes Test (Mumford et al., 1992). Mumford and Whitehouse (1988) and Dolan et al., (1990) find higher EAT scores among Asian girls in Britain than among Europeans but again no greater concern with fatness. Whilst Asian British students do seem similar to white students in terms of weight and shape dissatisfaction (Schmidt and Bakshi, 1993), they have a higher prevalence of clinical bulimia. Taking these studies together with Lee's data suggests that 'bulimia' among South Asians may be seen as something other than just a statistical reflection of general pressures against fatness.

Whether these findings in themselves argue for personal recourse to eating disorders as a specific and instrumental mode of self-determination is uncertain. Self-starvation might simply be the most accessible way of generally expressing distress and soliciting others, particularly parents and family members, in any context where food refusal denotes illness, and where past nurturance and current solidarity are articulated through an idiom of shared food prepared and distributed by women. Whether in all societies eating restriction is particularly salient in articulating conflicts about female autonomy, in subjective identity or as an instrumental communication in the family milieu, is uncertain. However, given the Jaipur study, and similar studies of schoolgirls elsewhere in northern India which found high scores on the Eating Attitudes Test (King and Bhugra, 1989), one might consider whether something like the cultural preconditions for 'ascetic self-starvation' already hold for South Asian societies and thus provide an available model for severe food restriction quite independently of any fear of fatness, what Lee terms non-fat phobic type .

Without the sort of detailed studies on local ethnopsychologies, gender and sexuality, body symbolism and eating patterns which have developed over the last few years in the West, and in the relative absence of an anthropology of the idioms, recognition and consequences of personal distress, it would be premature to draw any definitive conclusions, but a common theme which appears is that it is through bodily denial that South Asian women can instrumentally achieve relative self-determination or resolve ambivalent demands. Following Lee's suggestion of an anthropological dimension, I would note that under the rubric of chantage masochiste (Devereux, 1970), 'strategies of everyday resistance' (Scott, 1990), or 'the power of the weak' (Littlewood and Lipsedge, 1987), such patterns, like spirit possession or dissociative states, have been argued as the women's expression of limited personal agency through which some self-determination is achieved without overtly challenging accepted norms, whether publicly or in their personal understanding (Spanos, 1989). Also, these patterns are shaped and legitimated by local religious or medical practice, framing the loss of personal agency as caused by an intruding spirit, as a disease or as a distorted perception of the body. In 'involuntary' spirit possession, individual agency is experienced as diminished; what might be seen as motivated demands on others are attributed by individuals and their associates to some external power. Whilst this may be an appropriate model for certain Western illnesses (Littlewood and Lipsedge, 1987), the diminished agency being attributed to illness or overwhelming impulse (agoraphobia, hysterical dissociation, shoplifting), eating disorders seem characterised by a sense of heightened personal agency yet a disavowal of their strategic value. And if dissociative patterns recall spirit possession, the heightened agency of eating disorders is still reduced medically to a distorted perception. In terms of practical instrumentality, the final consequences of eating disorders seem poor, those of possession states relatively good.

We cannot presume that the final common pathway of self-starvation is reached in India, Hong Kong, Britain or elsewhere by the identical antecedents, but at a high level of generality we might argue for analogous subjective and objective renunciations by women, a limited self-determination through extreme self-denial. And that it is precisely in the ambiguous shift to 'modernity', with the loss of other instrumental strategies of personal resistance and with the ubiquity of potentially unlimited consumption, that these become heightened through the medicalised emphasis on a purified and self-sufficient body as the locus of personal agency.

References

Bhadrinath BR (1990). Anorexia nervosa in adolescents of Asian extraction. *British Journal of Psychiatry*, **156**, 565–8.

Bordo S (1993). *Unbearable Weight: Feminism, Western Culture and the Body*. Berkeley: California University Press.

Brown PJ, Konner M (1987). An anthropological perspective on obesity. *Annals of the New York Academy of Sciences*, **499**, 29–46.

Bryant Waugh R, Lask B (1991). Anorexia nervosa in a group of Asian children living in Britain. *British Journal of Psychiatry*, **158**, 229–33.

Demaret A (1991). De la grossesse nerveuse à l'anorexie mentale. *Acta Psychiatrica Belgica*, **91**, 11–22.

Deutsch E (ed) (1991). *Culture and Modernity*, Cambridge, MA: Harvard University Press.

Devereux G (1970). *Essais d'Ethnopsychiatrie Generale*. Paris: Gallimard.

Dolan B, Lacey JH, Evans C (1990). Eating behaviour and attitudes to weight and shape in British women from three ethnic groups. *British Journal of Psychiatry*, **157**, 523–8.

Furnham A, Alibhai N (1983). Cross cultural differences in the perception of female body shapes. *Psychological Medicine*, **13**, 829–37.

Giddens A (1991). *Modernity and Self-Identity: Self and Society In The Late Modern Age*. Oxford: Polity.

Good B, Good M-JD (1992). The comparative study of Graeco-Islamic medicine: the integration of medical knowledge into real symbolic contexts. In *Paths to Asian Medical Knowledge*, edited by Leslie C, Young A. Berkeley: University of California Press.

Hall JA, Jarvie IC (eds) (1992). *Transition to Modernity: Essays on Power, Wealth and Belief*. Cambridge: Cambridge University Press.

King MB, Bhugra D (1989). Eating disorders: lessons from a cross cultural study. *Psychological Medicine*, **19**, 955–8.

Lee S, Hsu LKG, Wing YK (1992). Bulimia nervosa in Hong Kong Chinese patients. *British Journal of Psychiatry*, **161**, 545–51.

Littlewood R (1990). From categories to contexts: A decade of the 'new cross cultural psychiatry'. *British Journal of Psychiatry*, **156**, 308–27.

Littlewood R (1995). Psychopathology and personal agency: modernity, culture change and eating disorders in South Asian societies. *British Journal of Medical Psychology*, **68**, 45–63.

Littlewood R, Lipsedge M (1987). The butterfly and the serpent: culture, psychopathology and biomedicine. *Culture, Medicine and Psychiatry*, **11**, 289–335.

MacCrae DG (1975). The body and social metaphor. In: *The Body as a Medium of Expression*, edited by Polhemus T. London: Allen Lane.

Morris B (1991). *Western Conceptions of the Individual*. Oxford: Berg.

Mumford DB, Whitehouse AM (1988). Increased prevalence of bulimia nervosa among Asian schoolgirls. *British Medical Journal*, **297**, ii, 718.

Mumford DB, Whitehouse AM, Platts M (1991). Sociocultural correlates of eating disorders among Asian schoolgirls in Bradford. *British Journal of Psychiatry*, **158**, 222–8.

Mumford DB, Whitehouse AM, Choudry IY (1992). Survey of eating disorders in English medium schools in Lahore, Pakistan. *International Journal of Eating Disorders*, **11**, 173–84.

Nasser M (1997). *Culture and weight consciousness*. London: Routledge.

Nasser M (1986). Comparative study of the prevalence of abnormal eating attitudes among Arab female students in both London and Cairo Universities. *Psychological Medicine*, **16**, 621–25.

Polhemus T (1978). Preface. In: *Social Aspects of the Human Body*, edited by T Polhemus. Harmondsworth: Penguin.

Ritenbaugh C, Weiss M, Parron D *et al.*, (1993). Eating disorders. In: *Revised Cultural Proposals For DSM IV*: edited by Mezzich JE, Kleinman A, Fabrega H *et al.*, Submitted to the DSM IV Task Force by the Steering Committee, NIMH Sponsored Group on Culture and Diagnosis, ms.

Russell GFM (1990). Metamorphose de l'anorexie nerveuse et implications pour la prevention des troubles du comportement alimentaire. In *Les Nouvelles Addictions*, Venisse J L. Paris: Masson.

Schmidt U, Bakshi N (1993). Personal communication.

Scott JC (1990). *Domination and the Arts of Resistance: Hidden Transcripts*. New Haven: Yale University Press.

Spanos N (1989). Hypnosis, demonic possession, and multiple personality: strategic enactments and disavowals of responsibility for actions. In: *Altered States of Consciousness and Mental Health*, edited by Ward C. New York: Sage.

Turner B (1992). *Regulating Bodies: Essays in Medical Sociology*. London: Routledge.

Commentary 2

Horacio Fabrega, Jr
Professor of Psychiatry and Anthropology,
University of Pittsburgh, Pittsburg, PA, USA

Professor Sing Lee has been involved in a continuous line of research on anorexia nervosa for well over five years. The current article constitutes a clear, informative, and penetrating summary of his arguments regarding the character of anorexia nervosa. Professor Lee's initial intuition about the cultural characteristics of this disorder in Chinese communities has been supported in a series of empirical studies. These and critical reviews of literature have progressively strengthened his reservations about the way anorexia nervosa has been described and how it is conceptualized in the international psychiatric community.

I support Professor Lee's intuition and position regarding the character of anorexia nervosa. Furthermore, I believe assumptions implicit in his argument, and which he confines to anorexia nervosa, need to be made more explicit. Moreover, they also need to be generalized. In my estimation, an argument about the 'differentness' of anorexia nervosa in China is but part of an argument about the cultural character of all psychiatric disorders (Fabrega, 2000). The argument underscores and brings to light the problems attending the internationalist enterprise regarding psychiatric diagnosis and classification. In what follows I present a sketch of why and how Professor's Lee's intuition, argument, and empirical validation regarding anorexia nervosa constitute a stepping stone towards an exposition about the special character of psychiatric disorders and urge one to examine and clarify their epistemology.

The general term that I use to cover the domain of interest of psychiatry is psychopathology. I consider the problems it describes as human universals. Analysis of knowledge in evolutionary biology and psychology as well as primatology suggests that psychopathology has a phylogenetic basis (Fabrega, in press). Psychiatry is a modern medical discipline that has as its concern a distinctive class of sickness problems. Examination of great traditions of medicine about which there is significant information (for example, India, China, Islamic) reveals the presence of a philosophy of disease or sickness that takes into account disturbances of body as well as of behavior, broadly conceived. This encompasses what among Western researchers is ethnocentrically referred to as 'mind and body'.

Interpreters of the 'Great' (non-Western) medical traditions have had no difficulty in 'finding' contemporary psychiatric disorders represented in ancient classics of medicine (but, interestingly, have as of yet found no clear cut references to disorders suggesting a 'match' with anorexia nervosa). These medical classics 'embody' a time-refined (that is, culturally evolved) wisdom about the integrated, holistic character of disease and sickness that should not be overlooked. Body and mind as well as basic cultural, existential assumptions about person and society are represented in the delineation of medical problems and sickness pictures of Great medical traditions. Because of this, there are intellectual quandaries in equating ancient culturally realized 'disorders' (that is, sickness pictures) with modern ones as stipulated in biomedicine. Our focus presently is purely on psychopathology, a form of sickness that as psychiatric disorder is very much bound to the history of modern European societies and to European medicine. A mix of factors pertaining to political economy and scientific development (a contested problem area in academic discourse) played an important role in bringing into prominence what later evolved into the discipline of psychiatry.

Examination of material on the history of Western psychiatry discloses that right from the beginning the 'mental' or 'psychic' sphere was singled out prominently as constituting an important locus of the set of problems that were of major concern to society and that were entrusted to and became the focus of the burgeoning profession. Of course, this by no means excluded general physiological manifestations as well. This is a chapter in the story of psychiatry that is beyond the scope of this commentary. The important point is that the sphere of human psychology, involving parameters such as thinking, feeling, world images, and the nature of personhood and personal identity, constitutes an integral part of the genealogy and architecture of the sickness problems that psychiatry seems destined to uphold in its theory and practice. Of course, from a general point of view, a society's social and behavioral ecology has to be accorded a central place in explaining clinical pictures of psychiatric disorders along with features of human biology. However, so does human psychology, not only for historical reasons but also for ontological and epistemological ones as well, as I shall elaborate upon in what follows.

Medical disciplines are cultural, historically contingent products. The medical disciplines or specialties that define the institution of medicine today are paradigmatic examples of this truism. Human psychology has as legitimate a claim to be considered as a criterion of a medical discipline's central area of concern and expertise as does any other criterion, such as causal agent, body location of pathology, technical means of treatment, or genes. This, of course, is a generalization consistent with the great non-Western medical traditions, as mentioned earlier: their disorders or sickness conditions reflected their construction of human psychology (along with many other things, of course). In short, human psychology plays a central role in all of the considerations that beg a clinically useful and valid organization of medicine or sphere of expertise of a discipline like psychiatry within it.

In the rest of modern, contemporary, Western medicine, human psychology has been excluded since definitions of disease make of the latter a mechanical, impersonal object or 'thing' with a life of its own that invades or takes root in an allegedly objective body. However, with respect to psychiatry and psycho-pathology, characteristics of human psychology play a determinate role in their essential features. This touches on an important, largely implicit assumption in Professor Lee's arguments about anorexia nervosa. This is that the psychological representation of alimentation is of central importance in the definition of anorexia nervosa as a variety of psychopathology. However, an argument as to whether or not fat phobia should constitute a criterion of definition makes no sense and comes close to 'nonsense'. If a system of classification purports to be universal, then any one specific way in which a deregulation of alimentation is represented psychologically and behaviorally is of no avail. Precisely how the alimentation mechanism/adaptation breaks down, in other words, how it is configured and enacted from a meaning centered point of view, has to be left open and free to vary in relation to local cultural conventions. Professor Lee's chapter and his previous articles, particularly those linking anorexia nervosa to other cultural themes of importance (for example, feminist issues), establish convincingly the importance of cultural variability in the way human psychology is represented in anorexia nervosa.

In short, a people's psychology has to be considered in a definition of anorexia nervosa. Furthermore, I would claim that any disorder that purports to 'be psychiatric', that 'belongs' within the territory and, indeed, socially mandated sphere of influence of psychiatry, has to have significant roots in a human psychology that allows for cultural variability. This is the case because a fundamental characteristic of psychopathology generally and psychiatric disorders more specifically is the domain of personal experience, social behavior, and associated alterations of bodily function. How a people's psychology is represented in the system of psychiatric disorders is a critical question that allows many valid answers. However, one of the factors that have probity and validity, it seems to me, is that of cognitive structures or models. By the latter I mean to single out the role that the cultural sphere plays in human psychology, making it a cultural psychology. Cognitive structures and models, the internalized conventions about mental representation that produce the cultural picture that the individual carries about the world, influence the configuration and enactment of sickness or disease as well as its 'real', objective parameters; for example, as a cause, (mental) 'organ' of pathology, manifestation, aspect of natural history, or response to treatment.

I believe that it is precisely in this area that resides the special message or meaning of Professor Lee's present summary chapter on anorexia nervosa. In it he reviews knowledge that makes it difficult to refute an argument to the effect that how (culturally specific) ideas, world views, sense of personal identity, notion of sickness, perspectives, perceptions, and orientations (that is, cognitive structures or models) are 'played out' in cases of anorexia nervosa is of less importance than the fact that they do 'play' a central and significant role.

It is generally regarded that anorexia nervosa constitutes prima facie evidence that psychiatric disorders are culture bound. I do not think this is 'wrong', merely that it 'misses the point' or does not go far enough. In anorexia nervosa, one observes a sickness picture or disease (considered in its general meaning) of great antiquity. In fact, I believe that it is universal and anchored in the architecture of the brain and in psychological adaptations or algorithms that are a product of human biological evolution. The emergence of language, cognition, and culture during human biological evolution ensured that the symbolic dimension of adaptation, the incorporation of meanings into the equation of living, reproducing, and surviving, would of necessity play a role not only in why and how things were fitted in the economy and social ecology of experience, action, and behavior, generally, but also in the way any of the several disorders or disturbances pertaining to these particular realms of adaptation were played out.

Pursuing this evolutionary theme further is not appropriate here. Suffice it say that alimentation is an essential feature of living forms and that in humans it 'has to have' a cognitive structure, model, or component, as does virtually any other psychological adaptation that orchestrates how a behavior complex is configured and played out. I would be surprised if unusual, culturally deviant patterns of alimentation (for example, over-eating, under-eating, non-eating, deviant eating preferences) were not features of behavior regularly encountered in all societies and if disorders of the regulation of the alimentation adaptive complex (or mechanism, adaptation) did not take place such as to occasion social, familial as well as medical concern in any society as a matter of course.

If one holds that adaptive human behavior has a cognitive dimension, then it follows that maladaptive behaviors will also; and furthermore, if alimentation constitutes a fundamental adaptive behavior pattern, then it follows that it is vulnerable to abuse, un-regulation, malfunction, aberration, or dilapidation. These generalizations, in my estimation, hold for all adaptive behavior patterns and for disorders or disturbances that are the product of perturbations of the psychological mechanisms underlying a behavior pattern or routine.

In my estimation Professor Lee's chapter illustrates with respect to one corner of the domain of psychopathology a fundamental tenet regarding psychiatric taxonomy and nosology generally. This is that while psychiatric disorders have a claim to be considered universal medical categories, as exponents of the inter-nationalist diagnostic enterprise and agenda contend, the disorders have to be defined in such a way that they bring into clear focus not only the reality of cultural meaning systems but of their differences across societies having distinct histories and cultures. In stipulating a pan-cultural, universal validity about the character of psychiatric disorders, a validity the exact outlines of which need to be developed further, to be sure, it becomes necessary that the disorders also be accorded a measure of cultural relativity. This is the lesson taught by an analysis of the biological and cultural evolution of *Homo sapiens*, generally, that of psychopathology and psychiatry, more specifically, and to complete the circle, it is the central implication of Professor Lee's chapter that is worth appreciating. I would claim that any system of psychiatric classification as well as psychiatric taxonomy and nosology that purports to be general if not universal is required to include a human cultural psychology dimension.

The natural, biological variability inherent in psychopathology requires that cultural meaning systems be accorded a central importance. Professor Lee's 'campaign' about anorexia nervosa, in other words, applies to other disorders such as psychosis, depression, anxiety, somatization, personality, developmental, and the like. Central parameters of all of the major psychiatric disorders, for example, aspects of cause, manifestation, diagnosis, course, and response to treatment, require not only a consideration of human psychology per se but also of human cultural psychologies which, in turn, entail cultural differences. Stated baldly, the biological and cultural evolution of psychopathology, the history of psychiatry, and the ontology and epistemology of psychopathology all point to the logical necessity of including human cultural psychology as a central criterion of the science of psychiatric taxonomy and systems of psychiatric diagnosis.

Given the cultural variability attending how human psychologies are configured, in such areas as world views, general attitudes and values, conceptions of personhood, and ways of thinking and feeling, it follows logically that a universalist view of psychiatric classification entails that a provision be made for cultural differences in their basic morphology and design.

References

Fabrega H Jr (2000). Culture, spirituality, and psychiatry. *Current Opinion in Psychiatry*, **13**, 525–30.

Fabrega H Jr (in press). *The origins of psychopathology: The phylogenetic and cultural bases of mental illness*. Piscataway, NJ: Rutgers University Press.

Chapter 4

Eating disorders: Integrating nature and nurture through the study of twins

Cynthia M. Bulik
Associate Professor of Psychiatry, Virginia
Commonwealth University, Richmond, VA, USA

Debate question
How do we unravel the complex relationship between genetic and environ-mental forces that place an individual at risk for developing eating disorders? Furthermore, how do we conceptualize 'environment', which can refer to concepts as diverse as an isolated event in an individual's life to the culture in which she is reared.

I Introduction

How do we unravel the complex relationship between genetic and environmental forces that place an individual at risk for developing eating disorders? Furthermore, how do we conceptualize 'environment', which can refer to concepts as diverse as an isolated event in an individual's life to the culture in which she is reared? Twin studies and twin studies over time and across cultures can help us untangle these questions; however, twin studies on eating disorders are only in their infancy.

After reviewing the basic principles of genetic epidemiology, a case vignette will be presented to illustrate, at the level of the individual, how complex genetic and environmental forces could conceivably contribute to the development of anorexia nervosa. The chapter will then progress from the individual as the unit of analysis to the population, where data supporting the role of both genetics and environment in the etiology of eating disorders will be critically reviewed. In conclusion, the chapter will challenge eating disorders researchers to move beyond the nature/nurture debate to begin to ask the more precise questions of which genes and which environments contribute to eating disorders and how to address how these specific forces interact with both cultural and developmental forces to culminate in these debilitating illnesses.

2 Twin studies

The scientific study of twins is an important step in understanding complex disorders (Cederlof *et al.*, 1982; Martin *et al.*, 1997). Twin studies have provided valuable insight into the contribution of genes and environment to such disorders as schizophrenia (Kendler, 1983, for a review), autism (Folstein and Rutter, 1977; Cook, 1998), depression (Kendler *et al.*, 1993a; Kendler *et al.*, 1993b; Sullivan *et al.*, 2000) and to personality traits as well (Loehlin and Nichols, 1976, Plomin and Daniels, 1987; Eaves *et al.*, 1989).

Twinning

Monozygotic (MZ) or identical twinning occurs at some stage in the first two weeks after the first mitosis when the zygote separates and yields two genetically identical embryos. Therefore, any differences between MZ twins, who for most intents and purposes share all of their genes, provides strong evidence for the role of environment (Plomin *et al.*, 1994, pp. 171–2). Dizygotic (DZ) twinning results from the fertilization of two ova by different spermatozoa. DZ twins are no more similar genetically than non-twin siblings. They share, on average, half of their genes. Thus, differences between DZ twins can result from genetic and/or environmental effects. The goal of the classical twin study is to use the similarities and differences between MZ and DZ twin pairs to identify and delineate genetic and environmental causes for a particular trait.

There are many ways to analyze twin data. The essence of most analytic approaches is to compare the similarity of MZ twin pairs with the similarity of DZ twin pairs for the trait under study. A common measure of similarity used for these analyses is the correlation coefficient (r).

Genes and environment

Additive genetic effects (abbreviation 'A')

Although a number of different types of genetic influences can be studied in theory, for psychiatric disorders and individual traits or behaviors, we are usually concerned with complex traits that arise from the cumulative impact of many individual genes each of small effect. This is called additive genetic effects (A). The presence of A is inferred when the correlation between MZ twins is greater than the correlation between DZ twins. The heritability of a given trait is reflected in A and is specific to a given population at a given point in time. Heritability estimates can vary across cultures and they can vary within a culture across time.

Common environmental effects (abbreviation 'C').

Common environmental effects result from etiological influences to which both members of a twin pair are exposed regardless of zygosity. Thus, common environmental effects contribute equally to the correlation between MZ pairs and the correlation between DZ pairs. Examples of common environmental effects include the social class or religious preference of the family of origin, general parenting style, or the global culture in which one is raised.

Unique environmental effects (abbreviation 'E')

The second type of environmental effect results from etiological influences to which one member of a twin pair is exposed but not the other. Unique environmental factors serve to increase the difference between members of a twin pair. Examples include unique aspects of the relationship between parent and child, one twin suffering from head trauma, or one twin being exposed to a group of peers who use drugs.

Equal environment assumption (EEA)

One of the key assumptions of the twin study is that of equal environments. The EEA states that MZ and DZ twins are equally correlated for their exposure to environmental influences that are of etiologic relevance to the trait under study (Plomin *et al.*, 1994). If the EEA is incorrect, then the greater correlation between MZ twins in comparison to DZ twins could actually be due to environmental, not genetic factors. A violation of the EEA could lead to an overestimation of genetic effects. The majority of studies that have tested the EEA for psychiatric disorders (see Kendler and Gardner, 1998, for a review) have found little or no evidence for violations of the assumption.

3 Case vignette: The story of 'Autumn and April'

The following case vignette of a pair of MZ twins will now be used to illustrate the principles outlined above and to explore how, on an individual level, genes and environmental factors could potentially contribute to the liability to anorexia nervosa.

Autumn and April were watching the World Gymnastics Championships on TV on a Saturday afternoon when their mother returned home from her aerobics class. Autumn and April were 12-year-old monozygotic twins. They were both excellent students and well-behaved children. Their mother was a perfectionistic and high-strung woman who was very concerned about her own weight and appearance. Their father was a self-proclaimed 'workaholic' who also hated fat and claimed that fat people were just lazy. April had been playing soccer since she was 6 and was a bit of a tomboy. Autumn had not participated in organized sports, but rather focused on playing the flute. Autumn had recently gained some weight and was showing signs of entering puberty. Children at school were teasing her about her weight gain and developing body. She was hurt by their comments, but wasn't sure what to do. Her mother had also recently told her that she needed to be careful or she was going to 'balloon out'. Whenever Autumn ate something like pizza, her father would say 'Are you sure you want to eat that dear?'

Autumn admired the gymnasts' bodies. They were incredibly lean and toned. She imagined they never got teased about their weight. April thought they looked sickly. Autumn decided to start taking gymnastics lessons. Her mother happily drove her to the gym the next day to sign up and she began training in earnest. Autumn enjoyed the gym – especially what the training did to her body. She became very dedicated to the sport and began working out daily. In addition, she cut out fatty foods from her diet altogether and lost a significant amount of weight. Her coaches praised her disciplined training and eating. Even though she had become quite thin, she still thought she needed to lose weight. At the age of 14, she had still not started menstruating. At first, she had done very well in competitions. As her weight decreased, she started to be more fatigued and not have the stamina to complete the grueling routines. After suffering from two stress fractures, her pediatrician diagnosed Autumn with anorexia nervosa.

Unravelling the role of genes and environment in Autumn's life

There are several levels of hypotheses that can be plausibly forwarded about the role of genes and environment in the development of anorexia nervosa in Autumn.

We will start the analysis of Autumn's case with the most basic and simplistic hypotheses which attribute the emergence of anorexia nervosa to unilateral effects of either genes or environment.

Autumn's anorexia was entirely due to genetic effects

As Autumn and April were MZ twins, they shared the same genetic liability for anorexia nervosa. Subclinical traits of anorexia nervosa were observable in their mother, fat phobia in their father, and indeed, a closer look at her family history revealed a maternal aunt who displayed anorexic-like behaviors in her youth. It is of particular interest that even though Autumn and April are functionally genetically identical, that only one of them developed anorexia nervosa (that is, they are discordant). Of course it is possible that April will develop anorexia nervosa later in life and they will then become concordant for the disorder, but discordant for the age of onset. However, if they remain discordant, then a purely genetic hypothesis to explain the emergence of anorexia nervosa in Autumn is unlikely.

Autumn's anorexia was entirely due to common environmental factors

From this perspective, there were environmental factors that were shared by both Autumn and April that caused Autumn to develop anorexia nervosa. If common environment is the key contributor, the genotype and unique environmental factors would be seen as less important than environmental effects that were shared by both twins. For example, this hypothesis would suggest that living in an upper middle class neighborhood where substantial attention was placed on material wealth and physical appearance could have increased her liability to anorexia nervosa. Given that April and Autumn were exposed to the same common environments, from this perspective, April would have to be considered to be at equal risk. Thus, like the purely genetic hypothesis, the common environment alone hypothesis is also unlikely to be true.

Autumn's anorexia was entirely due to unique environmental factors

From this perspective, Autumn's anorexia nervosa was caused by environmental events that she alone experienced that were not shared by April. In this example, the teasing at school (if we consider it to be an environmental variable) could have been one such environmental factor. The taunting could have been the driving force that led her to begin to diet and start gymnastics. The second unique environmental factor that could be viewed as causal is exposure to a sport such as gymnastics which overemphasizes thinness and reinforces a culture of dieting and unhealthy weight loss practices. This perspective states that unique environmental events are the primary contributors to liability to anorexia nervosa.

Critique of the above interpretations

Clearly, each of these perspectives is simplistic, extreme, and probably false. Anorexia and bulimia nervosa are considered to be 'complex disorders'. Such disorders are likely to be caused by a number of genes and/or environmental factors of relatively small effect. The inheritance of a critical combination of predisposing genes does not guarantee the expression of the phenotype (that is, incomplete penetrance). The expression of the trait remains a probabilistic event. Siblings, even monozygotic twins of individuals with eating disorders, may remain unaffected.

The environment-only perspectives are equally improbable. If they were true, then all gymnasts would be at risk for the development of eating disorders, yet countless young people participate in the sport without developing anorexia nervosa or bulimia nervosa. The basic environmental perspectives are unable to account for the scores of individuals who are exposed to presumably 'anorexogenic' environments who remain symptom-free.

What are the other factors in Autumn's story that suggest more complicated and interactive contributions of genes and environment and how could they have contributed to her development of the disorder? There are many ways in which genes and environments can interact to influence liability. An important first step, but one that can be quite complicated, is to determine to what extent seemingly environmental variables may actually be under genetic control.

Is it environmental or might it be under genetic control?

Several studies of eating disorders have suggested that weight and appearance preoccupation is an environmental risk factor for dieting which is often the first step in the onset of anorexia nervosa (Attie and Brooks-Gunn, 1989; Leon *et al.*, 1993; Graber *et al.*, 1994). If we trace the developmental progression of Autumn's anorexia nervosa, we see that she and her sister were both exposed to their parents' preoccupation with weight, shape, and appearance. Traditionally, this type of preoccupation in the family has been considered to be an influential environmental variable. Recent twin studies suggest that not only are eating disorders under genetic control, but traits that are believed to be related to eating disorders such as drive for thinness also show substantial genetic effects (Holland *et al.*, 1988; Rutherford *et al.*, 1993; Wade *et al.*, 1998; Klump *et al.*, 2000). Thus to view the maternal drive for thinness as a purely environmental variable would overlook the genetic contribution to the familiality of this trait.

Tracing the developmental progression of her disorder, as Autumn gained a few pre-pubertal pounds she started to be teased at school. To what extent can teasing be viewed as an environmental variable? First, teasing would be considered to be a unique environmental variable, because this experience was not shared by her twin sister. In order to fully understand the impact of unique environmental events, one must also take into consideration characteristics (some of which may be under genetic control) of the individual who experiences them. The comments hurt Autumn's feelings. She was, perhaps, constitutionally sensitive to such environmental insults. Other children may have been able to ignore the comments or even retaliate without developing feelings of being hurt. The factors that made Autumn sensitive to the environment may be genetically mediated such as interpersonal sensitivity or low self-esteem. This process is called genetic control of sensitivity to the environment (Kendler and Eaves, 1986).

Working with eating disorders one often hears of salient trigger experiences – being teased, being the recipient of a cat call, having one's weight criticized. It is imperative to ask whether individuals with eating disorders are actually exposed to such experiences more often or whether they are perhaps more sensitive to such comments than others who are not genetically predisposed?

Thus, for many of these variables, which on the surface appear to be environmental in origin, one must allow for the possibility of their being influenced, at least in part, by genes.

Additive effects of genes and environment

The effect of genes and environment may also be additive. In the case of Autumn and April, Autumn not only possessed the predisposing genotype, but was also exposed to the high risk environment. This cumulative exposure raised her above the liability threshold for the development of anorexia nervosa. In contrast, April, who had the same genotype, did not experience the additional effect of the gymnastics environment and therefore remained below the critical threshold.

Gene × environment correlation

Another way in which genes and environment can interact is referred to as gene × environment correlation. This effect focuses on those genetically determined aspects of the individual that influence their selection of environments. In Autumn's case, a trait such as drive for thinness, which has shown to be moderately heritable (Holland *et al.*, 1988; Rutherford *et al.*, 1993; Wade *et al.*, 1998; Klump *et al.*, 2000), may have propelled her to choose an environment such as gymnastics. An individual's genotype may strongly influence what type of environment to which she chooses to be exposed. In this case, April had clearly already made an early choice of an environment that was associated with high energy output and successful weight control. On the surface it may have appeared that the twins were discordant for choice of sport; however, April's early decision to pursue soccer may have placed her on a different developmental trajectory. Because she was already involved with athletics, she may have avoided the pre-pubertal weight gain, taunting, and ultimate choice of gymnastics that her sister encountered.

Gene × environment interaction

An unresolved question in the field of eating disorders is why, given near universal exposure to the collective cultural drive for thinness, do only a small percentage of individuals develop eating disorders whereas others seem resistant to the societal pressures? In the case of gene × environment interactions, the environment can act as a 'releaser' for a genetic predisposition. In this case, exposure to a 'high-risk' environment poses a greater risk to an individual with the predisposing genotype. Likewise, an individual at genetic risk may not express the trait unless or until they are exposed to the high-risk environment. In this model, the existence of an interaction increases liability beyond the simple additive effect of genes and environment. Had Autumn gone to the gym the next day only to find that they were booked up for the season and never gotten around to signing up the next year, even though she carried the susceptibility genes, in the absence of the releasing environment and its interaction with her genotype, she may never have developed the disorder. This particular mechanism can explain why so many young women diet, but for only a few does dieting become pathological. In addition, this can explain the rapid increase of eating disorders in cultures undergoing rapid Westernization (see below).

The role of culture

So far, we have considered environmental variables that vary within a given culture. What would be likely to happen to Autumn and April and the expression of their underlying genetic predisposition to anorexia nervosa if we include another environmental variable in the equation – namely the culture in which they are reared? For the sake of argument, let us say that our identical twins were separated at birth. Autumn remained in the United States and developed anorexia nervosa much as we described above. April was adopted into a family who lived on a remote Pacific Island where there was no television, no teen magazines that emphasized thinness, and most importantly, the people were robust and viewed body size as a symbol of *mana* or good fortune. During her development, April never thought twice about her body size. She ate well, developed normally, and remained at a healthy weight. When she reached the age of 16, something momentous took place on her island. Satellite television became widely available. Soon, she was watching Western television shows and admiring all of the thin beauties as portrayed on those programs. She began doubting her looks and wondering how she could change her body to look more like the girls on TV. She went on her first diet and found that she could excel at food restriction. She was not alone. Other young girls on the island also started experimenting with dieting. Indeed, some of them went on to develop eating disorders; however, April was the first incident case.

Given that the incidence of eating disorders increases sharply in countries that undergo rapid Westernization, these effects cannot be due to genes alone as it takes generations and generations for genetic effects to emerge in a population. Western cultures do not export genes; however, they do export permissive environmental factors that enable the expression of latent genetic traits that have been present all along, but not expressed.

What is inherited?

Even once we have determined that anorexia nervosa and bulimia nervosa run in families, we do not yet know precisely what is inherited. Although it remains a possibility that the disorders (that is, anorexia nervosa and bulimia nervosa) are inherited directly, there may also be more fundamental behavioral, biological, or temperamental traits (that is, endophenotypes) that are the actual features that are passed down in families. In the case of anorexia nervosa, traits such as drive for thinness, perfectionism, persistence, and harm avoidance have been posited as possible predisposing phenotypes. For bulimia nervosa, appetite, affective dysregulation, and novelty seeking are traits under consideration. These more fundamental traits may themselves increase the risk of developing anorexia and bulimia nervosa.

Protective factors?

Even if an individual has the critical mass of susceptibility genes as well as exposure to high-risk environments, there may be other genetic or environmental factors that play a protective role against the expression of the phenotype. In Autumn's case, a gymnastics coach who emphasized the positive aspects of exercise and discouraged dieting and unhealthy weight loss practices could have altered the developmental trajectory of her eating disorder. Alternatively, high self-esteem could have led Autumn to question the emphasis of her sport on thinness and allowed her to recognize her accomplishments regardless of her weight. Likewise, April's participation in a sport that emphasized strength and speed rather than thinness may have protected her from following the route of her sister.

Heterogeneity

Although dissecting the environmental and genetic sources of liability in an individual case can be illustrative, our hypotheses about etiology remain merely speculative. Clinical details can be readily molded to fit a favored theory. Like the blind men and the elephant, the geneticist and the sociologist might attach relevance to different aspects of the case. Even if we were able to determine with certainty the nature and magnitude of the individual contribution of genetic and environmental events to Autumn's case, our observations may only apply to her, or to a small number of cases. There are most likely many different etiological pathways to the emergence of anorexia nervosa which cannot be determined on an individual level. It is for this reason that we must turn to large population-based studies in order to determine which of these aforementioned hypotheses are most consistent with the observed data.

4 Empirical studies of the role of genes and environment in the etiology of eating disorders

Genetic epidemiology

What empirical evidence do we have to support the mechanisms outlined above through which genes and environment contribute to eating disorders in populations rather than individuals? In genetic epidemiology, the first step is to determine whether a particular disorder or trait aggregates in families. This question is addressed using the traditional family study design. These studies ask the question of whether there is a statistically greater lifetime risk of eating disorders in relatives of individuals who have an eating disorder in comparison to relatives of individuals without eating disorders.

Most (Gershon et al., 1983; Hudson et al., 1987; Kassett et al., 1989; Strober et al., 1990; Lilenfeld et al., 1998; Strober et al., 2000), but not all (Gershon et al., 1983; Halmi et al., 1991; Stern et al., 1992) controlled family studies, have found a significantly greater lifetime prevalence of eating disorders among relatives of eating disordered individuals in comparison to relatives of controls. In the two most methodologically sophisticated family studies to date (Lilenfeld et al., 1998; Strober, 1998), family members of women with anorexia nervosa and bulimia nervosa were at markedly increased risk for eating disorders. Intriguingly, several studies have found increased rates of both anorexia nervosa and bulimia nervosa (that is, co-aggregation) in relatives of individuals with anorexia nervosa as well as individuals with bulimia nervosa, compared to rates among relatives of controls

(Gershon *et al.*, 1983; Hudson *et al.*, 1987; Kassett *et al.*, 1989; Strober *et al.*, 1990, Strober *et al.*, 2000), suggesting that anorexia nervosa and bulimia nervosa share transmissible risk factors. Moreover, relatives of individuals with anorexia nervosa and bulimia nervosa have also been found to have a significantly increased rate of sub-threshold eating disorders compared to relatives of controls (Lilenfeld *et al.*, 1998; Strober *et al.*, 2000), suggesting that the eating disorders do not 'breed true', but are expressed in families as a broad spectrum of eating-related pathology. There are limits to the interpretation of family studies, however. One cannot, on the basis of a family study alone, determine whether the familiality of a trait is due to genetic or environmental factors. Far too few researchers who study families are aware of this one critical limitation.

Twin studies of anorexia nervosa

Beyond isolated case reports, the first systematic study of clinically ascertained twins with anorexia nervosa (Holland *et al.*, 1984; Holland *et al.*, 1988; Treasure and Holland, 1989) found that the concordance for MZ twins was substantially greater than for DZ twins. Our re-analyses of these data (assuming a population prevalence of anorexia nervosa of 0.75%) revealed evidence of familial aggregation with parameter estimates of 88% for additive genetic effects, 0% for common environmental effects, and 12% for unique environmental effects. What this means is that the observed familial aggregation for anorexia nervosa appears to be influenced most strongly by additive genetic effects, with some contribution from unique environment, but little or no contribution from the common environmental factors. Given the small sample size, however, these results must be viewed as preliminary.

Population-based studies of anorexia nervosa have been difficult to conduct given the relatively low prevalence of the disorder. We were able to successfully apply the twin method to the study of anorexia nervosa in the context of studying the nature of the comorbid relationship between anorexia nervosa and major depression (Wade *et al.*, in press). This study revealed that the heritability of anorexia nervosa was approximately 58% (95% CI; 33–84%). Moreover, we found that there was substantial overlap between the genes that contribute to liability to anorexia nervosa and those that contribute to liability to major depression. Although the best fitting model indicated a substantial contribution of additive genetic factors, the role of common environment in the familial transmission of anorexia nervosa could not be entirely ruled out.

On balance, we can conclude from these twin and family studies of anorexia nervosa (Lilenfeld *et al.*, 1997, for a review) that the disorder is familial. However, the definitive resolution of the independent contribution of genetic and shared environmental factors to the observed familiality of anorexia will require more ambitious collaborative efforts to obtain larger sample sizes with sufficient statistical power.

Twin studies of bulimia nervosa

Twin studies of bulimia nervosa have been more successful than twin studies of anorexia nervosa given the reported higher prevalence of the first. Initial case series of twins with bulimia nervosa revealed consistently greater concordance for bulimia nervosa in MZ than DZ twin pairs (Treasure and Holland, 1989; Fichter and Noegel, 1990; Hsu *et al.*, 1990). Pooling data from these case series for twin modeling and assuming a population prevalence of bulimia nervosa of 2.5% revealed evidence of familial aggregation with 47% (95% CI; 0–66%) of the variance accounted for by additive genetic effects, 30% (95% CI; 0–56%) by shared environmental effects, and 23% (95% CI; 9–44%) by unique environmental effects. However, the sample sizes were small and, as can be inferred from the wide confidence intervals, the estimates imprecise.

Population-based studies of bulimia nervosa have been conducted in the US (Kendler *et al.*, 1991; Bulik *et al.*, 1998) and Australia (Wade *et al.*, 1999). We have recently re-analyzed the data from these twin studies in order to provide a detailed comparison of results across studies (Bulik *et al.*, 2000).

Figure 4.1 presents results of the major twin studies of bulimia nervosa. Two studies are from the Virginia Twin Registry at different waves of data collection (Kendler *et al.*, 1991; Bulik *et al.*, 1998) and one study from the Australian Twin Registry (Wade *et al.*, 1999). There is reasonable consistency across these studies. The point estimates for additive genetic effects are somewhat variable, but range between 31 and 54%; however, the 95% confidence intervals are overlapping suggesting reasonable consistency across studies. For common environment, the point estimates are all near zero, but the confidence intervals are broad and consistent across studies. There is a more substantial contribution of unique environment (ranging from 46 to 68%) (which includes measurement error), and the confidence intervals did not contain zero.

We have learned, however, that bulimia nervosa is not a terribly reliable diagnosis (Bulik *et al.*, 2000). One way to improve reliability is to interview an individual on more than one occasion about, for example, their lifetime history of bulimia nervosa. Two of the studies presented in the figure took that approach (Bulik *et al.*, 1998; Wade *et al.*, 1999). The effect of this strategy was to increase the accuracy of the estimates (smaller confidence intervals). Both studies found that when correcting for unreliability, the estimates of heritability actually increased (59 and 83%). Again, the contribution of common environment remained negligible and the remaining variance came from unique environmental effects.

In summary, from twin and family studies, we can conclude that bulimia nervosa is familial and that there appears to be a moderate to substantial contribution made by genetic factors and a moderate contribution of unique environment to liability to the disorder. The contribution of shared environment is smaller and perhaps zero. This means, at a given point in time, in a given culture, those environmental influences experienced by both members of a twin pair (for example, socio-economic status, school system) do not play a major role in the development of eating disorders.

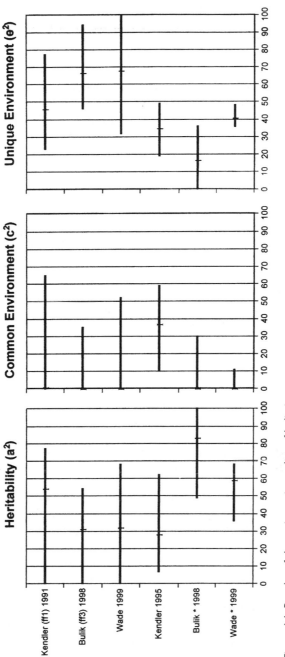

Figure 4.1 Results of the major twin studies of bulimia nervosa.

Twin models of component behaviors and continuous measures of disordered eating and attitudes

In addition to eating disorders, the twin method has also been applied to personality, attitudinal, and behavioral measures that are believed to be associated with the development of eating disorders.

The earliest twin study of eating disorders attitudes or behaviors (Holland *et al.*, 1988) examined the Eating Disorder Inventory (EDI) (Garner *et al.*, 1984) and only reported a heritability estimate for the 'drive for thinness' scale which was 'near 1.0', although the standard errors were large. Rutherford *et al.* (1993) also studied the EDI in twins and reported heritability estimates ranging from 28 to 52% for subscales. Shared environment was not included in any of the best-fitting models. In two samples of adolescent twins from the Minnesota Twin Family Study aged 11 and 17 years, there were marked differences between the two cohorts on the EDI (Klump *et al.*, 2000). For the younger adolescents, both genes and environment contributed to most subscales. For the older group, however, additive genetic effects appeared to supersede any contribution of common environment. These results suggest the influence of developmental age effects on the structure of genetic and environmental sources of liability to eating disordered behaviors and attitudes.

Studies from the Australian Twin Registry examined measures of dietary restraint and concern about eating, weight, and shape from the Eating Disorders Examination (EDE) (Wade *et al.*, 1998). For all subscales of the EDE, except concerns about weight, the best-fitting models included substantial contributions of additive genetic effects and unique environmental effects with no contribution from common environment. Only for the weight concern measure did common environment make a substantial contribution.

The extant twin studies have shed some light on the relative contribution of genes and environment to the liability to eating disorders. Although there is much more basic research to be done, it is not premature to begin to explore the next level of questioning which addresses specifically which genes and which environments contribute to liability to eating disorders.

Which environments?

That the contribution of additive genetic effects appears to be more prominent than shared environmental effects for both anorexia nervosa and bulimia nervosa is surprising given the historical focus on cultural and social factors in the study of eating disorders. There are several plausible explanations for this consistent finding. First, environmental experiences that are shared by members of a family may quite simply have little bearing on risk to eating disorders. Thus, the environmental factors that are important in increasing risk for eating disorders may be those experiences that are unique to the individual, possibly acting to increase the likelihood of body dissatisfaction, or initiating weight control practices. Second, if familial factors exert effects in concert with an individual's genetic propensities, the main effects of familial environment will be weak but effects operating in gene–environment interaction might be considerable.

Finally, the environmental risk conferred by the culture in which one is reared cannot be overlooked. By conducting twin studies in countries that are predicted to undergo Westernization now and again after cultural change has occurred, one could conceivably trace the change in heritability as prevalence of the behaviors increase. Kendler *et al.* (2000) explored so called gene × cohort effects for regular tobacco use in Swedish female twins in three age cohorts (born between 1910–1924, 1925–1939, and 1940–1958). The prevalence of tobacco use rose considerably across those three cohorts. Similarly the estimated heritabilities for tobacco use were 0 for those born between 1900–1924, 21% for those born between 1925–1939, and 64% for those born between 1940–1958. Thus, even though the genetic predisposition to smoking existed in those women born in the earliest cohort, social sanctions against smoking in women prevented genetic factors that influenced smoking from being expressed as both prevalence and heritability were near 0. This example illustrates dramatically how heritability estimates must be considered to be specific to a given population, in a given culture, at a given point in time. As we become more sophisticated and begin to identify susceptibility genes for eating disorders, we may then be in a position to identify those individuals who are at greatest risk of developing eating disorders in countries undergoing Westernization.

Risk factors

Whether common environmental factors are relevant will continue to be debated. However, studies have consistently observed a significant contribution of unique environmental factors in the liability to eating disorders. An important next step is to determine which sorts of unique environmental events contribute the greatest risk to liability to eating disorders. Although not yet extensively addressed in twin studies, a series of population-based risk factor studies from England have identified a rather large number of variables that distinguish women with eating disorders from healthy controls, and a smaller number of factors that distinguish between women with eating disorders and control women with other psychiatric disorders (Fairburn *et al.*, 1997; Fairburn *et al.*, 1999).

The variables found to distinguish between women with bulimia nervosa and psychiatric controls were low parental contact, high parental expectations, critical comments by the family about weight, shape, or eating, negative self-evaluation, parental alcoholism, childhood obesity, and parental obesity. In terms of anorexia nervosa, the only variables that differed significantly between women with anorexia nervosa and psychiatric controls were negative self-evaluation and perfectionism. Although some of these identified risk factors from these studies are likely to have environmental components, some, such as obesity (Maes *et al.*, 1997) and alcoholism (Kendler *et al.*, 1994; Schuckit, 1999) have been clearly shown to be under genetic control.

Specific environmental factors in twin models

These risk factor studies provide direction for future twin studies which attempt to determine the relative impact of different environmental variables on liability to illness. The flexibility of the twin modeling approach allows one to incorporate specific environmental variables into a twin model in order to determine the magnitude of the impact of that specified environmental variable. One such study has been conducted which explored whether marital conflict acts, at least partially, as an environmental risk factor for bulimia nervosa. Indeed, marital conflict, as reported by the mother of the twins, accounted for approximately 3% (95%CI; 1–8%) of the variance of liability to bulimia nervosa, which was a highly statistically significant contribution (Wade *et al.*, in press).

Co-twin control design

An additional approach to tease out the contribution of environment to the etiology of a disorder involves the use of monozygotic twins who are discordant for a particular trait or disorder – the co-twin control design. The elegance of this design rests with the fact that MZ twins are, for most intents and purposes, genetically identical. In addition to providing the ideal genetic control, MZ twins who are reared together also experience the same common or familial environment. Whereas differences between dizygotic twins could be a function of either genes or environment, differences between reared-together MZ twins must be attributed to the effects of unique environmental factors.

We studied female monozygotic twins who were discordant for bulimia nervosa (excluding the frequency and duration criterion) and the co-twin either reported some symptoms of bulimia nervosa but never met full diagnostic criteria ($n = 20$ pairs), or the co-twin reported no symptoms of bulimia nervosa ($n = 10$) (Bulik *et al.*, 2001). We compared the twins on demographic, developmental, personality, and psychiatric dimensions using self- and maternal report. Affected twins were more likely to report lifetime generalized anxiety disorder and were described by their mothers as more anxious and fearful as children. They also had significantly lower mastery, optimism, and self-esteem, and significantly greater obsessive and compulsive symptoms than their unaffected co-twins. Affected twins recalled greater discord in their families but viewed their parents as more warm toward them than toward their unaffected co-twin. Given that MZ twins are genetically identical and share a common family background, differences between them must be attributable to unique environmental factors. Although it is difficult to disentangle predisposing risk factors from sequelae of psychiatric illness in a retrospective co-twin control design, the affected twins were perceived to have been more anxious as children by their mothers – possibly reflecting a predisposing trait. More extensive interviews are required to determine the nature of environmental events that contribute to the expression of the observed personality, behavioral, anxious, and eating-related traits in the affected twins.

Which genes?

The status of genetic research in anorexia nervosa and bulimia nervosa is in its infancy in comparison to other complex disorders such as insulin-dependent diabetes mellitus (Todd, 1999), schizophrenia (Moldin, 1997), and bipolar disorder (Risch and Botstein, 1996). There are two basic approaches that can be applied in order to detect the genes that are implicated in a complex disorder: association studies using candidate genes and genome-wide searches for susceptibility loci. In part, progress in these areas is hampered because the genetically 'correct' phenotype is unknown. Is a propensity to anorexia nervosa or bulimia nervosa directly inherited or are there more fundamental factors such as temperamental traits or abnormalities in appetite regulation that are inherited and increase the chances of developing anorexia nervosa or bulimia nervosa?

The most likely candidate genes to be studied in eating disorders are related to those systems that have been shown to be abnormal in women with eating disorders. To date, the primary focus has been on genes involved in serotonergic (5HT) neurotransmission. Collier *et al.* (1997) conducted an association study of 81 women with anorexia nervosa and 226 controls, finding a modest increase in the frequency of the 5HT2A-1438/A allele in anorexia nervosa compared to controls. These results have since been replicated by Sorbi *et al.* (1998) and by Enoch *et al.* (1998). Interestingly, in the Sorbi *et al.* study the increased frequency of this allelic variant was seen only in the subset of non-purging restricting anorexics, whereas in the Enoch study this genotype was not found to discriminate BN patients from controls, yet was also more common amongst patients with obsessive compulsive disease.

Two studies have failed to replicate the 5HT2A finding. Campbell *et al.* (1998) studied 157 anorexic patients and 150 controls, finding no association of this polymorphism with anorexia nervosa. However, stratification by the presence or absence of purging was not performed and the frequency of the 1438A genotype in their controls was higher than in other reported controls samples. Still, Hinney *et al.* (1997) studied 100 anorexics, with 100 underweight but non-anorexic controls, and 100 obese controls and found no inter-group differences in the frequency of this genotype. They also failed to find an influence of alleles of the DRD4 on the development of any of these three conditions (Hinney *et al.*, 1999).

Other candidate genes awaiting further study that are possible mechanisms include those systems related to metabolism, appetite regulation and dysregulation, affective dysregulation, activity level, and the temperamental traits of harm avoidance, novelty seeking.

In terms of genome-wide searches, an on-going international collaborative study designed to detect susceptibility genes for anorexia nervosa is nearing completion and a parallel study for bulimia nervosa is underway (Kaye *et al.*, 1999).

5 Conclusions and future directions

An increasing body of evidence supports the notion that anorexia nervosa and bulimia nervosa have a strong familial component. Moreover, twin studies suggest a substantial contribution of additive genetic effects to the observed familiality of both disorders. In contrast, the magnitude of the contribution of common environmental effects appears to be less prominent. Moreover, both family and twin data suggest there is at least a moderate familial-genetic correlation between anorexia nervosa and bulimia nervosa, which may both reflect and explain the common development of bulimia nervosa during the natural course of anorexia nervosa.

Although preliminary genetic epidemiological studies have now been performed in several countries, there remain several gaps in our understanding of the role of genes, environment, and culture in the etiology of eating disorders. The majority of twin studies on eating disorders have been retrospective. This design inadequately addresses the developmental nature of these disorders. Only a limited number of studies have attempted to characterize behavioral features in childhood that portend the development of eating disorders (Marchi and Cohen, 1990; Stice *et al.*, 1999). Moreover, the risk of illness is strongly influenced by certain developmental periods—especially puberty. Furthermore, there is preliminary evidence that the nature and magnitude of genetic and environmental contributions to eating disorders may change over time, with shared environmental factors playing a greater role in pre-adolescence only to be superceded by genetic factors in later adolescence (Klump *et al.*, 2000). Unfortunately, there are no published developmental studies of twins that have assessed salient prepubertal environmental, biological, and temperamental variables in order to determine their effect on the emergence of eating disorders. Although we can speculate on an individual level, such as with Autumn in the beginning of this chapter, our knowledge of the developmental cascade through which genetic and environmental risk factors influence liability to eating disorders remains, at best, fragmentary. Comprehensive, large-scale developmental investigations using genetically informative samples are required in order to further illuminate the nature, magnitude, and developmental cascade of genetic and environmental factors that contribute to and protect against the development of anorexia nervosa and bulimia nervosa in young women. Likewise, longitudinal studies of genetically informative samples in countries undergoing Westernization, although expensive and difficult to time accurately, could assist in unravelling how genes, environment, and culture interact through time to lead to changes in both the prevalence and heritability of these disorders.

References

Attie I, Brooks-Gunn J (1989). Development of eating problems in adolescent girls: a longitudinal study. *Developmental Psychology*, **25**, 70–9.
Bulik C, Sullivan P, Wade T, Kendler K (2000). Twin studies of eating disorders: a review. *International Journal of Eating Disorders*, **27**, 1–20.

Bulik C, Wade T, Kendler K (2001). Characteristics of monozygotic twins discordant for bulimia nervosa. *International Journal of Eating Disorders*, **29**(1), 1–10.

Bulik CM, Sullivan PF, Kendler KS (1998). Heritability of binge-eating and broadly defined bulimia nervosa. *Biological Psychiatry*, **44**, 1210–18.

Campbell DA, Sundaramurthy D, Markham AF, Pieri LF (1998). Lack of association between 5-HT2A gene promoter polymorphism and susceptibility to anorexia nervosa [letter]. *Lancet*, **351**, 499.

Cederlof R, Rantasalo I, Floderus-Myrhed B *et al.*, (1982). A cross-national epidemiological resource: the Swedish and Finnish cohort studies of like-sexed twins. *International Journal of Epidemiology*, **11**, 387–90.

Collier DA, Arranz MJ, Li T, Mupita D, Brown N, Treasure J (1997). Association between 5-HT2A gene promoter polymorphism and anorexia nervosa. *Lancet*, **350**, 412.

Cook EH (1998). Genetics of autism. *Mental Retardation and Developmental Disabilities Research Reviews*, **4**, 113–20.

Eaves LJ, Eysenck HJ, Martin NG (1989). *Genes, Culture and Personality: An Empirical Approach*. London: Oxford University Press.

Enoch MA, Kaye WH, Rotondo A, Greenberg BD, Murphy DL, Goldman D (1998). 5-HT2A promoter polymorphism -1438G/A, anorexia nervosa, and obsessive-compulsive disorder. *Lancet*, **351**, 1785–6.

Fairburn CG, Cooper Z, Welch SL (1999). Risk factors for anorexia nervosa. *Archives of General Psychiatry*, **56**, 468–76.

Fairburn CG, Welch SL, Doll HA, Davies BA, O'Connor ME (1997). Risk factors for bulimia nervosa. A community-based case-control study. *Archives of General Psychiatry*, **54**, 509–17.

Fichter MM, Noegel R (1990). Concordance for bulimia nervosa in twins. *International Journal of Eating Disorders*, **9**, 255–63.

Folstein S, Rutter M (1977). Infantile autism: a genetic study of 21 twin pairs. *Journal of Child Psychology and Psychiatry*, **18**, 297–321.

Garner D, Olmsted M, Polivy J (1984). *Eating Disorders Inventory Manual*. New York: Psychological Assessment Resources.

Gershon E, Schreiber J, Hamovit J *et al.* (1983). In: *Childhood psychopathology and development*, edited by Guze SB, Earls FJ, Barrett JE. New York: Raven Press, pp. 279–84.

Graber J, Brooks-Gunn J, Paikoff R, Warren M (1994). Prediction of eating problems: An 8-year study of adolescent girls. *Developmental Psychology*, **30**, 823–34.

Halmi K, Eckert E, Marchi P, Sampugnaro V, Apple R, Cohen J (1991). Comorbidity of psychiatric diagnoses in anorexia nervosa. *Archives of General Psychiatry*, **48**, 712–18.

Hinney A, Schneider J, Ziegler A *et al.* (1999). No evidence for involvement of polymorphisms of the dopamine D4 receptor gene in anorexia nervosa, underweight, and obesity, *Neuropsychiatric Genetics*, **88**, 594–7.

Hinney A, Ziegler A, Nšthen M, Remschmidt H, Hebebrand J (1997). 5-HT2a receptor gene polymorphisms, anorexia nervosa and obesity. *Lancet*, **350**, 1324–5.

Holland AJ, Hall A, Murray R, Russell GFM, Crisp AH (1984). Anorexia nervosa: a study of 34 twin pairs and one set of triplets. *British Journal of Psychiatry*, **145**, 414–19.

Holland AJ, Sicotte N, Treasure J (1988). Anorexia nervosa: evidence for a genetic basis. *Journal of Psychosomatic Research*, **32**, 561–71.

Hsu GLK, Chesler BE, Santhouse R (1990). Bulimia nervosa in eleven sets of twins: a clinical report. *International Journal of Eating Disorders*, **9**, 275–82.

Hudson JI, Pope HG, Jonas JM, Yurgelun-Todd D, Frankenburg FR (1987). A controlled family history study of bulimia. *Psychological Medicine*, **17**, 883–90.

Kassett J, Gershon E, Maxwell M *et al.* (1989). Psychiatric disorders in the first-degree relatives of probands with bulimia nervosa. *American Journal of Psychiatry*, **146**, 1468–71.

Kaye W, Lilenfeld L, Berretini W *et al.* (1999). A genome-wide search for susceptibility loci in anorexia nervosa: Methods and sample description. *Biological Psychiatry* **47**, 794–803.

Kendler KS (1983). Overview: a current perspective on twin studies of schizophrenia. *American Journal of Psychiatry*, **140**, 1413–25.

Kendler KS, Eaves LJ (1986). Models for the joint effect of genotype and environment on liability to psychiatric illness. *American Journal of Psychiatry*, **143**, 279–89.

Kendler KS, Gardner CO Jr. (1998). Twin studies of adult psychiatric and substance dependence disorders: are they biased by differences in the environmental experiences of monozygotic and dizygotic twins in childhood and adolescence? [In Process Citation]. *Psychological Medicine*, **28**, 625–33.

Kendler KS, MacLean C, Neale MC, Kessler RC, Heath AC, Eaves LJ (1991). The genetic epidemiology of bulimia nervosa. *American Journal of Psychiatry*, **148**, 1627–37.

Kendler KS, Neale MC, Heath AC, Kessler RC, Eaves LJ (1994). A twin-family study of alcoholism in women. *American Journal of Psychiatry*, **151**, 707–15.

Kendler KS, Neale MC, Kessler RC, Heath AC, Eaves LJ (1993a). The lifetime history of major depression in women: Reliability of diagnosis and heritability. *Archives of General Psychiatry*, **50**, 863–70.

Kendler KS, Neale MC, Kessler RC, Heath AC, Eaves LJ (1993b). A longitudinal twin study of 1-year prevalence of major depression in women. *Archives of General Psychiatry*, **50**, 843–852.

Kendler K, Thornton L, Pedersen N (2000). Tobacco consumption in Swedish twins reared apart and reared together. *Archives of General Psychiatry*, **57**, 886–892.

Klump KL, McGue MK, Iacono WG (2000). Age differences in genetic and environmental influences on eating attitudes and behaviors in adolescent female twins. *Journal of Abnormal Psychology* **109**(2), 239–51.

Leon G, Fulkerson J, Perry C, Cudeck R (1993). Personality and behavioral vulnerabilities associated with risk status for eating disorders in adolescent girls. *Journal of Abnormal Psychology*, **102**, 438–44.

Lilenfeld L, Kaye W, Greeno C *et al.* (1998). A controlled family study of restricting anorexia and bulimia nervosa: comorbidity in probands and disorders in first-degree relatives. *Archives of General Psychiatry*, **55**, 603–10.

Lilenfeld L, Kaye W, Strober M (1997). In: *Balliere's Clinical Psychiatry*, vol. 3 , pp. 177–97.

Loehlin J, Nichols R (1976). *Heridity, Environment and Personality: A Study of 850 Sets of Twins*. Austin: University of Texas Press.

Maes H, Neale M, Eaves L (1997). Genetic and environmental factors in body mass index. *Behavior Genetics*, **27**, 325–51.

Marchi M, Cohen P (1990). Early childhood eating behaviors and adolescent eating disorders. *Journal of the American Academy of Child and Adolescent Psychiatry*, **29**, 112–17.

Martin N, Boomsma D, Machin G (1997). A twin-pronged attack on complex traits. *Nature Genetics*, **17**, 387–92.

Moldin S (1997). The maddening hunt for madness genes. *Nature Genetics*, **17**, 127–9.

Plomin R, Daniels D (1987). Why are children in the same family so different from one another? *Behavioral and Brain Sciences*, **10**, 1–16.

Plomin R, DeFries JC, McClearn GE, Rutter M (1994). *Behavioral Genetics*, Third Edition, New York: W.H. Freeman & Co.

Risch N, Botstein D (1996). A manic depressive history. *Nature Genetics*, **12**, 351–3.

Rutherford J, McGuffin P, Katz R, Murray R (1993). Genetic influences on eating attitudes in a normal female twin population. *Psychological Medicine*, **23**, 425–36.

Schuckit MA (1999). New findings in the genetics of alcoholism. *Journal of the American Medical Association*, **281**, 1875–6.

Sorbi S, Nacmias B, Tedde A, Ricca V, Mezzani B, Rotella C (1998). 5-HT2A promoter polymorphism in anorexia nervosa. *Lancet*, **351**, 1785.

Stern S, Dixon K, Sansone R, Lake M, Nemzer E, Jones, D. (1992). Psychoactive substance use disorder in relatives of patients with anorexia nervosa. *Comprehensive Psychiatry*, **33**, 207–12.

Stice E, Agras W, Hammer L (1999). Risk factors for the emergence of childhood eating disturbances; A five-year prospective study. *International Journal of Eating Disorders*, **25**, 375–87.

Strober M (1998). Presented at the Eating Disorders Research Society, Boston, MA.

Strober M, Freeman R, Lampert C, Diamond J, Kaye W (2000). A controlled family study of anorexia nervosa and bulimia nervosa: Evidence of shared liability and transmission of partial syndromes. *American Journal of Psychiatry* **157**(3), 393–401.

Strober M, Lampert C, Morrell W, Burroughs J, Jacobs C (1990). A controlled family study of anorexia nervosa: evidence of familial aggregation and lack of shared transmission with affective disorders. *International Journal of Eating Disorders*, **9**, 239–53.

Sullivan P, Neale M, Kendler K (2000). Genetic epidemiology of major depression: A review and meta-analysis. *American Journal of Psychiatry* **157**(10), 1552–1562.

Todd JA (1999). From genome to aetiology in a multifactorial disease, type 1 diabetes. *Bioessays*, **21**, 164–74.

Treasure J, Holland A (1989). In: *Child and Youth Psychiatry: European Perspectives*, edited by Remschmidt H, Schmidt M. New York: Hogrefe & Huber, pp. 59–68.

Wade T, Bulik C, Kendler K (2000). Anorexia nervosa and major depression: An examination of shared genetic and environmental risk factors. *American Journal of Psychiatry*, **157**, 469–71.

Wade T, Bulik C, Kendler K (in press). An investigation of marital conflict as a risk factor for bulimia nervosa.

Wade TD, Martin N, Neale M *et al.* (1999). The structure of genetic and environmental risk factors for three measures of disordered eating characteristic of bulimia nervosa. *Psychological Medicine*, **29**, 925–34.

Wade T, Martin N, Tiggemann M (1998). Genetic and environmental risk factors for the weight and shape concerns characteristic of bulimia nervosa. *Psychological Medicine*, **28**, 761–71.

Commentary I

Senior Lecturer in Anthropology, The University of
Auckland, New Zealand

Social anthropologists are used to approaching alien knowledge systems with respect in the hope of reaching understanding through hermeneutic[1] dialogue with the text or interlocutor. Bulik's paper is about as far from an ethnographic[2] approach to women's health or the meaning of food in society as one can get. Yet its lucidity and the author's careful sifting through the recent evidence for and against genetic and environmental effects in the etiology of eating disorders, her attempts to tease apart and then reintegrate the interactions between genes and environment, have made such a dialogue possible.

Gone from this account is the mess of life: accounts of frantically busy parents trying to accommodate the demands of their growing twins; the visceral realities of eating disorders; the sense that the research participants and their families have ethnic and gender identities, class affiliations, social networks, dreams and fears. Instead, we have an elegant and formal *pas de deux* which gives the necessary control to examine 'gene' and 'environment' separately and together. Absent also are questions of political economy:[3] whose are the bodies in question or why are eating disorders in affluent countries of concern at the same time that the global food system delivers starvation to the Horn of Africa and elsewhere? (Mintz, 1996).

---

[1] Hermeneutics describes an approach to understanding and interpretation. It assumes that interlocators bring pre-judgements to an encounter with a text or a person; that truths are always from a vantage point; that the aim of dialogue is to challenge one's pre-judgements in order to arrive at an understanding of how and why the other's views are formed (see Gadamer, 1975).

[2] Ethnography is a characteristic mode of enquiry in social and cultural anthropology. It stresses the researcher's immersion in a cultural context, engagement in everyday affairs of the research participants and serious attempts to understand the 'other's' point of view. Ethnographic fieldwork employs a range of research methods including a variety of types of interview, surveys, observations, diaries, and so on, all in the context of participant-observation. It is valued because of the contextual richness and depth of the resulting accounts, called ethnographies.

[3] Political economy is a theoretical approach which recognises the historical production of society and culture in the context of global political and economic forces. It directs attention to global–local interaction and the interrelationship of meaning and power (see Roseberry, 1989).

However, complexities are acknowledged. For example, in the paper and the studies it reviews, genetic inheritance does not necessarily refer to the inheritance of the disorders themselves but may include the inheritance of predisposing factors. The search for which genes might be involved is underway but not complete. Both genes and environment may play protective as well as precipitative roles. The small number of prospective studies mean the interactions between these factors in a dynamic developmental framework are not yet well understood. Yet there is some evidence to suggest that the quantitative and qualitative relationships between the influence of genes and environment may differ during different developmental periods.

The upshot of this, to my mind, is to reinforce the futility of asking generally how much genes and environment each contribute, and the utility of asking specific questions. These include 'genetic questions' such as, which combinations of genes influence which combination of predisposing or protective features, and 'environmental questions', such as which features of which environments increase and decrease the liability for eating disorders. They also should include questions of timing or development. Despite the present relative lack of developmental information, models situated in a developmental/ecological framework, for example, as proposed by Bronfenbrenner (1979), Harkness and Super (1994), that ground observations and interpretations in a dynamic and interactive approach that takes account of interpersonal and societal processes could be helpful. Such models would lead to more refined and specific questions about the role of ecology and development in the etiology of eating disorders and lives of the individuals and families who suffer with and from them.

In terms of its own aims, this paper succeeds very well. But there are important questions touched on within the paper which can be advanced only by other approaches. For example, reporting on the Australian Twin Registry study, Bulik notes that common environment made a contribution 'only' to the weight concern measure. In a general discussion, she suggests several reasons for the low showing of common environment in many of the studies: it may have little effect on eating disorders, compared to unique environmental effects, or its effects may be masked by gene–environment interaction. Study designs which include careful cross-cultural and cross-class comparisons may be more effective in shedding further light here.

In a series of ethnographic studies of 2000 New Zealand women from a range of different cultural backgrounds (Park, 1991) substantial differences in interest and anxiety about eating, food and body size and shape were noted between the *Pakeha* (people of mainly British background who are descendants of immigrants or long-term residents themselves), *Maori* (indigenous people descended from Polynesian ancestors) and *Pacific Islanders* (more recent immigrants from the Pacific, especially Polynesia). The study was about the place of alcohol in New Zealand women's lives, but women talked so much about food, and the multifarious dimensions of food were so important in women's lives, that food became an additional focus of the study. Food was perceived ambivalently by Pakeha women:

as friend and enemy – a dangerous comfort. One quotation from a Pakeha woman will suffice:

> *If I have [alcohol] in the house, I don't drink it. With me, [it's] a very different situation, for instance, if I have cake or biscuits ['cookies'] . . . in the house. That is far more dangerous. I would be much more likely to eat those than . . . to drink leftovers* (Herda, 1991, p. 145).

Food was a field of gender and generational battles and of individual battles for control, as well as being a source of status and a medium of love and care. Yet Maori and Pacific Islands women, with the exception of some of the youngest who identified with Pakeha ways, voiced no concerns about their eating or their body shape, although they too, like Pakeha, talked about other aspects of food, for example, in hospitality, sociability and as labour. At the time, the disorders of anorexia and bulimia were of infinitesimal importance in the health concerns of Maori and Pacific Islands women, whereas for Pakeha women they were a grave issue. In the study population, the vast majority did not have clinical eating disorders. It was this majority that was most alarming. As Herda (1991, p. 145) noted, these 'normal' women spoke about food in similar ways to their contemporaries who had been diagnosed with eating disorders, described in another ethnographic study (Austin, 1987). Thus, it seems that if questions are asked in different ways the environment common to a particular ethnic (or class or gender) group can be shown to raise or lower the ambient 'pathology'.

Broadening the frame further, Foucault's work on governmentality and the disciplinary society of our era prevents us from neglecting the historicity of the relations between the body and the body politic (Lock and Scheper-Hughes, 1990; Foucault, 1991). The insights derived from these theories of the politics of embodiment enable us to see that the terrain referred to so neutrally by Bulik as 'environment' is suffused with power, and, although it has local manifestations, is part of intensifying globalisation. Food is both symbol and agent of this globalising process as Mintz (1996) has brilliantly demonstrated. Thus, as well as the developmental/ecological framework, I would urge an analysis from political economy, with attention to gender, culture and class. We readily acknowledge the complexity of the human genome. So should we with that 'black box' concept, *environment*.

References

Austin C (1987). *Food for Thought: A Social Analysis of Bulimia*. Unpublished MA Thesis in Anthropology. Auckland: The University of Auckland.

Bronfenbrenner U (1979). *The Ecology of Human Development: Experiments by Nature and Design*. Cambridge: Harvard University Press.

Foucault M (1991). In: *The Foucault Effect: Studies in Governmentality*, edited by Burchell G, Gordon C, Miller P. London: Harvester Wheatsheaf, pp. 87–104.

Harkness S, Super C (1994). The Developmental Niche: A Theoretical Framework for Analysing the Household Production of Health. *Social Science and Medicine*, **38**, 217–26.

Herda P (1991). In: *Ladies a Plate: Change and Continuity in the Lives of New Zealand Women*, edited by Park J. Auckland: Auckland University Press, pp.144–72.

Gadamer HG (1975). *Truth and Method*. New York: Crossroad Press.

Lock M, Scheper-Hughes N (1990). In: *Medical Anthropology: Contemporary Theory and Method*, edited by Johnson TM, Sargent CF. Westport, CT: Praeger, pp. 47–72.

Mintz S (1996). *Tasting Food, Tasting Freedom: Excursions into Eating, Culture and the Past*. Boston: Beacon Press.

Park J (ed) (1991). *Ladies a Plate: Change and Continuity in the Lives of New Zealand Women*. Auckland: Auckland University Press.

Roseberry W (1989). *Anthropologies and Histories: Essays in Culture, History and Political Economy*. New Brunswick, NJ: Rutgers University Press.

Commentary 2

Phillipe Gorwood
Psychiatrist, Faculty Paris VII, France

Anorexia nervosa is a complex and severe disorder, with a large variety of factors contributing to the explanation of risk. Bulik pinpointed the importance of genetic factors in the risk of anorexia nervosa and bulimia nervosa through family and twin studies and a brief paragraph on the candidate genes already analysed. The strength of the evidence raised by numerous studies, clearly summarised by the author, on the importance of genetic factors in eating disorder may minimise the fact that genetic factors have been placed in the foreground only recently. Even 20 years ago, genetic factors were considered as non-significant in eating disorders and there were no molecular genetic analyses. Heritability in the broad sense of anorexia nervosa nevertheless ranges between 30% and 80%, averaging 50%.

We now know that genetic factors have one of the most important roles in its vulnerability. The discrepancy between the large heritability of the disorder and the very recent interest in the genetics of anorexia is probably explained by the strong influence of familial, cultural and psychosocial factors, factors that even 'pure' geneticists do not deny. In fact, anorexia nervosa has been considered as reflecting sexual difficulties (that is, a way of delaying sexual maturity) and/or a familial disorder (that is, a response to a threatening relationship with parents). In families with one affected relative, severe abnormality of relationship and difficulties with the female body image are in fact almost systematically observed.

However, striking clinical traits are not systematically equivalent to vulnerability traits. The risk of confusing explaining factors and indirect consequences is important. One has to compare, for example, the way autism was generally considered just a few decades ago as reflecting maternal incompetence; autism is now viewed as a much more neurogenetic disorder. Twin studies have not only showed that genetic factors explain a large part of the total variance of the vulnerability for anorexia nervosa, but they also consistently illustrated that the role of familial environment is much lower than was generally believed.

Many cannot understand how such a voluntary behaviour (starving) could be influenced by genes. Understanding the role of genetic factors in anorexia nervosa is probably difficult for clinicians and families because of the shift between the famous concept of 'Mendelian genetic disorders' (for which one disorder is completely explained by one defective gene) and the unknown and obscure concept of 'multifactorial phenotype with partial genetic determinism' (for which different genetic polymorphisms interact to increase the global vulnerability) (Gorwood, 1999)

One of the original and creative ideas of Bulik was to use twin studies both at the clinical and at the scientific levels to show the complex interaction between genetic factors, common familial environment and specific personal events. We met the case of a non-concordant twin pair with anorexia nervosa that highlighted presence of incomplete penetrance, a phenomenon that is defined by the fact that not all subjects with the vulnerability genes show the phenotype (Gorwood *et al.* 1998). This monozygotic twin sister of an anorexic patient was a married dentist with two children and did not meet the criteria of anorexia nervosa. Nevertheless, she was greatly concerned by her body image, and could not stand eating any food associated with milk. She had frequent dieting periods and her weight fluctuated precisely between 47 and 50 kg, for a height of 1.60 m. She explained that she was shocked by her sister developing anorexia nervosa. She therefore decided to watch her weight in order to avoid falling below 47 kg, the weight at which her twin sister began to lose control of her eating behaviour.

This observation shows that if inheritance of vulnerability factors increases the risk for the disorder, the expression of this vulnerability can be counteracted by different factors such as avoiding a critical weight loss. Further complex features interacting in genetic analysis of eating disorders may concern the circuit of appetite control, obsessive-compulsive concerns, perfectionism as a cognitive trait, childhood obesity, complex links with alcoholism and/or mood disorders. Regarding such a large spectrum of interactions, integration of different domains of research is absolutely necessary to further explain the risk factors involved, just as a large variety of specialists take account of eating disorders in clinical practice.

The true 'sociocultural debate' that needs to be held concerning the genetics of anorexia nervosa is how we are going to deal with the (hypothetical) discovery of the mutations (modification of the genes involved that leads to abnormal proteins). There are many potential benefits in such a finding, for example treating earlier borderline eating disorders, discovering new targets (and thus new treatments) through the proteinic expression of the genes involved, and matching treatment to the genetic polymorphisms that characterise each patient. On the other hand, the recent history of psychiatric genetics has shown us that the worst is always possible, such as the sterilisation of vulnerable persons and the attempt to create pure ethnic groups.

In our present society, while hopefully more responsive to individual rights, some drifts may nevertheless be possible. A private insurance company may be interested in detecting vulnerability for a very expensive disorder before they insure somebody. Some specific examinations (such as for models or dietitians who are supposed to be at higher risk) may use this information for specific recruitment. Some parents may try to analyse the genes involved prenatally for an eugenic purpose. This debate has been raised previously for intelligence, and some clues were given because the research on the genetic compound of intelligence is more advanced. A recent review proposed that 'finding genes associated with general intelligence detected by IQ tests, does not mean that we ought to put all of our resources into educating the brightest children. Depending on our values, we might worry more about children falling off the low end of the normal distribution in an increasingly technological society, and decide to devote more public resources to those in danger of being left behind' (Plomin, 1999).

This could also be proposed for eating disorders, using genetic analysis to help patients with a handicapping disorder rather than stigmatising vulnerable persons. Another fact that puts our mind at ease for the discovery of relevant genes in eating disorders is the limited power of such finding. The genes involved explain part of the genetic variance (if we know all the genes, their expression and interactions), and the genetic variance represents only part of the total variance of the disorder. In this view, it has to be remembered that although the genes involved in the genetic vulnerability are incredibly stable over a lifetime (and through generations), these genes probably have a significant impact only when specific trigger conditions, familial, personal and affective environments are present. There is thus no genetic 'determinism', and the importance of heritability does not reduce the potentially benefit of social, psychological, familial or psychiatric interventions.

Whatever the pessimistic phantasms described, looking for the genes involved is a powerful way to discover new treatments and understand further this complex disorder, much more than giving weapons to irresponsible companies or persons.

References

Gorwood P (1999). Genetic association studies in behavioral neuroscience. In: *Molecular Genetic Techniques for Behavioural Neuroscience*, edited by Cruzio W, Gerlai R. Amsterdam: Elsevier, pp. 944.

Gorwood P, Adès J, Parmentier G (1998). Anorexia nervosa in one monozygotic twin. *American Journal of Psychiatry*, **155**(5), 708.

Plomin R (1999). Genetics and general cognitive ability. *Nature*, **402**(S): C25–C29.

Chapter 5

Post-communism and the marketing of the thin ideal

Günther Rathner
Assistant Professor, Department of Paediatrics, Eating
Disorders Unit, Leopold-Franzens University of Innsbruck.
Innsbruck, Austria

> *Debate question*
> The transition of former socialist Central and Eastern European countries
> to Western market economy is now reflecting on many aspects of human
> life. One of the main features of this market economy is the selling via media
> images of the illusion of possible re-production of the human body. This
> clearly applies to the question of eating disorders, which may increase
> in the future or be replaced by cosmetic surgery. It is the selling of a
> mechanism that promotes the infinite malleability of the human body which
> serves as an antidote to aging and dying and a futile answer to personal
> and psychosocial problems.

> *'Bodily discipline is the instrument par excellence of every kind of
> "domestication" . . . Thus is explained the place that all totalitarian regimes
> give to collective bodily practices.'*
>
> *Piere Bourdieu (1990)*

Introduction

In Eric Hobsbawn's (1996) book on the 20th century, he suggests that the most
significant period of that century was that between the First World War and the
fall of the Berlin Wall. The fall of the Berlin Wall was a totally unforeseen event
that ushered in the decline of the former communist system in the countries of
Central and Eastern Europe (CEE). This led to a departure from the state-socialist
systems that governed virtually all these countries to a Western-style market
economy, with an unprecedented transition and transformation that included every
aspect of human life. One of the main features of this Western-style economy is
individualism, that is, the tendency for social conflicts and social inequality to be
individualised. Arguably, within the framework of this social system, problems

and conflicts are easily translated into socially accepted and communicable individualised morbidities. This is done through the psychological (re-)structuring of the human being, both body and soul. In an effort to adapt to continously changing social realities, it becomes possible and perhaps even encouraged for social distress to become articulated through medical or psychiatric terminology. Depression and anxiety disorders are commonly acknowledged as indicators of such individually experienced life strains. In Western industrialised countries, the tremendous increase in rates of depression during the last five decades has been explained in terms of the cultural tendency towards individualisation and the fragmentation of social bonds (Seligman, 1990). It has even been suggested that any rapid and enduring cultural change is likely to be associated with an increase in psychological strain, which can be at times of epidemic proportions (Reykowski, 1994; Arnetz, 1996).

Hysteria, the most prevalent psychiatric disorder among women at the end of the 19th century, was seen as reflecting the kind of social pressures that were facing women at the fin-de-siècle in Europe (Shorter, 1987). It has been argued that pathological eating behaviours, collectively known as eating disorders, such as anorexia nervosa and bulimia nervosa are now seen as having taken the place of hysteria particularly in industrialised/individualised Western economies. Some have suggested that eating disorders can been compared to a litmus test that measures the degree of cultural change and its impact on human beings (Rathner *et al.* 1995).

The transition in Central and Eastern Europe and its discontents

Since 1989, the reform countries and the new independent states in CEE have experienced gross economic, social, political and cultural change. All of the long-standing socialist countries have been moving in a capitalist direction. Politically, new democracies developed in some instances and authoritarian regimes in others. The reform countries in CEE face a double challenge, which includes first, the transition to capitalism with all the imponderables of early capitalist accumulation within a few years, and second, the immediate confrontation with globalisation and modernisation with their attendant disruptions. These changes were specifically disturbing for the large agrarian sector that still existed in these countries and forced people there to rapidly adapt to new values and lifestyles. This unique historical situation in Eastern Europe can be seen as a quasi-natural experiment that provides a unique opportunity for research, an opportunity that up till now has not been fully taken advantage of (Oyen, 1992).

It is the contention of this essay that transitional processes produce a number of ill effects on mental health and attitudes, particularly among the younger population in the short-term. These effects are most likely responses to Westernisation, in particular to the escalating exposure of the population to new cultural norms and values which destabilise the society's old and traditional norms. The resulting sociocultural defence mechanisms can be both adaptive and maladaptive (Hinkle, 1974). It is likely that the transition has created and will continue to create an anomic situation for the vulnerable groups of the society. The effect of an anomic situation on the individual was originally articulated in Durkheim's seminal work (1997) on suicide and alcoholism and continues to be a major paradigm for understanding the impact on individuals of disruptive change. In addition to psychological difficulties, the losers of the transitional process could also experience long lasting ill-health, including a fall in fertility rates that could possibly result from the stress of social insecurity as well as an increase of mortality rates and drug abuse. However these long-term effects of the transition remain to be investigated.

It has long been suggested by numerous authors that eating disorders are one of the most sensitive barometers of culture change (Prince, 1985; Swartz, 1985; Di Nicola, 1990; Rathner et al. 1995; Nasser, 1997; Gordon, 2000). Hence the change and the ongoing transition process in CEE could be seen as posing a heightened risk for eating disorders in the populations of these countries, specifically adolescents and young adults.

Eating disorders in Central and Eastern Europe before the political changes in 1989: Empirical evidence

Until recently, comparative epidemiological studies into eating disorders that employed consistent methods, sampling procedures and diagnostic criteria were rare even in Western countries. The majority of these studies compared rates in one of the West European countries with those in North America. Typically, disturbed eating attitudes were found to be more common in North America than in West Europe (Steinhausen, 1984; Norring and Sohlberg, 1988; Thiel and Paul, 1988). However, recent studies showed striking similarities of test scores in Austria with those North America, suggesting period and cohort effects and indicating a globalisation of attitudes (Rathner and Rainer, 1997; Rathner and Waldherr, 1997).

Comparative cross-cultural studies in socialist European countries were almost non-existent before 1989, with few exceptions. This could reflect the absence of prevalence studies of eating disorders in the CCE. However, to preclude Western- or Euro-Centrism, one has to keep in mind that methodology in Western countries has typically followed a characteristic sequence: first case reports, then screenings in schoolgirls or students because of easier sampling, then general population screenings, and finally proper epidemiological two-stage studies. Research on eating disorders in developing countries has followed exactly the same sequence, albeit with a time lag. Although in the 1980s some clinical reports emerged from Czechoslovakia, Poland and Russia (Faltus, 1986; Zok-Jaroszweska, 1988; Krch, 1991; Korkina et al., 1992), they were mainly on anorexia nervosa, and it seems that bulimia nervosa was scarcely known in these countries. Perhaps this difference can be explained by the fact that an emphasis on consumption was far less in the East compared to the West.

One exception to the general trend, however, was a screening study carried out in Berlin in the second half of the 1980s, that is before unification. Berlin, before the fall of the Berlin Wall, was a city with shared history and similar cultural roots but more than 40 years of different political/economic systems. The study compared the eating attitudes of East and West Berlin schoolgirls and nursing students. The results revealed similarity between the two groups but showed the possibility that over-identification with Western ideals could perhaps be even greater among the East Berliners (Neumarker et al., 1992).

In a further notable exception, a two-stage epidemiological survey conducted in 1988 on female college students in Hungary showed a 1.3% prevalence of bulimia nervosa, a rate comparable to that reported in Western countries (Szabs and Tzry, 1991). It is possible that the results reflected the nature of the Hungarian society at that time, which was relatively more liberal than the rest of communist Europe. In this regard, the Hungarian system was often referred to rather jokingly as 'Goulash Communism'!

In 1988, a year before the changes that befell Europe, a collaborative research study was carried out between Hungary, the German Democratic Republic and Austria, comparing eating attitudes and eating disorder prevalence rates in large student samples (Rathner et al., 1995). Since no one at that time could imagine the scale and the magnitude of the change in CEE, the data of this study clearly provide a unique source of information in understanding the psychosocial precursors and sequelae of culture change on eating disorders. All the samples from East and West European students showed very similar weight indices. Desired weight was almost identical and prevalence rates of eating disorder morbidity were also the same in the three countries. Disturbed eating attitudes and behaviours (as measured by the Eating Disorder Inventory) were nonetheless somewhat higher in Hungary than in East Germany. Thus different levels of identification with the West existed before the political changes.

This study showed that eating disorders have been in existence in CEE before the political changes and perhaps were not all that different from those found in Western Europe. One possible interpretation might be that the countries in this study have been more or less through similar stages of industrialisation, though they are politically and economically different. The infiltration of Western-style media images through the Iron Curtain may have been there all along (in East Germany even in the same language) and sensitised student groups to the thinness ideal. Obviously, this pre-1989 level of advertisements was not comparable to the flood of first only translated Western advertisements and then Westernised national advertisements directed at the public in the reform countries in the 1990s. In contrast to the West, eating disorders did not receive adequate professional and public attention in Eastern Europe before the changes. This neglect might have been due to an erroneous identification of eating disorders as upper class or bourgeois afflictions. This characterisation may have been at one time correct in Western countries, but has changed since 1950 (Gard and Freeman, 1996).

Eating disorders in Central and Eastern Europe after the political changes in 1989

Comparative studies between Eastern and Western Europe have recently been carried out, resulting in a number of published studies. The comparative study referred to earlier (Rathner *et al.*, 1995) was replicated in the mid-1990s on large general population samples from Austria and the reform countries Hungary, the Czech Republic and Poland. This is the first population-based epidemiological study of eating disorders in the reform countries. No significant differences in eating attitudes (measured by Eating Attitudes Test scores) were found between the different countries and no clinical cases of anorexia nervosa were detected. The prevalence rates for full and sub-clinical cases of bulimia nervosa among the female population was in the range of 0.5–1.5% in all four countries. This meant that disturbed eating attitudes and rates for bulimia nervosa were the same for the adult female population in the European countries in transition as they were in Western Europe. An interesting and possibly significant finding was the emergence of dieting on this occasion among the male population in the four countries, a phenomenon which was non-existent in the pre-1989 study. This points to the possibility of the spread of the cult of thinness to the male gender in both Western and former Eastern bloc countries (Rathner *et al.*, 2001).

The Berlin study, referred to earlier, was also replicated following German unification in 1990, but only in former East Berlin. The girls were more preoccupied than boys with issues of body dissatisfaction, dieting and quest for thinness. Their eating attitudes (measured by EAT scores) were pretty similar to those of East Berliners in the mid-1980s, with a notable exception of an increase in the levels of body dissatisfaction (Hein *et al.*, 1998). In a subsequent study in 1992, in which a school population in Bulgaria was compared to the East Berlin group, the Bulgarian girls (nearly half of them attending private/Western-oriented schools) showed higher rates of eating disturbances (measured by Eating Attitudes Test scores) than their East Berlin counterparts (Boyadjieva and Steinhausen, 1996). One possible interpretation is that Bulgarian adolescents have perhaps more difficulties adapting to post-communist changes than the East Berlin girls.

Poland provided another case in point. Two groups of adult Polish women (factory workers and students) were studied in 1990 for their eating attitudes (using the Eating Attitudes Test and the Bulimia Investigatory Test). The students showed five times higher levels of disordered eating attitudes and bulimic symptoms than factory workers. Bulimia nervosa was noted to be unknown and it was even difficult to find suitable Polish phrases for terms such as diet food or bingeing. The study concluded, however, that the student female population in Poland was more at risk because of their increased Western orientation (Wlodarczyk-Bisaga *et al.*, 1995). Since then, the changes in popular culture in Poland and all the former socialist countries have followed the Western tendency to overvalue thinness as desirable and equivalent to feminine attractiveness. New women's magazines carry advertisements for diet foods ('Slimfast') and thin models advertise clothes, cosmetics and Western lifestyle (Dolan, 1993). There seems to be a nationalisation of the Western ideal of thinness as magazines in their respective languages prosper in each reform country. As the Western fashion industry is always in need of new faces and bodies, famous Central and Eastern European models now fill the insatiable stock of West European/US-American elite model firms. This Westernised popular culture might be the main cause for the development of Western prevalence rates for eating disorders in reform countries. In 1992/93, the same researchers conducted one of the rare longitudinal two-stage epidemiological study in female Polish adolescents. The prevalence rates of eating disorders were very similar to West European/US adolescents (Rathner and Messner, 1993; Wlodarczyk-Bisaga and Dolan, 1996). Upon assessing the natural history of their cases, their results showed a somewhat higher improvement rate in Poland than in the West (Rathner, 1992).

Altogether, there is a developing body of evidence that even before the political changes in Europe in 1989, eating disorders were as common in the East as in the West, but only in specific segments of society, specifically the student population (Rathner *et al.*, 1995). After the political changes, the vulnerability for eating disorders may have spread in other segments of the (female) society in the reform countries and eating disorders may now be as common in the reform countries as in West Europe. This was particularly demonstrated by the first adult population-based study in these countries (Rathner *et al.*, 2001) and a Polish female adolescent study (Wlodarczyk-Bisaga and Dolan, 1996). The former provided similar prevalence rates for bulimia nervosa in Eastern and Western Europe, while the latter revealed prevalence rates comparable to Western levels in Polish schoolgirls. Some screening studies have showed even more disturbed eating attitudes in reform countries than in West Europe due to over-identification. As revealed in the last years before the changes, differences between the reform countries still exist. The prediction of an increase in eating disorders in the reform countries (Rathner *et al.*, 1995) still has to be substantiated, as no general population comparison data are available for the stage before transition that took place in 1989. However, screening data do point in that direction. For example, although 3% of Polish female workers scored above the EAT cut-off score in 1990 (Wlodarczyk-Bisaga *et al.*, 1995), 7% of Polish general population females did so in 1995 (Rathner *et al.*, 2001).

Thus, the spread of Western ideals of thinness, dieting and their erroneous equation with 'success' in the reform countries may follow the same course as we have experienced in the West in the last five decades, although at increased speed in Eastern Europe. Additional studies, and especially longitudinal studies, are urgently needed to demonstrate the connection between the culture changes that are characteristic of the transition and the important public health problem of eating disorders.

New economy, new images

In the 20th century, society and culture have witnessed wrenching transformations: from full-blown industrial society via imperialism to globalisation, from colonialism to post-colonialism, from industrial production to the post-modern information age. Globalisation might be the 21st century synonym for imperialism, that is, the concentration of economy and power on a previously unknown level. These dramatic changes have been accompanied by similar changes in social and family life, social relations, and new forms of human embodiment. Both the transition of former communist countries in Central and Eastern Europe and globalisation are part of the same process. Globalisation is not an 'out there' phenomenon removed from the concerns of everyday life, but rather it is an 'in here' matter which affects or rather is dialectically related to even the most intimate aspects of our lives. Whilst these sociocultural changes allowed for an increase in the range of options available to the individual, they also meant the loss of other social provisions afforded previously. This was bound to lead to the splitting of societies, an increase of the policy of exclusion of certain parts of society as well as an increase of health inequality. The core conflict of modernisation and transition stems from the increase in possibilities coupled with diminishing social criteria for choice and decision making. The recent rise of nationalism, racism, xenophobia, but also religious fundamentalism can be seen as counter-movements to re-establish certainty against the ambivalence and ambiguity of modernity (Bauman, 1991; Giddens, 1991; Beck, 1992; Nasser, 1997).

One aspect of modernisation is the progressive management, surveillance and regulation of the human body by market forces. Whereas in the 1920s in the United States the ideal of thinness was mainly centred in the upper social classes, beginning in the 1960s it spread to all layers of society. A market needs its masses! Besides TV as the new mass medium, heightened opportunities for female education and labour may have played a role in spreading the thinness ideal. In the 1960s and 1970s a major post-industrial shift was made from production towards consumption. 'Shop till you drop' is the right slogan for the 'industry of human happiness'. Interestingly, during the same period, a new eating disorder, bulimia nervosa, was first noted and appeared to be occurring in epidemic proportions. The conflicting production–consumption dialectic in Western societies is reflected in conflicting mass communication messages (control, diet, starving versus consumption; not to eat versus to eat), forming a parallel to the dilemma of starving and bingeing in eating disorders (Smith, 1993; Fine 1995, 1998).

The notion of body control through the marketing of the thin ideal has been at the core of the discussion of the impact of sociocultural factors on the psychopathology of eating disorders for some time. There was an early focus on the role of the media in disseminating the thinness ideal. At the present time, the majority of models still are thin white girls and women, although there is an increasing trend aiming to find new faces and bodies in non-Western models. Models grow ever younger and prepubescent girls are selling labels for adult women. At the same time that movie stars and models became ever thinner in the last decades (compare Marilyn Monroe and Kate Moss; Gagnard, 1986), the average weight in Western countries has increased. Celebrities with an eating disorder are frequently portrayed in the media, thereby glamorising these conditions and possibly fostering imitative behaviour (Gordon, 2000).

Unfortunately, the medical profession has supported this thinness ideal by selling ideal weight formulas. Thus, a Procrustean bed for weight was created. This bed (taken from a giant in Greek mythology) was always the right size: anyone too tall would have his feet cut off, anyone too short would be stretched to fit. Altogether, the effect of media influences might take place through the combination of waif-like supermodels as well as other forms of media depiction, particularly through thin pictures in women's magazines which were found to have greater influence than television shows in inducing abnormalities of eating behaviours (Harrison, 1997; Harrison and Cantor, 1997).

Relevant as well is the suggestion that the effect of this exposure is also likely to be dose-related (Field *et al.*, 1999). The social learning process of modelling has been put forward as an explanation for the effects of the media in this context. However, it would be simplistic to assume linear causality in this case. The media influence is clearly not acting in isolation from other sociocultural influences such as family and peer groups. The major effect of the media might be indirect: weight/shape-preoccupied subcultures significantly contribute to the predilection of the individual to body image concerns as well as disturbed eating (Paxton *et al.*, 1999).

The thinness gospel currently promoted by the Western media goes hand in hand with advertisements and commercials of fattening junk foods targeted mainly at the younger consumer. This in essence represents the unity of opposites in contemporary society. The massive spread of the cult of thinness through the media is perhaps the reason for the infiltration of this 'body ideal' from the upper socio-economic strata to all social classes, thus highlighting the interface between markets and media.

The curious relationship between economy and the media has been the subject of recent analysis and investigation. Becker and Hamburg (1996) posited that, 'it is not so much which images are presented as ideal but how they are rendered so compelling'. There is a circular relationship between consumers and media industry. Every media representation, be it a photograph, film, video or advertise-ment is a function of someone's investment in selling a message coded as an image. The consumer of an image is therefore not a passive victim but an active participant. The body is portrayed as a product that can be personally re-created or even purchased, just like buying a new car. The media's role here is selling the very possibility of re-manufacturing one's self through the medium of its image (Becker and Hamburg, 1996).

The problem is not the image *per se* (nowadays unnaturally thin), but the selling of the illusion of infinite technological or medical re-production of the human body. Accordingly, Turner (1992) defines the current Western social system as a 'somatic society in which the body . . . is the principal field of political and cultural activity. The body is the dominant means by which the tensions and crises of society are thematized'. Plastic bodies are also now creating plastic selves (Rogers, 1999). Society purports false assumptions that the body is infinitely malleable and that an imperfect body reflects an imperfect self, hence the necessity to perfect the human body.

The pursuit of thinness, physical activity and the expansion in cosmetic surgery are nonetheless symptoms of the centuries-old mind–body dualism in Western culture. The more medicine and technology claim to control the body through its potential and literal construction, both fixing bodies and improving them, the less control people sense they have over their bodies (Shilling, 1993). Loss of control predisposes people to medical/technical solutions, thus starting a vicious circle. It is likely that the 21st century will witness a tremendous rise in the use of the cosmetic surgery industry, perhaps paralleling the rise of eating disorders in the 20th century (Rathner 1999). Cosmetic surgery tries to reclaim the 'whole self' through 'technologies of the self'. In an era where markets flourish, 'standardisation' becomes society's main motto. The whole range of cosmetic surgery favours the 'sameness principle' from the nose job and breast enlargement to liposuction and even the change of the colour of the skin to remove bodily racial features and signs to approach Caucasians (Gilman, 1999). All ironically seem to be varieties of cloning, but in individualistic Western societies!

Western society can be characterised by a predominance of the visual and coincidentally, it is usually the surface of the body, which is the target of cosmetic surgery. Cosmetic surgery has an almost instantaneous effect. Why diet for weeks, months, and years, or engage in bingeing–purging cycles, if similar results can be achieved within hours by surgery? Anti-aging clinics are prospering and advertising for cosmetic surgery can be found even in tiny local newspapers. Only recently, an Austrian TV company started a women's lottery for breast enlargement for the coming summer/bikini season. Reading through those bodily procedures, it is obvious to see that they do not only impart messages of health or beauty, but also the antidote to aging and the 'guarantee to everlasting youth'. These young bodies are literally constructed against aging, but in the end in vain, of course. In Western societies, this image of endless youth coincides with the denial of the frailty of human beings and the denial of death.

Markets and their media are therefore recreating new identities through body manipulation, which in turn serves the market philosophy. The case of Eastern Europe following the economic transformation has been used in this essay as a paradigm for the impact of economic transformation on the human body, which is regarded within this context as a sellable/malleable commodity. The sociocultural transformation of the self through the body under these economic forces passes through stages of production to reproduction to simulation (Baudrillard, 1993). Historically this progression is mirrored in the journey from anorexic asceticism to bulimic consumption to simulation via cosmetic surgery (Rathner, 1999).

References

Arnetz BB (1996). Causes of change in the health of populations: a biopsychosocial viewpoint. *Society, Science and Medicine*, **43**, 605–8.

Baudrillard J (1993). *Symbolic exchange and death*. London: Sage Publications.

Bauman Z (1991). *Modernity and ambivalence*. Cornell: Cornell University Press.

Beck U (1992). *Risk society. Toward a new modernity*. London: Sage Publications.

Becker AE, Hamburg P (1996). Culture, the media, and eating disorders. *Harvard Review of Psychiatry*, **4**, 163–7.

Bourdieu P (1990). *In Other Words. Essay towards a Reflexive Sociology*. Cambridge: Polity Press.

Boyadjieva S, Steinhausen HC (1996). The eating attitudes test and the eating disorders inventory in four Bulgarian clinical and nonclinical samples. *Inernational Journal of Eating Disorders*, **19**, 93–8.

Di Nicola VF (1990). Anorexia multiforma: Self-starvation in historical and cultural context. Part II: Anorexia nervosa as a culture-reactive syndrome. *Transcultural Psychiatric Research Review*, **27**, 245–86.

Dolan B (1993). Eating disorders: A Western 'epidemic' spreads East? *European Eating Disorders Review*, **1**, 71–3.

Durkheim E (1997). *Suicide: A study in sociology*. New York: Free Press.

Faltus F (1986). Anorexia nervosa in Czechoslovakia. *International Journal of Eating Disorders*, **5**, 581–5.

Field AE, Camargo CA Jr, Taylor CB, Berkey CS, Colditz GA (1999). Relation of peer and media influences to the development of purging behaviors among preadolescent and adolescent girls. *Archives of Pediatric and Adolescent Medicine*, **153**, 1184–9.

Fine B (1995). Towards a political economy of anorexia? *Appetite*, **24**, 231–42.

Fine B (1998). *The political economy of diet, health and food policy*. London: Routledge.

Gagnard A (1986). From feast to famine: depiction of ideal body type in magazine advertising: 1950–1984. *Proceedings of the American Academy of Advertising*, **27**, 461–70.

Gard MCE, Freeman CP (1996). The dismantling of a myth: A review of eating disorders and socioeconomic status. *International Journal of Eating Disorders*, **20**, 1–12.

Giddens A (1991). *Modernity and self-identity: self and society in the late modern age*. Cambridge: Polity Press.

Gilman SL (1999). *Making the body beautiful. A cultural history of aesthetic surgery*. Princeton: Princeton University Press.

Gordon RA (2000). *Eating Disorders: Anatomy of a Social Epidemic*. Oxford: Blackwell Publications.

Harrison K (1997). Does interpersonal attraction to thin media personalities promote eating disorders? *Journal of Broadcasting and Electronic Media*, **41**, 478–500.

Harrison K, Cantor J (1997). The relationship between media consumption and eating disorders. *Journal of Communication*, **47**, 40–67.

Hein J, Neumärker KJ, Neumärker U (1998). Untersuchungen zum Eßverhalten in einer unselektierten Schülerpopulation der 7. bis 10. Klasse einer Berliner Schule. *Z Kinder-Jugendpsychiat*, **26**, 21–33.

Hinkle LR (1974). The effect of exposure to culture change, social change, and changes in interpersonal relationships on health. In: *Stressful life events: Their nature and effects*, edited by Dohrenwend BS, Dohrenwend BP. New York: Wiley, pp. 9–44.

Hobsbawn E (1996). *The age of extremes. A history of the world 1914–1991.* Vintage Books.

Korkina MV, Tsyvilko MA, Marilov VV, Kareva MA (1992). Anorexia nervosa as manifested in Russia. *International Journal of Psychosomatics*, **39**, 35–40.

Krch FD (1991). Epidemilogie Téchslovaquie des troubles des conduites alimentaires en Tchicoslovaquie. *Neuropsychiatrie de l'Enfance*, **39**, 311–22.

Nasser M (1997). *Culture and weight consciousness.* London: Routledge.

Neumärker U, Dudeck U, Vollrath M, Neumärker KJ, Steinhausen HC (1992). Eating attitudes among adolescent anorexia nervosa patients and normal subjects in former East and West Berlin. *International Journal of Eating Disorders*, **12**, 281–9.

Norring C, Sohlberg S (1988). Eating Disorder Inventory in Sweden: description, cross-cultural comparison, and clinical utility. *Acta Psychiatrica Scandinavica*, **78**, 567–75.

Oyen E (1992). *Comparative methodology. Theory and practice in international social research.* London: Sage Publications.

Paxton SJ, Schutz HK, Wertheim EH, Muir SL (1999). Friendship clique and peer influences on body image concerns, dietary restraint, extreme weight-loss behaviors, and binge eating in adolescent girls. *Journal of Abnormal Psychology*, **108**, 255–66.

Prince R (1985). The concept of culture-bound syndromes: Anorexia nervosa and brain fag. *Social Science and Medicine*, **21**, 197–203.

Rathner G (1992). Aspects of the natural history of normal and disordered eating and some methodological considerations, In: *The course of eating disorders. Long-term follow-up studies of anorexia and bulimia nervosa*, edited by Herzog W, Deter HC, Vandereycken W. Berlin: Springer, pp. 273–303.

Rathner G (1999). *The colonization of the body.* Invited plenary paper read at the 4th London International Conference Eating Disorders 1999, April 20–22, 1999, London, UK.

Rathner G, Messner K (1993). Detection of eating disorders in a small rural town: an epidemiological study. *Psychological Medicine* **23**, 175–84.

Rathner G, Rainer B (1997). Normen für das Anorexia-nervosa-Inventar zur Selbstbeurteilung bei weiblichen Adoleszenten der Risikoaltersgruppe für Eßstürungen. *Z Klin Psychol Psych*, **45**, 302–18.

Rathner G, Tury F, Szabo P, Geyer H, Runpold G, Forgaces A, Sollner W, Plottner G, (1995). Prevalence of eating disorders and minor psychiatric morbidity in Central Europe before the political changes in 1989: A cross-cultural study. *Psychological Medicine* **25**, 1027–35.

Rathner G, Tury F, Szabo P, Krch FD, Namyslowska I (2001). How common are culture-change syndromes such as eating disorders in European post-communist countries? (under review).

Rathner G, Waldherr K (1997). Eating Disorder Inventory-2: Eine deutschsprachige Validierung mit Normen für weibliche und männliche Jugendliche. *Z Klin Psychol Psych*, **45**, 157–82.

Reykowski J (1994). Collectivism and individualism as dimensions of social change. In: *Individualism and Collectivism. Theory, Methods, and Applications*, edited by Kim U, Triandis HC, Kagitcibasi C, Choi SC, Yoon G. London: Sage Publications, pp. 276–92.

Rogers MF (1999). *Barbie culture.* London: Sage Publications.

Seligman MEP (1990). Why is there so much depression today? The waxing of the individual and the waning of the commons. In: *Contemporary Approaches to Depression*, edited by Ingram RE. New York: Plenum Press, pp. 1–9.

Shilling C (1993). *The body and social theory*. London: Sage.

Shorter E (1987). The first great increase in anorexia nervosa. *Journal of Social History*, **21**, 69–96.

Smith RJ (1993). Eating disorders and the production-consumption dialectic. *New Ideas in Psychology*, **11**, 95–104.

Steinhausen HC (1984). Transcultural comparison of eating attitudes in young female and anorectic patients. *European Archives of Psychiatric and Neurological Science*, **234**, 198–201.

Swartz L (1985). Anorexia nervosa as a culture-bound syndrome. *Society, Science and Medicine*, **20**, 725–30.

Szabs P, Tzry F (1991). The prevalence of bulimia nervosa in a Hungarian college and secondary school population. *Psychotherapy Psychosomatics*, **56**, 43–7.

Thiel A, Paul T (1988) Entwicklung einer deutschsprachigen Version des Eating Disorders Inventory (EDI). *Z Different Diagnost Psychol*, **9**, 267–78.

Turner BS (1992). *Regulating bodies*. London: Routledge.

Wlodarczyk-Bisaga K, Dolan B (1996). A two-stage epidemiological study of abnormal eating attitudes and their prospective risk factors in Polish schoolgirls. *Psychological Medicine* **26**, 1021–32.

Wlodarczyk-Bisaga K, Dolan B, McCluskey S, Lacey H (1995). Disordered eating behaviour and attitudes towards weight and shape in Polish women. *European Eating Disorder Review*, **3**, 205–16.

Zok-Jaroszweska U (1988). Kliniczne i psychologiczne aspekty anorexia nervosa. *Psychoterapia*, **3**, 7–16.

Commentary I

Noah E. Gotbaum
Senior Vice President and Head of European Corporate
Development, Level 3 Communications, Inc., London, UK

I must begin by saying that as one of the American capitalists charged with instigating turmoil in Eastern Europe, I may be too critical and unsympathetic to Günther Rathner's chapter 'Post-communism and the marketing of the thin ideal'. Although Dr Rathner posits that globalization, and the permeation of 'Western' (read: American) economic ideals of capitalist consumerism and the associated force-fed cultural ideals of 'thinness', are the root cause of most problems of the post-communist countries of Central and Eastern Europe including an increased incidence of eating disorders, I found little to support his assertions.

Certainly Dr Rathner is correct in pointing out that loosened state and societal bonds in Central and Eastern Europe, including the wholesale disappearance of cradle to grave employment and economic safety nets that were keys to the communist system, have led to an increased and forced reliance on the individual rather than the state. It is also fair to say that these economic and political transitions have been extremely difficult for much, if not most, of the citizenry and have led to measurable psychological stress. Whether these transitional strains are in any way comparable to those brought on by day to day life under the previous Stalinist regimes including surveillance, purges, environmental ruin and the like is debatable. But there is no question that the sociological and psychological impact of the region's recent changes have been underestimated and under analyzed. Witness surprising, if temporary, election victories by resurgent Communist parties in virtually every country in the region outside of Russia and it is clear, to turn the Clinton dictum on its head, that there is more going on than 'the economy, stupid'. And as Rathner points out, the long-term effects of the former political, economic and sociocultural structures on physical, mental and social health need to be investigated.

I could not agree more. The transition in Central and Eastern Europe from a one-party political and centrally planned economic system to one based on democracy and free-market economics has been neither easy nor complete. The political transition has caused much pain and many physical and psychological hardships, including perhaps a rise in the incidence of eating disorders. I would have appreciated the inclusion of additional research on the psychological responses generally to political and economic changes. This argument, however, was not fully developed.

True, Rathner does point out that massive cultural changes lead to 'significant changes in health' and that 'the losers of the transition process will experience longer lasting ill-health'. One need only to point to the increased incidence of heart disease and the huge lowering of male life expectancy in the former Soviet Union post-transition to know this to be a possibility. What continues to plague me, however, is exactly how eating disorders are produced in such a period of economic and political transition. Perhaps this cannot be answered by anyone at the present.

The data provided in the argument supports Rathner's general thesis that the 'Western media's thinness ideal' is responsible for all the ills faced by citizens of transitional economies. However, the pre-transition studies referred to in Rathner's argument show that the incidence of anorexia nervosa was roughly equivalent in the West and the East. Yet such findings fly in the face of his expectation of a lower incidence of eating disorders in the East prior to the assumed deleterious effects of the economic changes and the increased exposure to 'Western style media images' that accompanied those changes.

With the Western media as the bogeyman, Rathner does not entertain the possibility that other factors might have led to 'Western' levels of anorexia nervosa in the pre-transition Communist countries, factors including the Soviet deification of thin female athletes (weight lifters excluded) and even thinner ballerinas, for example. Given the manner in which the Communist political structures controlled all flows of information, particularly that which showed their countries in an unfavorable light, it would not surprise me that the true incidence of eating disorders in the pre-transition Soviet 'bloc' was even higher than in the West.

Equally frustrating is Rathner's tendency to oversimplify the research. When Rathner finds a 1996 study showing an unusually high proportion of positive EAT scores in Bulgaria, he automatically assumes that 'Bulgarian adolescents have perhaps more difficulties adapting to the post-Communist changes than the rest of Eastern Europe'. Since, however, he has no data from the pre-Communist Bulgarian era his assumption is based on little other than conjecture as the Bulgarian sample might have had high prevalence rates prior to the changes. Rathner has, however, chosen to compare the high Bulgarian scores to those lower ones found in studies of other post-Communist countries, namely Poland and Hungary. In so doing, he might benefit from at least recognizing the potential effects of timing differences (not to mention country differences) on the research he cites. While, for example, the 1993 Polish studies he references show a relatively low incidence of eating disorders, it is possible that studies from Poland in 1996, at which time the economic transition, and its associated psychological effects, were much further along, might have shown a similarly high proportion of EAT scores as in Bulgaria. Such a possibility, however, is never entertained.

Certainly Rathner is ambitious and perhaps even a trail blazer in his efforts to understand the psychological situation in Eastern Europe and to be fair his ability to draw conclusions suffers from the general lack of credible research, both pre- and post-transition, a failing for which he cannot be blamed. Yet I would have prefered it had he proposed a wider range of possible interpretations.

Another fascinating, but unanswered, question is Dr Rathner's prediction that the future may see an increase in cosmetic surgery. What does that have to do with the earlier question of the effects that the economic and cultural changes in the East will have on the incidences of eating disorder? Perhaps he is saying that since the all powerful Western media ideal is changing from one of thinness to one of standardization and malleability of the body, the easily influenced East will naturally assume this new (negative) ideal as well.

In the end, however, this point, and those which preceded it, may be just side shows to Rathner's dogmatic assertion ' . . . globalization . . . means . . . following the paths of imperialism and neo-colonialism'. After unsuccessfully blaming the Western capitalist media for all the woes in the region, and specifically an (unproven) increase in eating disorders and ill health, the author broadens the attack to encompass globalization as a whole. As an alternative to this (exploitive capitalist) globalization, Rathner would, he says, like to find the famous 'Third Way' which calls for the 'revival of the local'. An admirable goal perhaps, but only after Rathner is able to provide more proof that the democratic capitalist 'First Way', which most countries of the former Soviet bloc now embrace, has failed its citizens. I find little in the argument so far to convince me that it is the case!

Commentary 2

Katarzyna Bisaga
Department of Child Psychiatry, Columbia
University-New York State Psychiatric Institute,
New York, USA

The impact of the recent socio-economic and political changes in Central and Eastern Europe upon societies undergoing this transition is a timely and important topic for exploration. As Dr Günther Rathner rightly states, such times of transition offer a unique opportunity to disentangle the interaction between the societal changes and the expression of individual suffering. Yet, understanding this transition is contingent upon adequate descriptions of ongoing processes of cultural change so that comparisons can be made across former socialist/communist countries. Westernization appears to be one of the processes involved but its impact upon the Eastern European societies may be variable according to cultural, religious, and political diversity in the former Eastern block countries. Thus, the introduction of a free market economy may have led to different responses both at national and individual level in each of the countries undergoing the transition. For example, since the early 1970s Poland and Hungary became relatively open to foreign travel, with Western fashion and stereotyped expression of femininity present in the mass media (for example, in movies). Yet, other countries, such as Romania or former Soviet Union countries, remained more isolated. Therefore, assessment of a degree of already present Westernization in those countries prior to the change in addition to screening for eating problems would be necessary to determine the impact of the dramatic changes since 1989.

Not only should the exposure to Western pressures be established in any research but also the adherence to indigenous values, including religion, needs to be taken into account. For example, the Catholic faith has been strongly endorsed in Poland but not so much in other Eastern European countries. Dr Rathner, to his credit, mentions some aspects of the cultural diversity of Eastern European countries that need to be spelled out clearly in any discussion of the recent transition. Any unitary concept of one 'Eastern block' culture needs to be challenged.

Understanding the impact of cultural changes in Eastern Europe on eating disorders requires the establishment of the baseline rates of eating disorders prior to the change. For example, Rathner shows that rates of eating disorder symptoms in two Eastern European countries prior to the change were found to be comparable with those reported in Western countries (for example, rates of bulimia nervosa in Hungary and GDR). These studies showed that the vulnerability for the development of eating problems had been present in Eastern Europe prior to the change. Yet the degree of this vulnerability remains unknown. In general, eating disorders were under-studied in most of these countries. Poor identification of mental health problems, including eating disorders during the communist era, was perhaps related to the government denial of problems, since such recognition would threaten the system designed to provide happiness to all.

The intuitive notion expressed by Dr Rathner that the unprecedented exposure to a thinness ideal in the media could lead to an increase in the rates of eating disorders remains to be substantiated, since no study to date has documented an increase in the rates of eating disorders. Furthermore, most studies at hand rarely investigated community samples and the majority used self-report questionnaires in lieu of diagnostic assessments. For example, higher EAT scores among Bulgarian adolescent girls could be related to the postulated over-identification with the Western ideal, and yet the lack of diagnostic assessment and unexplored cultural identity status of subjects limit the conclusions regarding the prevalence of actual eating disorders as well as the impact of Westernization. The increased presentation for treatment described in Hungary might not reflect the community trends but rather suggests a change in service utilization practices. Studies of Polish university students and adolescent schoolgirls have indicated the stability of rates of eating problems (as reflected by proportion of EAT-26 high scorers) at least during the initial (3 year) period following the changes (Wlodarczyk-Bisaga et al., 1995; Wlodarczyk-Bisaga and Dolan, 1996).

Moreover, assuming that risk factors (such as the media idealization of thinness) associated with development of a disorder in Western setting would operate in a similar fashion in an Eastern European setting as they do in Western countries has to be questioned. In fact, the role of media exposure in the development of eating problems among Western women is still debated. Most studies that have focused on this relationship have used cross-sectional designs, thus precluding any conclusions regarding cause and effect relationships.

It has also been argued that while there appears to be an association between the media images of thinness and eating disorders, it may be that women who already have disordered eating are more vulnerable to the images of thinness than non-eating disordered women (Hamilton and Waller, 1993). The only prospective study to find a positive relation between the media exposure and abnormal eating attitudes was carried out in Fiji during 36 months following the introduction of television on this island (Becker and Burwell, 1999). Any state-of-the-art study of the impact of cultural change upon eating symptoms in Eastern European countries should prospectively measure a degree of cultural change/identification along with development of eating symptoms. One could thereby index the impact of a change in eating disorders to relevant psychosocial variables.

Further, any study of the impact of cultural change upon development of psychopathology should determine if there is a specific factor operating within a particular culture such as one exemplified by media idealization of thinness or whether cultural change itself constitutes a non-specific risk factor. A recent study of Mexican immigrants in the US found that, contrary to the previous notions, psychiatric morbidity was not higher among immigrants compared to their native counterparts (Escobar, 1998). Yet, some of the worrisome trends reviewed by Dr Rathner such as a decrease in life expectancy, a decrease in fertility rates, and increased rates of alcohol abuse/dependency indicate increased health risks occurring during the transition in Eastern Europe.

References

Rathner G, Tury F, Szabo P *et al.* (1995). Prevalence of eating disorders and minor psychiatric morbidity in Central Europe before the political changes in 1989: a cross-cultural study. *Psychological Medicine,* **25**, 1027–35.

Boyadjieva S, Steinhausen HC (1996). The eating attitudes test and the eating disorders inventory in four Bulgarian clinical and nonclinical samples. *International Journal of Eating Disorders,* **19**, 93–8.

Wlodarczyk-Bisaga K, Dolan B (1996). A two-stage epidemiological study of abnormal eating attitudes and their prospective risk factors in Polish schoolgirls. *Psychological Medicine,* **26**, 1021–32.

Wlodarczyk-Bisaga K, Dolan B, McCluskey S, Lacey H (1995). Disordered eating behaviour and attitudes towards weight and shape in Polish women. *European Eating Disorders Review,* **3**, 1–12.

Hamilton K, Waller G (1993). Media influences on body size estimation in anorexia and bulimia. An experimental study. *British Journal of Psychiatry,* **162**, 837–40.

Becker AE, Burwell RA (1999). *Acculturation and Disordered Eating in Fiji.* Presented at the 152nd Annual Meeting of the American Psychiatric Association, 1999.

Escobar JI (1998). Immigration and mental health. *Archives of General Psychiatry,* **55**, 781–2.

Chapter 6

Emerging markets: Submerging women

Ana Catina
Research Fellow, Center for Psychotherapy Research, Stuttgart, Germany

Oltea Joja
Clinical Psychologist & Research Fellow, Institute of Endocrinology, Bucharest, Romania

Debate question
The economic transformation in Eastern Europe following the decline of communism and the adoption of a market philosophy is bound to affect women's perception of themselves and of their societal roles. This theoretically should increase their confusion over gender roles and subsequently their propensity to develop eating disorders.

I Gender ambivalence and eating disorders

'Gender ambivalence' is a term coined by Silverstein and Perlick (1995) to describe the ambiguities in the female role during periods of historical and cultural transition that leave women vulnerable to eating disorders. The issue of gender ambivalence has been central to the sociocultural debate on eating disorders for nearly the past decade. The pursuit of thinness in the anorexic syndrome has been seen as metaphorical to woman's struggle to formulate a new identity in the face of changing social roles (Orbach, 1986; Gordon, 1999).

In *Culture and Weight Consciousness*, Nasser (1997) raised the issue of the apparent split between gender and culture in feminist discourse. She pointed to the fact that the position of women in other cultures was not taken into account in the gendered analysis of the problem, which was by and large exclusively limited to the Western culture. She specifically drew attention to the position of women in countries that had socialist regimes, in an attempt to explore the impact of the economic transformation on women in these societies. These included the nations of Eastern Europe after the decline of communism and other societies which underwent a socialist experience. Given the tight social networks in these societies, women were protected in their education, employment and child care. However, with the adoption of market economies many of these provisions were threatened, and this in turn rendered women vulnerable to gender role confusion.

It has been argued that temporary reversals of gender roles with an increase in gender ambivalence occurs in response to macroeconomic developments (Silverstein and Perlick, 1995). The gender ambivalence experienced by particular individuals appears to be secondary to societal ambivalence about its own expectations of women. The higher the degree of this ambivalence, the greater the ambiguity women would feel about their own role with subsequent increased risk to develop an eating morbidity (Nasser, 1997)

In this chapter these issues will be dealt with in more detail and in particular the following issues will be discussed:

- gender roles and communism: discussion of gender role definitions under communist regimes;
- differences between women's perception of their role in Eastern and Western Europe;
- market forces, gender and eating disorders: discussion of the impact of the economic transformation on the lives of women in Eastern Europe and whether these changes increase their risk of developing eating disorders.

2 Gender roles and communism

In Socialist Realist Art, the 'the new woman' was depicted as a successful student, a university academic, a collectivist peasant, or a qualified worker in an industrial plant. The 'hallmark' of communism was the involvement of the masses in the process of building a new social order. Each member of society, irrespective of gender, race or nationality, was expected to contribute to this process through an active professional, social and above all political commitment. Millions of women stepped out of the traditional bourgeois role that limited them to the care of children and serving of the needs of men and entered the labour force.

The nationalised means of production which followed the communist revolution in Russia (1917), and the Second World War in the rest of Eastern Europe, meant the takeover by the state of all sources of economy. The productive branch, especially heavy industry, as well as state defence and the public sector were ideologically and financially considered to be top priorities. As communist regimes had to increase the labour force to develop those aspects of heavy industry, employment among women rose dramatically. What feminists in the West had long been struggling for became a reality in Eastern Europe almost overnight, despite the fact that women's duties up until then had not strayed beyond the confines of home and hearth (Young, 1996).

The society created an economic infrastructure geared to encourage women to work outside their homes. Relatively convenient day care and nursery schools as well as a complex system of leaves, concessions and allowances were made available, in order to permit women to work full time. The communist ideology promoted an ideal image for a new type of woman, who would be an active social agent. The symbolic image of the new woman was robust with an enthusiastic face, lifted upwards, as if standing firmly against the wind. Women's physical and sensual beauty that was traditionally integral to art was redefined by the communist ethic to mean sober simplicity. This set the communist woman at a distance from the capitalist decadent emphasis on external image and outer appearance.

The 'new woman' was politically active, fighting tirelessly against class enemies and the remnants of bourgeois ideology. She would sacrifice her personal needs to exceed the work quota required by the five-year plan and to secure an overall increase in national productivity. The national presses highlighted women's professional achievements, commending those who had won the socialist competition at work. The socialist woman worker was also mother and a head of the family, on equal footing with her husband. The worker/mother enjoyed the highest social esteem and received generous state support, while the housewife/mother was seen as not taking part in the socialist project and their domestic responsibilities were largely discounted (Staikova and Gedeleva, 1992).

On International Women's Day, the communist government celebrated this newly emerging woman: the mother, wife, and active communist. Kindergartens, schools and political youth associations were instrumental in preparing young girls for this complex role that society expected of them. Women were expected to be 'professional, mother and wife', and this was the case for almost four generations in the Soviet Union and for nearly two generations in Eastern Europe. Women in Russia were reported by the World Bank to be on the whole better educated than their male counterparts (Young, 1996). According to one-year statistics (1989), 47% of the women had completed secondary and higher specialised or technical education, with nearly half of all university academic posts occupied by women.

In communist Czechoslovakia 97% of all employable women were at paid work (Siklova, 1997). However, these figures applied mainly to women living in cities who had opportunities for growth and possible development. Women in very small towns or villages remained by and large 'traditional', dependent upon older prescribed gender roles.

Thus, as far as women were concerned, there were still 'two cultures' operating within the unified socialist regime, that is urban and rural. The collectivisation of agriculture and the escalating need for a workforce to fuel the industrialisation project led to massive internal migration from villages to cities. Young uneducated rural women with little or no qualifications were by and large causalities of this massive migration. Dramatic changes in women's roles and identity took place among the rural populations secondary to this internal migration, and yet city life still carried with it the hope for better education, better life prospects and even possible participation in party politics.

Notwithstanding any urban/ rural differences in women's position in former socialist Europe, the fact remains that the societal image promoted by the party of 'the new woman' seemed on the whole a reconciled one, embracing the woman worker and the woman nurturer. The 'double role' stress, often mentioned in the

Western feminist literature, was not unknown to Eastern European women. However, both men and women were operating within similar social structures and no sharply different societal roles were prescribed for either gender. Women and men shared the same responsibilities and both were expected to be equally assertive in the face of the challenge for progress. It is relevant to note that the official party ideology played down the old notions of femininity, even if women continued to see themselves as intrinsically different from men, being more emotional or more skilled in rearing children.

Socialist women also continued to pay attention to their appearance, not as a reflection of dependency on standards of social desirability or social approval, but stemming from a personal preference to maintain a degree of individuality within the boundaries of a more or less homogeneous fashion. These 'feminine' qualities were not perceived by women as a disadvantage or a weakness and were not regarded as hindrance to women's progress in the public arena (Svendsen, 1996; Drakulic, 1999).

3   Gender roles: Between left and right

Some empirical investigations have been carried out to substantiate the assumed differences in the perception of gender roles between Eastern and Western Europe (Catina et al., 1996; Catina et al., 1997; Joja and Vasilescu, 1998; von Wietersheim and Pecova, 1998).

The aim was to illustrate the impact of different socio-economic models on young women's perception of themselves and their role in society. These studies were conducted on groups of female German students, representing Western Europe, and comparable female students from Bulgaria, Romania and the Czech Republic, representing Eastern Europe. The results pointed to the fact that young German women saw the combined role of a mother and a successful professional as contradictory. They considered that the society's preference is for women to adopt the mother/wife role which curtailed women's potential and limited their opportunities for growth, development and self-actualisation. The German girls also expressed ambivalence towards their social role(s), and felt torn between what is seen as domestic and public.

In contrast, the Czech, Bulgarian and Romanian female students appeared to accept both roles, that is, the woman/mother and the woman/worker, and both roles were viewed as complementary and not contradictory. These views were very much in keeping with the communist ethos and social ideal in this respect. Accordingly, their acquired new self-image matched their expectation of carrying out multiple social roles. In contrast to German girls, the Bulgarians, the Czechs and the Romanians perceived themselves as competitive and goal-oriented and did not view this in any way as interfering with or diminishing their femininity.

When the views of the four groups were compared regarding women's attractiveness, both the Eastern and Western European girls considered attractiveness as important to social success. The German young women saw women's attractiveness exclusively in terms of physical appearance, while the Eastern European girls described it in terms of psychological gifts and attributes of mental and social intelligence and the issue of physical appearance was not even mentioned. It does seem ironic that young German women who enjoyed living in a culture which respects individual rights and freedom seemed to have remained internally restrained in exercising their own individual choices and therefore still appeared tied to traditional views of femininity while young women living under restrictive communist regimes seemed psychologically more able to take advantage of party rhetoric and free themselves from the restrictive notions of historical femininity. Most likely their more flexible view was facilitated by the practical social provisions for women that were enshrined within the socialist system.

4 Market forces, gender and eating disorders

To those living under former communist regimes, however, the West was the beacon for individual freedom and democracy. Men and women of Eastern Europe admired the Western European ideals and waited nearly half a century for this perceived utopia to become a reality for them. The ending of the communist political regimes in Europe in the late 1980s generated a great deal of optimism (Olsen, 1996). Yet the reality was very difficult, and a state of political and economic instability became symptomatic of the transition from state to market economy. One of the most recognisable side-effects of economic liberalisation was unemployment and as a result, women's presence in the workforce became undesirable. Significant changes to the position of women in the labour force followed, as the high ideals of gender equality fostered by socialism could no longer be sustained. Impoverished states had to withdraw the support traditionally granted to the social sector, with subsequent closure of many day care centres and child care facilities. What remained of the existing infrastructure for child care became costly and largely unaffordable under the new economic climate. Many regional and local authorities in Russia declared that if women would retreat from the labour forces to take care of their children, the social infrastructure could be used for other commercial goals (Kliatchko, 1994).

Health care provisions which had supported women's active participation in the public life were also considerably reduced. The state of Hungary suspended national maternity leave benefits, possibly at the recommendation of the World Bank and International Monetary Fund (Acsady, 1995/96). As a consequence of this cut in benefits and the introduction of private health systems, a drop in the national birth rate and rise in the rates of abortion was noted in Bulgaria. These statistics seemed not to cause concern but rather were welcomed by the state as helping to resolve current economic problems (Kanev, 1999).

In Ukraine there was a significant decrease in medical services, with a particular decline in support for child care facilities (Rudneva, 1999). In Russia alone, 80% of the first wave of unemployed workers were women, among them doctors, teachers and scientists (Afanassieva, 1992). In the early 1990s sterilised women in East Germany were rumoured to stand a better chance of obtaining or maintaining employment than non-sterilised ones.

In Bulgaria, Poland, Lithuania and Slovakia the percentage of female unemployment rose rapidly (Wyzan, 1998). Employment figures among women in Hungary dropped from 90% to 63% in the course of eight years (1987–1995) (Acsady, 1995/96). In accordance with the new economic strategy, societal perceptions and expectations of women inevitably changed and the accepted gender definitions were questioned. A revival of the ideal image of the woman as housewife and mother took place. However the housewife model belonged to a different economic structure in which gender roles were traditionally defined with the man being the economic power of the household and the woman economically dependent on him.

The women of Eastern Europe in the post-communist era had to face an unfamiliar situation that conflicted with their former values and the principles they were brought up to believe. These changes were coupled with the fact that husbands could no longer be sole providers as many families could not survive on a single wage or salary (Staikova and Gedeleva, 1992). They were reinforced by a stream of media images disseminating new values concerning women's role in the family. The entire phenomenon, which preached the social desirability of a newly reformulated woman who is dedicated to domestic tasks and the care of her children (Zareva 1992), was referred to as women's 'restoration' phase. At the same time the professional was portrayed as a 'false'/ pseudo-social or pseudo-political woman, one who needed to give up on her personal life to pursue a career (Lipovskaya, 1992; Acsady, 1995/96).

These new market definitions of gender elicited varied and ambivalent responses from Eastern European women. Their reaction differed according to each individual's experience prior to the 1990s economic and the political reform. For some, the communist regimes gave women no choice and their entrance into the labour market was perceived as a kind of obligation or even a national duty. Their attitude towards this forced emancipation, which in their opinion was detrimental to them and their families, was understandably negative (Jalusic, 1992; Zareva, 1992). For many of those women, work did not fulfil any personal aspirations and their preference was clearly to stay at home if they were given the chance. In a survey conducted in Russia nearly 30% of the women expressed their wish to remain at home (Chinyaeva, 1999; Drakulic, 1999). However, this was not the case for all women. Others perceived the post-socialist trend as threatening to their rights, undermining their position and constituting a serious regression in women's standing in society (Acsady, 1995/96).

The communist 'culture' with its specific set of models has been subjected to a major transformation in the name of development and against a background of economic chaos and poverty. The rhythm of transition was fast, even precipitous. National leaders were eager to receive international recognition, financial support and the long-awaited integration with the rest of Europe. Transition, said Sampson, is 'people's perception of what the world out there offers and their place within it'

(Sampson, 1995). For women of Eastern Europe the transition in post-socialist Europe meant 'gender ambivalence'. There was an acute conflict between the gender in which they were previously socialised and the new gender identity dictated by market forces and largely imported from America (Svendsen, 1996).

These changes resulted in an excessive concern among Eastern European women with being 'feminine' in the Western sense, that is, equating femininity with physical attractiveness. This meant the re-entry of the body into the newly formulated definition of gender. Being physically attractive was seen as a vehicle towards social mobility. Women felt the need to reshape their bodies and recast old identities, hoping perhaps to remould old values to suit the new economic realities they now live in (Svendsen, 1996). However Western-style femininity and Western feminism, which idealised the independent physically attractive politically and environmentally conscious American woman, was not necessarily appealing to all the women in Eastern Europe. Some of the writings on Eastern European women showed a kind of passive resistance to these changes, sometimes amounting almost to withdrawal from the public arena (Drakulic, 1999).

In theory, women who opted to reshape their bodies for the purpose of reshaping their identity would be vulnerable to develop eating morbidity, for both reasons of gender role confusion and susceptibility to media influences. In one investigation, Romanian women translated their desire to look and behave in a 'feminine way' into an obsession with 'fitness', with a tendency to emulate models. Krch (1994) predicted a steady increase in the rates of obesity among women in Prague, secondary to changes in diet and lifestyle following the political and economic reform. He foresaw this tendency towards obesity as a significant risk factor for eating disorders within the framework of societal changes and increased orientation towards a Western lifestyle. Also research in other Eastern European countries, particularly Hungary, showed the rates of eating disorders to be comparable to those in Western Europe. However, bulimia, which was practically unknown until 1990, was shown to be on the increase (Rathner *et al.*, 1995; see also Rathner, chapter 5, this volume).

It is still important to be careful about overinterpreting the vulnerability of Eastern European women to eating disorders in the light of what has been discussed. For older women in Eastern Europe who were exposed to both communist and post-communist definitions of gender, this issue of vulnerability is questionable. These women are at possible risk of gender confusion, but it could still be argued that they may retain an earlier confidence in their roles and identity that could shield them against such problems. Older women in Eastern Europe were found to value social relationships based on connectedness and find socialising within a framework of individualism unattractive. These values could in theory continue to protect them from developing eating disorders, even if they fail to protect them against other psychological disturbances (Catina *et al.*, 1996).

The situation for the younger women, that is, the adolescent population in Eastern Europe, is different as they are now subjected to only one system of gender definition informed by Western ideals and in that sense their vulnerability to eating disorders should indeed be much higher (Catina and Kächele, 1995). However, these are pure speculations that need more investigation and analysis.

Acknowledgements

We wish to thank Mervat Nasser for her competent comments, her permanent support and for making this chapter publishable. We thank also Michaela Bergner, Heike Ulbrich and Camelia Ghita for being helpful in setting up the instruments and collecting data needed for this presentation.

References

Acsady J (1995/96). *The taste of disillusionment: Women perspectives in Hungary before Beijing*. Available in HTTP: **http://antena.nl.nl./ywd/Background/acsady.html** (20 December, 1999)

Afanassieva T (1992). Das Schicksal der Frau in Rußland der Umgestaltung. *Feministische Studie*, **2**, 75–84.

Catina A, Boyadjieva S, Bergner M (1996). Social context, gender identity and eating disorders in West and East of Europe: preliminary results of an comparative study. *European Review on Eating Disorders, 4*, 150–7.

Catina A, Boyadjieva S, Bergner M (1997). *Construing womanhood: teacher society and its bad students*. Presented at the 12th International Congress on Personal Construct Psychology, July 1997, Seattle.

Catina A, Kächele H (1995). Sviluppo adolescentiale, contesto sociale e disturbi alimentari: una possibile riposta a la domanda. Perche le adolescenti? *Adolescentia*, **4**, 299–310.

Chinyaeva E (1999). An identity of one's own. Online. Available in HTTP: **http://www.transitions-online.org** (15 December 1999).

Drakulic S (1999). What we learnt from Western feminists. Excerpted from the '*Lipstick and other feminist lessons*'. Online. Available in HTTP: **http://www.transitions-online.org** (15 December 1999).

Gordon R (2000). *Eating disorders: Anatomy of a social epidemic*. Oxford: Blackwell.

Jalusic V (1992). Zurück in der Naturzustand? Desintegration Jugoslawiens und ihre Folgen für die Frauen. *Feministische Studie, 2*, 9–21.

Joja O, Vasilescu PI (1998). *Body Dissatisfaction and Self Esteem in Eating Disordered females*. Presented at The International Conference on Eating Disorders, November 1998, the Hague.

Kanev P (1999). Loving but poor: motherhood after communism. Available in HTTP: Wysiwyg: //38/ **http:// www.geocities.com/Wellesley/3321/win8c.htm** (15 December 1999).

Kliatchko T (1994). *Russian Women back to stove*. Newsletter-ICP-20: Russian Women. Available in HTTP: **http://antena.nl/** (18 December 1999).

Krch F (1994). *Needs and possibilities of prevention of eating disorders in the Czech Republic*. Presented at the IV International Conference on Eating Disorders, New York.

Lipovskaya O (1992). Der Mythos der Frau in der heutige sowjetischen Kultur. *Feministische Studie*, **2**, 64–75.

Nasser M (1997). *Culture and Weight Consciousness*. London: Routledge.

Olsen M (1996). Pure relationships: the search for love among Hungarian academic women. *Anthropology of East Europe Review*, **14**, 1–14.

Orbach S (1986). *Hunger Strike: The Anorectic's Struggle as a Metaphor for Our Age*. New York: Norton.

Rathner G, Turi F, Szabo M, *et al*. (1995). Prevalence of eating disorders and minor psychiatric morbidity in Central Europe before the political changes in 1989: a cross cultural study. *Psychological Medicine*, **25**, 1027–35.

Rudneva S (1999). Queuing up for capitalism? Online. Available in HTTP: **http://www.worldwoman.net/** (30 October 1999).

Sampson S (1995). All is possible, nothing is certain: The horizons of transition in a Romanian village. In: *East European Communities*, edited by Kideckel DA. Boulder: Westview.

Siklova J (1997). Why we resist western style feminism. *Journal of Social Research*, Summer. Available in HTTP: **http://www.transition-online.org** (18 December 1999).

Silverstein B, Perlick D (1995). *The Cost of Competence: Why Inequality Causes Depression, Eating Disorders and Illness in Women*. Oxford: Oxford University Press.

Staikova R, Gedeleva S (1992). Die Frauen in Bulgarien – ihre Bestimmung heute und in Zukunft. *Feministische Studien*, **2**, 98–104.

Svendsen MN (1996). The post-communist body: beauty and aerobics in Romania. *The Anthropology of East Europe Review*, **14**, 8–13.

von Wietersheim J, Pecová V (1998). *Dieting Behaviour and Role Expectations in Female Students and their Mothers in Germany and Czech Republic*. Presented the International Congress 'The Treatment of Eating Disorders – research Meets Clinical Practice', June 1998, Stuttgart.

Wolf N (1990). *The Beauty Myth*. London: Chatto & Windus.

Wyzan M (1998). Unemployed unequally? Online. Available in HTTP: **http://www.transitions-online.org** (18 December 1999).

Zareva S (1992). Frauen in Südosteuropa: zwischen dem kommunistischen Modell und dem Orientalismus des Balkans. *Feministische Studie*, **2**, 56–63.

Young KE (1996) .Loyal wives, virtuous mothers. In: *Russian Life Magazine*, March Lead. Available in HTTP: **http://207.136.230.83./396.HTM** (18 December 1999).

Commentary I

Ivan Eisler
Senior Lecturer in Clinical Psychology, Institute of
Psychiatry, University of London, UK

Emerging markets or migrating cultures? Uncertainties
and opportunities (for both women and men)

I found this chapter thought provoking in spite of (or perhaps because of) the
fact that there was a great deal that I disagreed with. My initial response was that
the chapter gives a rather narrow account of how post-communist life has been
shaping women's experiences, based primarily on an economic analysis, taking
little account of the differences across the communist world. On second reading I
realised that my own view on this was no less restricted by my own particular
experiences (being male; growing up in Czechoslovakia; being bilingual and
identifying with two different cultures; moving to another country and experiencing
the effect of having to adjust to life in a new cultural context). My aim in this
commentary, therefore, is not to offer a polemic but rather to provide another voice
from my own particular perspective.

It is an oversimplification to think of Eastern and Central Europe as an homogeneous entity. The break up of the Habsburg Empire at the end of the First World
War led to the creation/re-emergence of nation states with very varied economic,
social and cultural compositions. Compare for instance Czechoslovakia which
was highly industrialised, politically relatively stable and had a fairly flat social
class structure with Romania, which was 75% agricultural at the beginning of the
interwar period but underwent major social and economic change leading to an
80% increase in industrial output and a major land reform, in which 30% of land
was redistributed. Or consider Hungary which, apart from a brief experiment with
communism in 1919, was dominated by a small but economically and politically
powerful nobility owning half the land in the country (Walters, 1988). The impact
of the social changes during the communist era cannot be fully understood without
taking some account of the historical contexts of these countries.

After the Second World War, Eastern Europe entered a Marxist ideological
straightjacket which certainly brought about major economic and social changes
but also stifled open political discussion. This undoubtedly blurred, or at least
submerged, some of the pre-existing social, cultural and economic differences but
the social experiences (of both women and men) of these apparently homogenised
societies continued to be shaped by these differences. Above all the effect of living
in an environment which was dominated by ideology, had a profound effect both
on those who espoused it and those who felt oppressed by it.

In Czechoslovakia after 1948, like elsewhere in Eastern Europe, equality for women became part of the official rhetoric and while it is true that some very real and important changes took place in access to education, possibilities for professional career development and child care, the reality generally did not match the rhetoric. Women were anything but equal, most of them having to juggle full-time household responsibilities with full-time work commitments. The International Women's Day, mentioned by Catina and Joja, may have officially celebrated the high achieving communist woman but for most it only served to contrast the ideology with everyday reality. This was seldom openly discussed other than in the occasional satirical portrayal of the few 'liberated' men who on this one day would wash the dishes or even cook dinner rather than just buy the traditional bunch of flowers. The lack of equality was of course much more fundamental when one considers the professional let alone the political arena. While the numbers of women who developed professional careers may have grown considerably, their opportunities to reach senior positions were no less restricted than was true in the West. In the political sphere there was virtually no meaningful place for women at all – certainly not in the top echelons of the party where it mattered.

However, as a number of women writers have emphasised (Drakulic, 1991; Siklová, 1997) these discrepancies were more likely to be experienced as conflicts with the system rather than as an issue of gender inequality. Any sense of discrimination that women might have felt was much more likely to be experienced as an aversion to the paternalism of the Communist Party. In Czechoslovakia this was particularly true after the 1968 invasion by the Soviet Union which took away any possibility of the Party standing for anything other than state control. Most people dealt with this by separating their public and private lives, not necessarily out of fear but as a way of protecting the (private) part of their lives which was central for maintaining their sense of self and individual identity. This sense of identity in opposition to the system was shared by women and men, whereas any questions of equality and emancipation for women were relegated to the public domain and therefore were not to be taken seriously. This has continued even after the 'Velvet Revolution' when many visitors from the West are surprised to find that any attempt to discuss gender issues tends to be greeted with suspicion as an example of quasi-Marxist dogma.

Women's position in society of course cannot be considered without also taking into account men's role. If there was little fundamental change during the communist era in attitudes towards women then the corollary of that was that both men and women had an expectation, mostly unspoken, that men would continue in the role of provider/protector of the family. Most families, however, found it economically unviable for the man to be the sole wage earner. This eroded men's sense of identity in two ways. Not only was their role as sole bread winner diminished but hand in hand with this came a diminution of their decision-making role in the family (Hanáková, 1999). In addition, the work setting lost much of its value for many people by being the place where you put on your public persona which was generally a mixture of conformity and cynicism. For many men this made it difficult to derive satisfaction from a 'traditional' male role, which perhaps created even more of a conflict with the traditional patriarchal attitudes than the rather superficial emancipation of women.

It is against this background that one has to consider the changes taking place in the post-communist societies. The economic pressures have varied considerably from country to country and while in some instances they have affected women more than men, in many the reverse has been the case particularly in areas where high levels of unemployment are the result of the closing down of large heavy industry complexes. The effect of the economic changes, while undoubtedly important, has been mediated by what I would argue has been a more universal experience of social change of a society in transition. For many this has been a culture shock that can be compared to the experience of migration – except that instead of moving from one culture to another they had the experience of the culture migrating around them (Eisler, 1992). The excitement and hope of the early days after the Velvet Revolution was rather quickly replaced by uncertainty, turmoil and a realisation that life was going to get harder at first and probably for longer than one anticipated. The loss of certainty, the disruption of social networks and personal relationships, being unable to rely on the familiar patterns of everyday life all have parallels for people who have moved from one culture to another. There is evidence that this is a time of psychological vulnerability both in immigrants (Ritsner and Ponizovsky, 1999) and in post-communist Eastern Europe (Sartorius, 1996).

For migrants the vulnerability is a transitional phenomenon typically lasting five years or more with a peak at two years (Ritsner and Ponizovsky, 1999) and one might expect that some of the same adaptive mechanisms might operate in societies in a process of transition. Like the situation of the migrant, the initial response to the uncertainty is likely to be a mixture of looking for things that are stable, giving a sense of coherence in past experiences (which has been very noticeable all over Eastern and Central Europe), and looking for ways of joining the new cultural context. But in the end one has to find a new sense of identity which is neither a simple retreat to the past nor a pure adoption of the new. I expect that the way in which this will happen may well be different for women and men and will vary from country to country and from one social group to another.

Accounts of the process of transition in post-communist countries often assume, at least implicitly, that the main problem facing these countries is the importation of all the ills of the capitalist West, be it in the economic or social sphere. The eating disorder literature has contributed to this sense of foreboding, warning about the dangers of recreating the often described conflicts that women experience growing up in the West. I have always been somewhat skeptical about this. Thinking about the chapter and writing the commentary has increased my skepticism that the process we are witnessing in the post-communist countries is best described as one of Westernisation. Dealing with transitions is about finding a way of feeling that one is in control of one's own future and being able to make use of the new opportunities. Opportunity and uncertainty are two sides of the same coin. As outsiders we may not always be able to appreciate fully what it is like living with such uncertainties and I suspect that we may have even greater blind spots when trying to understand the nature of the new opportunities.

References

Drakulic S (1991). *How We Survived Communism and Even Laughed*. New York: Norton.

Eisler I (1992). *Eastern Europe: 'Migrating' nations*. Paper presented at the European Families at Risk Conference, London.

Hanáková P (1999). The vicissitudes of Czech Feminism. **http://www.cddc.vt.edu/feminism/cz.html**

Ritsner M, Ponizovsky A (1999). Psychological distress through migration: The two-phase temporal pattern? *International Journal of Social Psychiatry*, **45**, 125–39.

Sartorius N (1996). Recent changes in suicide rates in selected Eastern European and other European countries. *International Psychogeriatrics*, **7**, 301–8.

Siklová J (1997). Feminism and the roots of apathy in the Czech Republic. *Social Research*, **64**, 258–80.

Walters EG (1988). *The Other Europe: Eastern Europe to 1945*. New York: Dorset Press.

Commentary 2

Cynthia King Vance
Economist and Management Consultant, New York, USA

This article presents a number of interesting observations about the interplay of economic, political and social forces and their influence on women's self image and psychological health in the former Eastern European communist countries. The historical description and sometimes sweeping assertions about women's feelings raise thought-provoking questions and have the potential to make a difference to the psychological health of women. However, the article at times creates a sense of frustration for a lay reader by not pushing the observations to practical recommendations for action and omitting some of the detail that would facilitate intervention.

The authors pose a strong hypothesis from an economic perspective. Market economies will seek to maximize production with the lowest input cost of labor and capital. Since women can be convinced to provide domestic and child-rearing services for free (or relatively low cost) society overall can earn the highest overall return from them doing so. The marginal value gained from employing women needs to be higher than the marginal cost of replacing these services.

When there is a shortage of labour and/or sudden demand for dramatically higher output, market economies, and affiliated political and social values, can adjust temporarily and can resemble the social model presented in this article. This happened during the early days of communism due to the need for rapid industrialization. It also happened in the US during the Second World War, when American women were needed in the factories – men were away at war and the country needed to produce supplies and weapons. 'Rosie the Riveter', an obviously feminine woman dressed in a factory worksuit and kerchief flexing her biceps, became a strong positive media icon, reminiscent of the working mother ideal under communism. This image not only made it acceptable for women to work outside the home, but made it their patriotic duty.

After the war, when jobs in America were needed for the returning troops, the ideal housewife image re-emerged with a vengeance, further reinforcing the hypothesis of links between the employment market and social identity. Under communism, as the employment demand subsided, or reached equilibrium, post-industrialization, political values and centralized control of employment and media sustained the working woman ideal. The high cost, however, could be one of the contributing factors to the collapse of the communist economic model and, as a result, the political system.

The US today provides an example of the limits of market forces alone. Two of the economic factors cited as catalysts for the improved gender identity in Eastern Europe – full employment and the need for families to have two incomes – exist in the US today. The number of working women, including mothers of young children, has increased due to necessity, opportunities and sometimes the efforts of needy employers to be more attractive. However, there does not seem to be a corresponding change in social values and media images to reflect this reality. Child care facilities, men's domestic responsibilities and other support have expanded, but not to the level implied in this article. Employers seem more inclined to invest in increased productivity to relieve the pressure on employment and wages rather than day care, probably because it is cheaper. Nor does increased participation necessarily lead to increased social status, achievement of high level positions or narrower wage gap.

Some of these factors could be captured in an economic model to illustrate the relationship between market forces and social change. For example one could examine whether there is a continuum, with varying degrees of economic or market pressures (for example, high employment, maximized productivity, wage pressure) resulting in matching degrees of social changes (for example, female employment, wage differential, unit investment in child care), or whether it is a step function with change only really occurring in times of crisis. It may also indicate how 'sticky' any changes are over economic cycles, or whether they evaporate as soon as the employment demand eases.

Despite the resonance of the underlying thesis, the article left a high level of frustration, at least for a professional outside of the mental health or eating disorders field, in three areas.

First, many of the assertions were not strongly supported with specific facts. Presumably, familiarity with the cited references would overcome this objection, since the evidence and statistics used were not always compelling on their own. Comparisons over time or between cultures would anchor some of the statements as would providing some segmentation of the population. The sweeping statements about women in general undermined credibility. The authors' picture of women today and in the past is painted with a broad brush. Large populations, at least for consumer marketing analysis, are rarely homogeneous. The authors suggest some underlying segmentation exists. Taking that further to propose groupings by key characteristics or behaviors would help untangle and clarify some of the arguments as well as potentially identify and quantify risk groups.

A second frustration is that the conclusion is so tepid. The authors seem to lose steam when they conclude that the environmental changes in Eastern Europe 'might' make women more prone to psychological disorders. Similarly, the confusing arguments supporting, then on the other hand refuting, this conclusion weakened the article.

Most frustrating, however, is that the authors did not answer the 'so what' question. In other words, their thesis may be true, but what should done as a result? As a management consultant, this is the acid test of any research. Having brought the reader along with their arguments, they leave a sinking feeling of circumstances beyond anyone's control and not much advantage from knowing this information.

Even when hedging about whether or not there is really a problem (that is that eating disorders and other psychological disorders will increase in women in Eastern Europe), the authors could push their analysis to recommend practical actions based on their observations. I would like to know how the increased risk of eating disorders and other psychological disorders in Eastern Europe, specifically among adolescents, should be managed. Presumably the authors know the education, health and mental health services and traditions in these countries and could identify areas that will need to change, what evidence will need to be shown in order to stimulate that change and the likely, possibly hidden, cost.

The authors could provide even more intriguing 'so whats' by suggesting applications of the apparently successful former communist strategies to address gender identity issues and psychological disorders more broadly. The authors imply that there were a number of concrete factors and experiences that reduced gender role conflicts. It would be useful to understand in more tangible detail how these were accomplished to explore copying or adapting them in other countries.

For example, efforts aimed at challenging media messages and cultural biases in other countries may be able to apply the techniques used previously in Eastern Europe to ensure that 'working women enjoyed the highest social praise' and that a 'sense of efficiency and social usefulness' is conveyed. Public and private sector investments in child care could benefit from a greater understanding of the former communist states' commitment to child care and leaves/allowances, their cost and the return gained from maternal labor. Educators concerned with the children's development could learn from what 'kindergartens, schools and political youth associations' did to 'prepare young girls for (their) complex role', as well as what these organizations do not do now after communism.

The issues raised in this article are thought-provoking and have the potential to make a difference, particularly the assertion that female role confusion is a major risk factor for psychological distress. However, more specific analytic evidence and clear suggestions of what to do are needed at least to enable mental health professionals in either Eastern Europe or North America to engage members of the business community and gain their valuable financial and political support. I look forward to the next article that builds on this research.

Chapter 7

One country, two cultures

Giovanni Maria Ruggiero
"Studi Cognitivi", Centro di Psicoterapia e Ricerca, and
Clinica Psichiatrica, Università di Milano, Milan, Italy

Debate question:
The process of modernisation in Italy has managed to produce two distinct cultural territories, the industrialised north and the rural south. This disharmonious cultural transition is speculated to create tension between old traditional values and modern ways of life in both areas. This could in turn reflect itself in the level of eating psychopathology in each territory, depending on the degree of exposure to culprit cultural forces.

Introduction

Culture does not always follow the boundaries drawn by ethnicity, language, religion or political forms, there are exceptions. The Italian people have their own intrinsic cultural differences, represented in a spectrum of regional variations of values and lifestyles. These differences are real despite the fact that Italy is linguistically, ethnically and religiously homogeneous as well as politically unified.

In modern times these cultural variabilities became so pronounced as to divide Italy into two distinctly different regions, the affluent industrialised north and the rural south. The case of northern and southern Italy is perhaps a rather unique example of the outcome of the robust demands of modernisation in our contemporary times. The process of modernisation has in fact created a state of disharmonious transition within Italy and produced strong tension between old-fashioned and modern ways of life, adding to changes in family structures and gender roles. This has ultimately culminated in what is now known as the 'two Italies'.

This peculiar situation lends itself to the study of the influence of the cultural evolutionary and transitional forces on human behaviour, particularly in the area of 'eating disorders'. Within the framework explanations of eating disorders, the role of culture is well acknowledged (Bruch, 1973; Selvini-Palazzoli, 1974; Garner and Bemis, 1985). In the cultural discourse the fundamental psychopathology of the pursuit of thinness and weight phobia has been linked to changes in aesthetic values and the standards of feminine beauty in the developed affluent and industrialised economies of North America and Western Europe. Media and mass culture is commonly seen to be behind the promotion of these new images of beauty.

Recently, other cultural conceptualisations of the phenomenon were put forward, specifically, the impact of culture change with its subsequent feelings of transition and disconnection on the individual. These forces are now thought to affect all cultures and societies calling for the importance of studying the eating disorders phenomenon outside the traditional boundaries of the Western world (Katzman and Lee, 1997; Nasser, 1997).

The Italian mixed cultural map with its northern and southern territories could possibly represent a shorthand version of what the whole world is currently going through. The discussion of the Italian situation in this respect could easily demonstrate the array of cultural forces claimed to be responsible for these transformations, be it media images or the more intricate forces of modernisation and urbanisation.

The north and south of Italy: A historical difference

Since the Middle Ages, Italy has developed a multicentric identity. In particular, southern territories precociously began to develop ways of life different from those belonging to northern Italy and northern Europe. The reasons behind this developmental division are political, geographical, economical and social.

In its political history, Italy has seldom been a unified country or a unified culture. Any unification was only for a brief period between ages of division. Before the Roman conquest, the north was inhabited by Gauls, from northern Europe; the central region by the Etruscans, Latins and other ancient Italic peoples, and the south, specially the coast by ancient Greeks and Carthaginians. Italy was again divided after the fall of the Roman Empire, with the north being invaded by German populations from northern Europe and the south dominated by Byzantines, from the East Mediterranean Roman Empire.

Geographically, the nature of Italian land varies between the north and the south. The land in the north is fertile alluvial plain crossed by rivers of steady regulation. In contrast, peninsular Italy is covered by the low, uneven, and dry Appenine mountains, and lacks rivers capable of irrigating the fields. This poor agricultural state is highly significant in understanding the value system of pre-industrial Italy. This may have been behind the 'poveristic' fasting culture of Saint Francis, the 'poverello' (poor man) of Assisi, the patron saint of Italy (Galli della Loggia, 1998).

Nonetheless, it is important to say that despite the nature of the land, the south of Italy in the 10th century was relatively in a better economic position than the rest of Europe. Southern Italy produced valuable goods, such as grain, indigo, henna, silk, wool, and cotton and had intense trade business with the Byzantine and Muslim Mediterranean areas. Its currency, the Tarì, was also internationally valued (Cipolla, 1995).

This relative affluence of the south did not last for very long. By the 12th century, southern Italy restricted its economy to a simple mono-agriculture producing mostly grain, whilst northern Italy began to develop high quality and brilliant textile handicraft. Within the course of a century, the south lost its financial autonomy and wealth, whilst the north gained economic supremacy. This evolution led to the economic dependency of the south and its backwardness relative to the north (Abulafia, 1977). It ushered in the economic structure of Italy that endures till today. The south of Italy still lives a harder life of poorer economy that is subsistent on agriculture while the north is making strides in the industrial realm, producing luxury goods that are sold all over the Western world (Petralia, 1995).

The socio-economic situation of the south continued to deteriorate up until the unification of Italy in the 19th century. A northern Italian politician who had not visited the south before, described the poor condition of the region in rather disparaging terms: 'This is not Italy! This is Africa: bedouins are civil people in comparison to these cafoni' (a derogatory term for 'peasants').

The 'questione meridionale' or the problem of southern Italy, was born. In-depth analysis of the social situation of the south followed and became in fact the subject of several publications (Villari, 1961). One of those was a paper published at the turn of the 20th century by Giustino Fortunato (1911) that had the title: '*Le due Italie*' (the two Italies).

The sociocultural configuration of the two Italies

The current economic map of Italy still shows this division, highlighting the lag of development in the south. According to the International Standard of Poverty Line (ISPL), 70% of Italian poor families live in the south, with four times more unemployment figures than the North (ISTAT, 1999).

This rich–poor division between the north and the south resulted into two different economic configurations of two different Italian societies with two different value systems, albeit sharing the same geographical land . Banfield (1958) showed that southerners lacked the traits of 'advanced Western societies'. The Italian people of the north had the tendency to act in groups by joining clubs or associations to achieve a goal or a purpose. The lower and middle class promoted social organisations such as workers' unions, Catholic charity and solidarity societies, referred to as '*the associative art of living*' creating a *horizontal* society with associative forms of solidarity (Leopardi, 1824–1906; Tocqueville, 1835; Weber; 1920–21). This pattern went hand in hand with another *vertical* form of associative solidarity, through the family where patronage was highly privileged, as it was the case with the upper classes who patronised the foundation of cultural clubs, journals and reviews. In fact, the northern economic development appeared to have run parallel to the principles of '*ancient civicness*', laid down by the Tuscan traders and bankers who nourished culture through their patronage of art and literature. The horizontal forms of social life in the north with the vertical structures of the family are sometimes seen to reinforce each other (Sciolla, 1997). The north of Italy therefore continues to enjoy a high degree of associative ways life and of public service accessibility (Putnam, 1993)

On the other hand, the centralised southern Kingdom of Naples showed features of social decline, with a classical feudal system of peasants who constituted the majority of the populace, who lack both initiative and autonomy, and few debauched landlords that belonged to the parochial aristocracy (Salvemini, 1908; Einaudi, 1911; Croce, 1924; Galasso, 1978).

In the past two decades, however, the south, similar to the north of Italy, began a new wave of civic associationism (Della Porta, 1996) with evidence in the 1990s of some economic success, largely seen as an achievement of a network of small family enterprises. According to Sciolla (1997), the optimistic scenario for true economic growth in the south would be for this vertical development through the family to finally integrate with new horizontal modes of association between the people themselves. In this way, people will move from merely having social obligations based on social relationships that are embedded in clan familiarity to develop a sense of individual competence and relate to other people according to formalised rules. However, if the vertical development is not accompanied with a horizontal one, the southern Italian society could remain only developed on the surface, that is, identifying mainly with the consumer's values of Western democracy albeit lacking true means of production.

Gender roles in the north and south of Italy

The historical and economic differences between the south and the north of Italy had, no doubt, its impact on gender definitions and gender roles in both regions. In the Middle Ages, women of Italy were the promoters of refined manners of 'Courteous Love', first adopted in the Sicilian court of the Holy Roman Emperor Frederick II who was later to abandon the south and move to Tuscany and the northern regions (Duby, 1994). The first feminist movement in Italy took place in the late 19th century and was predominantly active in the north and central parts of Italy. The feminist movement, however, only gathered momentum in the south in 1970s, almost a century later (Pieroni Bortolotti, 1987).

A vivid account of the recent social development of gender roles in southern Italy was given by Siebert (1991). This was based on her interviews of three successive generations of women living in Calabria, one of the poorest regions in southern Italy. The youngest generation was of female university students, while the two elder ones were the mothers and the grandmothers of these students. The interviews covered subjects including work, participation in public life, education, family and sex roles. The author described the difficulties encountered by these women in negotiating the issue of emancipation, which took place parallel to partial modernisation. She reported that the older generation of women were consistent in their lifestyle and outlook with the stereotypes of the conventional and rigid gender roles. On the other hand, the youngest of the three generations reported having better opportunities than their mothers or grandmothers, and yet showed some ambivalence towards this newly acquired liberation, expressing nostalgic sentiment about the past. They seemed to be going through the transition from the old vertical social order of the rural world where the rules are set and controlled by the family to horizontal modes of social interchange which have not yet gone beyond the infantile phase.

Research has shown that cultures could suffer during the process of modifying the society's vertical social order, with inevitable consequences on gender role definitions. This often results in maladaptive behaviours, particularly eating disorders. The majority of the studies that looked into this issue have in fact surveyed young immigrant populations of ethnic minorities (Ahmad *et al.*, 1994; Akan and Grilo, 1995; McCourt and Waller, 1995). The situation of southern Italian women, though not exposed to this geographical conflict of immigration, could still be seen as arguably similar to that of the immigrant group which demand an uneasy cohabitation of both old and modern values.

The epidemiology of eating disorders in Italy and its sociocultural determinants

Historically Italy is known for its 'starving girls'. From the 12th century onward a great number of girls practised fasting for religious purposes, demonstrating behavioural traits and eating patterns not dissimilar from modern anorexia. Bell (1987) hypothesised that fasting was probably used by medieval girls as a tool for social self-assertion and self-fulfilment. Vandereycken and Van Deth (1994) noted that the late Middle Ages was an age of cultural evolution and possibly confusion, where tension, disorientation and assimilation of new relational patterns between the sexes took place. They nonetheless warned against applying modern psychology to ancient behavioural patterns.

In the modern era, the presence of eating disorders in Italy followed more or less the same path as the rest of Europe. The first cases of anorexia nervosa reported in literature seem to have appeared in the late 19th century and during the first half of the 20th century. Mara Selvini-Palazzoli, while working as a resident at Milano General Hospital, observed a rapid increase of cases of anorexia immediately after the Second World War (1998, pp. 1–2).

In recent times a number of epidemiological studies were conducted for the purpose of assessing the rate of occurrence of eating disorders in Italy. Four of these studies were two-stage investigations, using the Eating Attitude Test (EAT-40) self-report questionnaire followed by clinical interviews. The studies covered the north of Italy (Santonastaso *et al.*, 1996), the central (Vetrone *et al.*, 1997) and the south (Dalle Grave *et al.*, 1997; Cotrufo *et al.*, 1998).

The study published from the southern region pointed to the fact that the prevalence rate of eating disorders there was comparable to what was found in other Western European countries. This finding initially appeared surprising, given the rural nature and limited modernity of southern Italy. However, this finding was substantiated after comparing the rates of the four epidemiological studies that covered the three Italian regions. The highest prevalence rates were found in the two studies conducted in the south, whilst the lowest was that from the north.

A special investigation was carried out in an attempt to explain this difference as well as explore the psychological and socio-cultural profile of eating-disordered girls in both the south and north of Italy. The degree of media exposure, level of self esteem and body dissatisfaction were all measured using the Eating Disorder Inventory (EDI). The study revealed that while the southern girls were less sensitive to mass media influences in relation to body ideals than their northern counterparts, they had nonetheless lower self-esteem and higher degree of emotional confusion and of maturational fears. This means that the impact of lower self-esteem and social insecurity could be just as powerful a psychological determinant for eating disorders psychopathology as body dissatisfaction and media influences (Ruggiero et al., 2000).

Eating disorders: Italy and the rest of the Mediterranean

A comparative analysis of the eating disorders situation between Italy and the rest of the Mediterranean region is relevant here, given the cultural and historical roots that are in common, particularly with southern Italy. In Egypt, Nasser (1986) found that Arab students attending London University had higher rates of eating disorders than Arab students of Cairo University and yet, the Cairo sample, contrary to expectations, showed higher rates of weight concerns. A similar finding was arrived at when the eating attitudes of a Greek immigrant population in Germany was compared to comparable groups in Greece and Turkey. Higher rates of disordered eating were found among the Greek immigrant sample, which was attributed to the demanding cultural change of immigration (Fichter et al., 1988).

In another Middle Eastern study, both Arab and Israeli girls were the subject of comparison. Among the Israeli schoolgirls, the kibbutz sample came first in terms of their level of eating disturbance, followed by the Arabs. The results were thought to be proportionate to the degree of exposure to Western media and Western body ideals (Apter et al., 1994). The role of the Western media in Mediterranean culture and its impact on increasing susceptibility to eating disorders was also highlighted in another study carried out in Spain (Toro et al., 1994)

Turkey was again at the heart of a recent study that compared the performance of two different Turkish groups, over a ten year period, on the Eating Attitude Test Questionnaire (EAT/ factor structure). The findings were interesting in as much as the 'bulimia' factor and 'ambivalence about eating' that were non-existent in the earlier study emerged in the later study (Savasir and Erol, 1989; Elal et al., 2000).

The 'ambivalence about eating' was interpreted as reflecting a deeper sense of ambivalence resulting from exposure to new modern values, clashing with the older Turkish traditional ones.

The social transformation of Italy: Is it a cultural factor for eating disorders development?

What do we really mean by social transformation? In her book *Culture and Weight Consciousness*, Nasser (1997) discussed the impact of global changes on eating disorders psychopathology. She referred to increased levels of urbanisation, modernisation and marketisation of the economy that are now taking place in a majority of societies, with subsequent major changes to individual lifestyle, to traditional family structure, to gender roles and to national identity.

These changes are rather typical of 'consumerist modernism', that is, cultures that appear to be superficially modern and yet lacking means of real development and production. As mentioned above, this is applicable to southern Italy. Though economically weak, southern Italy still features wealthy sectors that have easy access to mass media and are eager to consume.

The threat that modernity poses to traditional family structure is to be observed in the rising tension in modern Italian families. In Italy the family structure remains vital, even in the industrialised north (Piselli, 1981), and independence of the younger generation from the family is not economically viable, particularly in the south (Leccardi, 1995, 1997).

With demands of approaching adulthood and forced prolonged adolescent turmoil, the family is perceived by adolescents as a 'cultural prison', fostering serious intergenerational conflicts and discord (Cavalli and Galland, 1995; Cavalli, 1997).

The adolescents exposed to these conflicts are often caught between two processes, the ambivalent desire for independence and parental control (Bryant-Waugh and Lask, 1991; Mumford, Whitehouse and Platts, 1991). A clash of values is also likely to happen simply as a result of the cultural distance between the adolescents' value system, informed mainly by media, and parental values, derived from history and tradition (McCourt and Waller, 1995). This cultural distance could make the family overprotective or even intrusive towards their adolescents, constituting yet another factor predisposing to eating disorders (Selvini-Palazzoli *et al.*, 1998).

The role of cultural transition and disconnection is central to the hypothesis of Katzman and Lee (1997). This could render women vulnerable to develop eating disorders by reasons of the emotional pressure resulting from the process of cultural change itself, without concomitant conscious mediators such as body dissatisfaction or fear of fatness. The negative depressive emotions would therefore be the vehicle to starvation, which carries a message of protest to the family and society at large (Power and Dalgleish, 1997).

Conclusion

In this essay the focus was mainly on the relationship between gender role, societal development from vertical to horizontal structures, and the effect of all of this on eating disorders psychopathology. The argument was encapsulated as possibly resulting from the modernisation process with its tendency towards consumerism, the so-called 'consumerism without development' (Villari, 1961; Galasso, 1982). Intrinsic in this argument is the conflict between the demanding needs of the individual, particularly the personal need for self-fulfilment with the need for social harmony through effective interpersonal horizontal relationships. Eating disorders are known to flourish at times when there is a need for self-change, particularly when a sense of competence and effectiveness are lacking (Fairburn, 1997). Hence the social changes of modernity can act as both internal (psychological) and external (social) mediators as well as reinforcers of the psychopathology of eating disorders (Palmer, 1998).

Acknowledgements

The author acknowledges Raffaele Papa, Salvatore Freni, Mervat Nasser, Thomas Hillecke and Corrado Ruggiero.

References

Abulafia D (1977). *The Two Italies. Economic Relations between the Norman Kingdom of Sicily and the Northern Communes*. Cambridge: Cambridge University Press.

Ahmad S, Waller G, Verduyn C (1994). Eating attitudes among Asian schoolgirls: The role of perceived parental control. *International Journal of Eating Disorders*, **15**, 91–7.

Akan GE, Grilo CM (1995). Sociocultural influences on eating attitudes and behaviours, body image and psychological functioning: A comparison of African-American and Caucasian college women. *International Journal of Eating Disorders*, **18**, 181–7.

Apter A, Shah M, Iancu I, Abramovitch H, Weizman A, Tanyo S (1994). Cultural effects on eating attitudes in Israelei subpopulations and hospitalised anorectics. *Genetic, Social, and General Psychology Monographs*, **120**, 83–99.

Banfield EC (1958). *The Moral Basis of a Backward Society*. Chicago: Free Press.

Bell RM (1987). *Holy Anorexia*. Chicago: University of Chicago Press.

Bryant-Waugh R, Lask B (1991). Anorexia nervosa in a group of Asian children living in Britain. *British Journal of Psychiatry*, **158**, 229–33.

Bruch H (1973). *Eating Disorders: Obesity, Anorexia Nervosa and the Person Within*. New York: Basic Books.

Cavalli A (1997). The delayed entry into adulthood: Is it good or bad for society? *In: Jovens em mudança: Actas do Congreso Internacional 'Growing up between centre and periphery'*, Lisboa, 2–4 de Maio de 1996, edited by Machado Pais J, Chisholm L. Lisboa: Instituto de Ciências Sociais da Universidade de Lisboa.

Cavalli A, Galland O (eds) (1995). *Youth in Europe*. London: Pinter.

Cipolla CM (1995). Introduzione. In: *Storia Facile dell'Economia Italiana dal Medioevo ad Oggi*, edited by Cipolla CM. Milano: Mondadori.

Cotrufo P, Baretta V, Monteleone P, Maj M (1998). Full-syndrome, partial-syndrome and subclinical eating disorders: an epidemiological study of female students in Southern Italy. *Acta Psychiatrica Scandinavica*, **98**, 112–15.

Croce B (1924). *Storia del Regno di Napoli*. Bari: Laterza.

Dalle Grave R, De Luca L, Oliosi M (1997). Eating attitudes and prevalence of eating disorders: A survey in secondary schools in Lecce, southern Italy. *Eating and Weight Disorders*, **1**, 34–7.

Della Porta D (1996). *Movimenti Collettivi e Sistema Politico in Italia*. Bari: Laterza.

Duby G (1994). Il modello cortese. In: *Storia delle Donne*, edited by Duby G, Perrot M. Bari: Laterza.

Einaudi L (1911). Le speranze del mezzogiorno. *La Voce, III*, **11**, 535–6.

Elal G, Altug A, Slade P, Tekcan A (2000). Factor structure of the eating attitudes test (EAT) in a Turkish university sample. *Eating and Weight Disorders*, **5**, 46–50.

Fairburn CG (1997). Eating disorders. In: *The Science and Practice of Cognitive Behaviour Therapy*, edited by Clark DM, Fairburn CG. Oxford: Oxford University Press.

Fichter MM, Elton M, Sourdi S, Weyerer S, Koptagel-Ilal G (1988). Anorexia nervosa in Greek and Turkish adolescents. *European Archives of Psychiatry and Neurological Sciences*, **237**, 200–8.

Fortunato G (1911). Le due Italie. *La Voce, III*, **11**, 525–7.

Galasso G (1978). *Passato e Presente del Meridionalismo*. Volume I: Genesi e Sviluppi. Napoli: Guida Editori.

Galasso G (1982). *L'altra Europa*. Milano: Mondadori.

Galli della Loggia E (1998). *L'Identità Italiana*. Bologna: Il Mulino.

Garner DM, Bemis KM (1985). Cognitive therapy for anorexia nervosa. In: *Handbook of Psychotherapy for Anorexia Nervosa and Bulimia*, edited by Garner DM, Garfinkel PE. New York: Guilford Press.

ISTAT (1999). *Rapporto sull'Italia*. Bologna: Il Mulino.

Katzman MA, Lee S. (1997). Beyond body image: the integration of feminist and transcultural theories in the understanding of self starvation. *International Journal of Eating Disorders*, **22**, 385–94.

Leccardi C (1995). Growing up in southern Italy: Between tradition and modernity. In: *Growing up in Europe*, edited by Chisolm L, Brüchner P, Krüger H-H, du Bois-Reymond M. Berlin: Walter de Gruyter.

Leccardi C (1997). Youth and social change in the Italian Mezzogiorno. In: *Jovens em mudança: Actas do Congreso Internacional 'Growing up between centre and periphery'*, Lisboa, 2–4 de Maio de 1996, edited by Machado Pais J, Chisholm L. Lisboa: Instituto de Ciências Sociais da Universidade de Lisboa.

Leopardi G (1824–1906). Discorso sopra lo Stato Presente dei Costumi degli Italiani. In: *Giacomo Leopardi. Scritti Inediti dalle Carte Napoletane*. Firenze: Successori Le Monnier.

McCourt J, Waller G (1995). Developmental role of perceived parental control in the eating psychopathology of Asian and Caucasian schoolgirls. *International Journal of Eating Disorders*, **17**, 227–82.

Mumford DM, Whitehouse AM, Platts M (1991). Sociocultural correlates of eating disorders among Asian schoolgirls in Bradford. *British Journal of Psychiatry*, **158**, 222–8.

Nasser M (1986). Comparative study of the prevalence of abnormal eating attitudes among Arab female students at both London and Cairo Universities. *Psychological Medicine*, **16**, 621–5.

Nasser, M. (1997). *Culture and Weight Consciousness*. London: Routledge.

Palmer B (1998). Culture, constitution, motivation and the mysterious rise of bulimia nervosa. *European Eating Disorders Review*, **6**, 81–4.

Petralia G (1995). Nord e Sud: nascita di un contrasto plurisecolare. In: *Storia Facile dell'Economia Italiana dal Medioevo ad Oggi*, edited by Cipolla CM. Milano: Mondadori.

Pieroni Bortolotti F (1987). Per una cronologia del movimento delle donne e dell'emancipazione femminile. In: *Franca Pieroni Bortolotti. Sul Movimento Politico delle Donne. Scritti Inediti*, edited by Buttafuoco A. Roma: Cooperativa UTOPIA.

Piselli F (1981). *Parentela ed Emigrazione*. Torino: Einaudi.

Power M, Dalgleish T (1997). *Cognition and Emotion: From Order to Disorder*. Hove, UK: Psychology Press.

Putnam RD (1993). *Making Democracy Work. Civic Tradition in Modern Italy*. Princeton: Princeton University Press.

Ruggiero GM, Hannöwer W, Mantero M, Papa R (2000). Body acceptance and culture: A study in northern and southern Italy. *European Eating Disorders Review*, **8**, 40–50.

Salvemini G (1908). Cocò all'università di Napoli o la scuola della malavita. *La Voce, I*, **3**, 9–10.

Santonastaso P, Zanetti T, Sala A, Favaretto G, Vidotto G, Favaro A (1996). Prevalence of eating disorders in Italy: A survey on a sample of 16-years of female students. *Psychotherapy and Psychosomatics*, **65**, 158–62.

Savasir I, Erol N (1989). Yeme tutum testi: Anoreksiya nervosa bertileri indeksi. *Psikoloji Dergisi*, **7**, 19–25.

Sciolla L (1997). *Italiani: Stereotipi di Casa Nostra*. Bologna: Il Mulino.

Selvini-Palazzoli M (1974). *Self Starvation*. London: Chaucer.

Selvini-Palazzoli M, Cirillo S, Selvini M, Sorrentino AM (1998). *Ragazze Anoressiche e Bulimiche: La Terapia Familiare*. Milano: Raffaello Cortina Editore.

Siebert R (1991). *'È femmina però è bella'. Tre Generazioni di Donne al Sud*. Torino: Rosenberg and Sellier.

Tocqueville A de (1835). *De la Démocratie en Amerique*. Paris: Gosselin.

Toro J, Salamero M, Martinez E (1994). Assessment of sociocultural influences on the aesthetic body shape model in anorexia nervosa. *Acta Psychiatrica Scandinavica*, **89**, 147–51.

Vandereycken W, Van Deth R (1994). *From Fasting Girls to Anorexic Girls*. New York: New University Press.

Vetrone G, Cuzzolaro M, Antonozzi I (1997). Clinical and subthreshold eating disorders: Case detection in adolescent schoolgirls. *Eating and Weight Disorders*, **1**, 24–33.

Villari R (1961). *Il Sud nella Storia d'Italia: Antologia della Questione Meridionale*. Bari: Laterza.

Weber M (1920–21). *Gesammelte Aufsätze zur Religionssoziologie*. Tübingen: Mohr.

Commentary I

K.-J. Neumärker
Chairman and Professor
Department of Child and Adolescent Psychiatry and
Psychotherapy, Charité Hospital, Humboldt University of
Berlin, Germany

J. Hein
Research Staff, Department of Child and Adolescent
Psychiatry and Psychotherapy, Charité Hospital, Humboldt
University of Berlin, Germany

The questions raised in this chapter by Ruggiero are of continuing, even increasing, relevance to our knowledge about eating disorders. Due to the intense globalisation process and the ongoing political transformation following the end of the Cold War, the issue of cultural revolutions and changing gender roles will gain importance in the future. On the other hand, the standardised and structured assessment of cultural influences on eating disorders challenges widely held interpretations about pathogenic factors and provides important data for a better understanding of the condition. In the following we will briefly present some of our own findings on the subject from data assessed in Germany where 'cultural migration without moving to another country', as Ruggiero writes, has taken place repeatedly in the recent past.

After Germany had lost the Second World War, it became divided into West and East Germany, a process that began with the introduction of different currencies in the two parts of Germany in 1948. The erection of the Berlin Wall on August 13th 1961 was the final step in the political separation process and meant the permanent division of both German countries. Afterwards, differences in the formative influences on the individual became increasingly important. Independent of age, those factors affected people's biographies mainly on three levels:

- the notional level in the areas of ideology, science, contemporary culture, education, religion and socialisation;
- the interpersonal level in the areas of politics, partisan structure, public organisations, welfare systems and family structure;
- the material level in the areas of economy, technology and ecology.

The female image and self-concept in the society, determined by current sentiment, personality traits and emotional reactions, deviated in the two countries despite all the similarities. When the Berlin Wall came down in November 1989, the formerly insurmountable frontier between two countries disappeared.

Eating disorders in East Germany (GDR) and West Germany (FRG): The situation in East and West Berlin

Political and civil transformations have always caused discontinuities on notional, interpersonal and material levels (Ahrendt, 1963). They can be interpreted as positive or negative by each person, depending on that person's sensitivity and the ability to cope with new situations, as well as the particular form and content of the changes for the individual herself. As in the present chapter, the question of whether a linear and causal connection between the degree of transformation and psychiatric disorder exists has often been raised, but because of the difficulties in comparing the differing circumstances a conclusive answer has not been found. The separation and development of two countries in Germany provided a unique opportunity to examine these issues, for example in the field of eating disorders. What differences in prevalence and symptomatology existed between these two countries with a shared sociocultural background?

Eating disorders were well-known in Germany even before 1945, as is exemplified by numerous case descriptions in the archives of the Psychiatric and Neurologic Clinic of the Charité in Berlin (for example, Dührssen, 1950; Zutt, 1946/47, 1948). These case reports of the war and post-war period could be taken as archetypal descriptions of the condition.

In 1963 Karl Leonhard, head of the Psychiatric and Neurologic Clinic of the Charité in East Berlin from 1957 to 1970, laid out treatment principles for anorexia nervosa and compulsive vomiting (Leonhard, 1963). His co-worker von Trostorff published in the same year nine case reports of anorexia nervosa, including those of two male adolescents age 15 and 18 who had all grown up in East Germany before the erection of the Berlin Wall (von Trostorff, 1963). In 1985 von Trostorff compared these cases retrospectively with others that had been treated at the Charité from 1959 to 1969. She analysed a total of 15 patients, with an average age of 16.9 years at admission to the clinic (von Trostorff, 1985). The similarities of her case descriptions to those of Zutt (1946/47, 1948) are striking. The Charité in East Berlin continuously treated patients with eating disorders. Ehle et al. reported in 1985 about 69 female and 3 male patients treated for anorexia nervosa from 1975 to 1983 (Ehle et al., 1985). An increase in the number of eating disorder patients at the clinic was notable. In 1982 our eating disorder research group of Neumärker and colleagues could already report 21 inpatient cases (18 girls, 3 boys) between 12.0 and 16.11 years of age treated for anorexia nervosa (Döll and Neumärker, 1982), diagnosed according to the Feighner criteria (Feighner et al., 1972). Due to a steady increase in the number of patients with eating disorders in the following years, we were able to assess approximately 100 cases until the fall of the Berlin

Wall in 1989, with case histories of up to eight years. Our patients were not only from East Berlin, but from all of East Germany.

Naturally there was also a department of Child and Adolescent Psychiatry and Neurology at the University of West Berlin, headed by H.-Ch. Steinhausen. Although hardly tolerated by East and West German officials, there was a consistent academic exchange between the eating disorder research groups of Steinhausen and Neumärker since 1984. Both groups instituted a standardised documentation of clinical data. The remarkable result was the investigation of two comparable population samples of eating disorder patients across the Berlin Wall.

We analysed the different attitudes of the probands from East and West Berlin and other factors. Only after the fall of the Berlin Wall in 1989, were the two groups able to compare and analyse their data (Neumärker *et al.*, 1992, 1994; Steinhausen and Glanville, 1992; Steinhausen *et al.*, 1992, 1995).

Our data show some remarkable differences between the East and the West Berlin samples, including the significantly younger age of the patients from the East at the onset of disease as well as at the beginning of menstruation. The average weight loss and length of in-patient treatment were practically identical. Due to the exchange of ideas between our two centres and based on modern treatment standards, both samples were treated with a multi-dimensional approach including behavioural therapy. Outstanding was the small percentage of patients with bulimia in the West and the absence of such patients in the East Berlin sample. The patients from East Berlin ranked significantly lower on measures of introverted, anxious, depressive, and obsessive-compulsive personality traits, as well as somatic complaints. Passive-aggressive psychopathological features were salient in both samples. The higher IQ-scores of the East German patients is probably connected to differences in the educational systems. The parental level of education of the East Berlin sample was higher compared to the parents of the West Berlin probands. Marriage problems and divorce were more prevalent in the West. East German patients had significantly less complaints and reported a better state of health than their West German peers. Lower Eating Atttitude Test scores were found for both the East and West Berlin sample when compared with North American samples. East German patients scored significantly lower than their Western counterparts with regard to the majority of Eating Disorders Inventory scales.

Summary and Discussion

The study at issue provided an exceptional opportunity for the study of differences in the clinical picture of eating disorders and their development in children and adolescents under different political and medical care systems. For the present discussion we consciously put the issue of eating disorders in Berlin in relation to the end of the Second World War, since the pathogenic-clinical-psychopathological analysis of the case descriptions from 1945 to the present constitutes a homogeneous picture. In each singular case the core psychopathology of the eating disorder appears identical, even in extreme situations and under different political and economic conditions. In these cases the eating disorder reflects the qualities of a disease, dysfunctions of particular cerebral pathways, and not an abnormal reaction to stimuli per se. Thus, we firmly emphasise the historical context of Ruggiero's text.

The historical predominance of anorexia nervosa over bulimia nervosa in the diagnosis of eating disorders can be observed to the East–West study. Only in the last years did both groups observe patients with bulimic features whereas the distinct clinical picture of bulimia nervosa became rare. The fact that the East German patients were younger at admission than the patients from West Berlin could be due to the health politics in East Germany. Before the publication by Döll and Neumärker (1982), eating disorders were considered as diseases of people with a 'higher social status'. Such people were not a reality in the collective consciousness and public self-presentation of the 'worker's and peasant's state' East Germany. Consequently there was little resonance and public concentration on eating disorders. The younger age at the onset of disease in East German patients can be explained by the earlier onset of menstruation of these patients (Danker-Hopfe and Ostersehlt, 1990; Richter, 1990; Sommer, 1990). It could be argued that the East German patients represented a historically earlier form in the social history of eating disorders. Influences on anorexia nervosa such as racism, sexism, feminism, drug or sexual abuse, consuming or dieting behaviour, as described by Fine (1995) did not nearly have the importance in East Germany that they had in the Western countries, including West Germany. Such differences reflect dissimilar cultural influences and demonstrate their formative influence on the psychopathology. Nevertheless, between 1980 and 1989 the prevalence of in-patients treated for an eating disorder increased in East Germany from 3.4 to 5.4 per 100 000 female inhabitants (Nomos, 1993; Sieber and Schulz, 1988). The prevalence of male patients in the same period was unchanged with less than 1 person per 100 000.

Overall, our data support the ideas and standpoints expressed by Ruggiero. Eating disorders existed in both East and West Berlin. They present diseases with distinct clinical courses and core psychopathologies on the basis of specific, well-known vulnerabilities and puberty as their specific time of onset. Still there were differences in the clinical appearance of the eating disorders due to long-term sociocultural changes and differing personal histories of people in East and West Germany.

References

Arendt H (1963). *On Revolution*. New York: Viking Press.

Danker-Hopfe M, Ostersehlt D (1990). Probleme bei der Erfassung und Auswertung von Menarchedaten, aufgezeigt am Beispiel empirischer Daten aus zwei Bremerhavener Wachstums-Studien [Problems with the registration and analysis of menarche data, exemplified by empirical data from two growth studies in Bremerhaven]. *Ärztl. Jugendkd*, **81**, 396–401.

Döll R, Neumärker K-. (1982). Bemerkungen zur Therapie der Pubertätsmagersucht [Remarks on the therapy of anorexia nervosa]. *Dt. Gesundh.-Wesen*, **37**, 677–80.

Dührssen A (1950). Zum Problem der psychogenen Essstörung. Ein kasuistischer Bericht über die gemeinsame Erkrankung eines weiblichen Zwillings-paares an sogenannter 'psychogener Magersucht' [On the problem of psychogenic eating disorders. A casuistic report about the concurrent illness of female identical twins with so-called 'psychogenic anorexia']. *Psyche*, **4**, 56–72.

Ehle G, Preller I, Preller W (1985). Zur Klassifizierung des Syndroms der Anorexia nervosa [On the classification of the syndrome of anorexia nervosa]. *Z. Klin. Med*, **40**, 897–900.

Feighner JP, Robins E, Guze SB, Woodruft RA, Winokur G, Munoz R (1972). Diagnostic criteria for use in psychiatric research. *Archives of General Psychiatry*, **26**, 57–63.

Fine B (1995): Towards a Political Economy of Anorexia? *Appetite*, **24**, 231–42.

Garner DM, Garfinkel PE (1979). The Eating Attitudes Test: An index of the symptoms of anorexia nervosa. *Psychological Medicine*, **9**, 273–9.

Garner DM, Olmstead MP, Polivy J (1983). Development and validation of a multi-dimensional eating disorder inventory for anorexia nervosa and bulimia. *International Journal of Eating Disorders*, **2**, 15–34.

Indikatoren zum Gesundheitszustand der Bevölkerung in der ehemaligen DDR. Psychogene Essstörungen [Indicators of the status of health of the people of the former GDR. Psychogenic eating disorders]. Hrsg: *Der Bundesminister für Gesundheit* (1993). Nomos Verlagsgesellschaft, Baden-Baden, pp. 190–2.

Leonhard K (1963). *Individualtherapie der Neurosen*. Fischer Verlag, Jena.

Neumärker U, Dudeck U, Vollrath M, Neumärker K-J, Steinhausen H-Ch (1992). Eating Attitudes Among Adolescent Anorexia Nervosa Patients and Normal Subjects in Former West and East Berlin: A Transcultural Comparison. *International Journal of Eating Disorders*, **12**, 281–9.

Neumärker K-J, Steinhausen H-Ch, Dudeck U, Neumärker U, Seidel R, Reitzle M (1994). Eßstörungen bei Jugendlichen in Ost- und West-Berlin in den 80er Jahren. (Eating Disorders in East and West Berlin Adolescents in the Eighties). *Prax. Kinderpsychol. Kinderpsychiat*, **43**, 60–8.

Richter J (1990). Kontinuierliche Menarche-Beobachtungen einer geschlossenen Population. (Continuous menarcheal observation of a closed population). *Ärztl. Jugendkd.*, **81**, 402–8.

Sieber E, Schulz R (1988). Zum Verhältnis von ambulanter und stationärer Behandlungshäufigkeit in der Neurologie/Psychiatrie während eines Jahres. (On the proportion of out-patient to in-patient treatment frequency in one year of neurology and psychiatry). *Psychiat. Neurol. Med. Psychol.*, **40**, 150–8.

Sommer K (1990). Variationsbereiche der sexuellen Reifungszeichen. (Ranges of variation of the indicators of the sexual maturation). *Ärztl. Jugendkd.*, **81**, 412–22.

Steinhausen H-Ch, Boyadijeva S, Neumärker K-J (1995). Transcultural Comparisons of Adolescent Eating Disorders. In: *Eating Disorders in Adolescence. Anorexia and Bulimia Nervosa* edited by Steinhausen H-Ch. Berlin: de Gruyter, pp. 38–46.

Steinhausen H-Ch, Glanville K (1984). Der langfristige Verlauf der Anorexia nervosa. (Long-term course of anorexia nervosa). *Nervenarzt*, **55**, 236–48.

Steinhausen H-Ch, Neumärker K-J, Vollrath M, Dudeck U, Neumärker U (1992). A transcultural comparison of the Eating Disorder Inventory in former East and West Berlin. *International Journal of Eating Disorders*, **12**, 407–16.

von Trostorff S (1963). Praxis der Individualtherapie bei Anorexia nervosa und Zwangserbrechen. (The practice of individual therapy in case of anorexia nervosa and forced vomiting). *Psychiat. Neurol. Med. Psychol.*, **15**, 144–52.

von Trostorff S (1985). Katamnestische Untersuchungen bei Patienten mit Pubertäts-magersucht. [Catamnestic studies on patients with pubertal anorexia]. *Psychiat. Neurol. Med. Psychol.* **37**, 90–100.

von Zerssen D, Koeller DM (1976). *Die Beschwerden-Liste* (B-L) [*The complaints list*]. Weinheim: Beltz.

von Zerssen D, Koeller DM (1976). *Die Befindlichkeits-Skala* (Bf-S) [*The sentiments list*]. Weinheim: Beltz.

Zutt J (1946/47). Psychiatrische Betrachtungen zur Pubertätsmagersucht [Psychiatric reflections on pubertal anorexia]. *Klin. Wschr.*, 21–4.

Zutt J (1948). Das psychiatrische Krankheitsbild der Pubertätsmagersucht [The psychiatric symptomatology of pubertal anorexia]. *Arch. Psychiat.*, **180**, 776–849.

Commentary 2

Beatrice Bauer,
Head of Didasco, Verona, Italy and University of Milan
Breconi Business School, Milan, Italy

The importance of the impact of culture on behavior has been widely recognized (Hofstede, 1980, Segall *et al.*, 1990). Ruggiero reflects on one aspect often neglected in cross-cultural studies on behavior, namely the intra-cultural differences.

Italy is a country with striking regional differences. Due to diverse historical and economical development we find significant variations in the cultural values and norms in northern and southern Italy with different traditions, behaviors, language, and social structures. This split is one which is always at the center of Italian political debate, a division which persists in spite of the very large investments made by the government in attempts to eliminate it.

Ruggiero describes how the south of Italy is still embedded in more traditional values and role patterns, but experiencing at the same time a period of cultural change due to a strong exposure to northern and more 'modern' social developments.

If one is looking for a better understanding of the sociocultural dimensions determining eating disorders in southern Italy, it is essential to examine Italian family structures.

Ruggiero mentions briefly the importance of the patriarchal family in the past and talks about its implosion into a modern nuclear family. In my opinion the family still has a great impact on the whole of Italian society. As Barzini (1964) puts it, scholars have always recognized the Italian family as the only fundamental institution in the country, a spontaneous creation of the national genius, adapted through centuries of changing conditions, the real foundation of whichever social order prevailed. In fact, the law, the state and society function only if they do not directly interfere with the 'family's supreme interest'.

Family is the basis of Italian culture. The family enterprise is a fundamental of Italian capitalism. Family and business links are much more widespread than in other industrial countries, since in Italy most of the major private companies are family based. The family in Italy constitutes the main motivational basis for investment and for work and it also provides a way of handling the risks of economic activity, by offering protection and support in difficult situations (Gagliardi and Barry, 1993).

The special quality of the Italian family, as compared to other European countries is shown in a recent study (Istat, 2000). According to this research more than half of the young Italians between 20 and 34 years of age are still living in their parents' house (88% of the 20 to 24 years old, 54% of those between 25 and 29 years and 20% of those between 30 to 34). Asked why young Italian adults are not motivated to leave their parents' home the major reply was for economic reason, that is living with the family saves money. The second reason offered was 'not having to do the housework, cooking and ironing'. This explains also the strong mother figure and the fundamental role mothers play in everyday Italian social life.

In northern regions the role of family is changing at a quicker rate than in the south. In the south, with a high unemployment rate, the economic need to remain with the family is stronger than in the north. But probably basic cultural values rather than convenience are the major reason why Italians in general feel comfortable staying with their parents, even as adults.

Whereas in Anglo-Saxon and Nordic countries children leave their parents' place on average at the age of 17–18 years, independence, self-reliance and autonomy are not taught as major positive values to Italian children and adolescents. In Italy we observe the phenomenon of the 'prolonged family', that is to say that the family links do not change at a certain biological age or with completed professional education of the children. In Italy, actually, you never really leave the family context and if you do so it is only to create your own family. But still even then 11.3% of young married couples with or without children live in the same house as their parents and 42.9% at a maximum distance of 1 km from their parents' home (Istat, 2000).

In Italy we see 'familismo' as a life orientation. (Cerroni, 1996). The origin of the term familismo goes back more than 2000 years in Italian history and culture, when the Italian provinces had been conquered and governed by foreigners or dominated by their influence. This is a major reason why most Italians prefer to rely on their families for the conduct of their lives and the solution of problems. The term 'family' in southern Italy often also includes distant cousins, kinsmen, clients, and close friends.

The anthropologist Banfield (1985) analyses the problematic consequences of familismo in the rural areas of southern Italy. He speaks of 'unmoral familismo', because he observed that the sense of faith in the family is opposed to the civic sense. In fact the familismo of the Italian society is seen by various sociologists and cultural anthropologists as the origin of the difficult relationship of the Italians with the state and politics.

The lack of civic sense and the strong sense of familismo leads to the fact that numerous services, which in northern Europe are assigned to public institutions, get partially accomplished by the families in order to compensate for the non-function of the state structure. This means a substantial functional overload on Italian families.

It is easy to understand how this kind of family links resemble in part the families described in the literature of eating disorders treatment. Strong and prolonged dependency, unclear boundaries, and favoritism rather than isolated individual effort are needed in order to succeed (Eurisko, 1991). Especially in the south, where as Ruggiero explains very well economic difficulties make family ties even stronger, we observe a lack of trust in other people in general. The element of specificity reflects a preference for dealing with known individuals and for personal contacts which can be regarded as an extension of the family. It then becomes more difficult to place trust in those who cannot be located socially in this fashion.

When looking at trust in health services, research by Buzzi (1994) has shown that 35% of young people from the north versus 15% of the south express trust towards hospitals and doctors of all kind. The impact this strong relationship and dependency within the family have on the therapeutical relationship is evident, and makes empowering young women particularly difficult.

Many families from the south search for treatment in the north and only very recently has there been development of eating disorders treatment facilities in regions such as Campania, Puglia, and Sicily. There is little or no debate on differences a therapist experiences when working with these two populations even if there is a high sensitivity to the cultural characteristics of northern and southern families. Unfortunately it is part of Italian culture to hide these differences under a general pattern of paternalism in order to avoid conflict, even if my own experience in addressing assertively these topics with families has been very positive.

There exists another cultural orientation system in Italian social life, quite independent from the family orientation, but with old historical roots, the 'aesthetic principle' (Henning, 1996). The importance of the aesthetic form is very apparent in all aspects of Italian culture. For centuries the aesthetic of the Italian culture has been the experience of foreign travelers and tourists and is the central point of most books of travel (Wilton and Bignamini, 1996). But 'beauty' is not only an important part of the foreign perception of Italy, but also an important category for the Italian self-image in everyday life. The flair for design and visual appeal that grows out of the public concern with dress and the visual arts, is also associated with the special place of design and designers in Italian culture. 'Bello' and 'Bellissimo' are not, as it might look at a first glance, the exaggerated exclamation of emotional people, but rather a basic category of social interaction. For northern countries this is a difficult concept, since beauty is understood as an attribute, as a pleasant supplement to the 'serious things' in life. But for Italians the striving for 'bellezza' is a fundamental part of identity, on the collective as well as on the individual level. This might be compared with identification models of other nations such as the American's 'nice guy'/'nice girl' concept or that of the Germans, valuing accountability and moral reliability over communicative qualities. These kind of patterns give a specific style to social life: it gives the individual the feeling that by respecting these codes he or she belongs and is accepted within a certain group.

The social expression of this concept of 'bellezza' is 'fare bella figura', slightly similar to the Asian concept of 'face saving', but with reference to a 'beautiful appearance' which leaves a good impression on others.

This aesthetic principle appears at various levels in Italian everyday life. At the first view there is the importance of clothing. Independently from social class the Italians care a lot for the way one is dressed, emphasizing strongly the outer appearance. The ideal of 'bella figura' refers not only to the sensual exterior of things, but is also related to behavior, among which generosity is of great importance, especially in respect to guests and people important to the family.

Again, this aspect of Italian culture is more accentuated in the south than in the north, and is often linked to the tendency to invest a great part of one's resources into these aspects of life. Living in great financial difficulties but still spending a lot to 'fare bella figura' is for many families in the south a normal practice. Women in the families have to learn how to make ends meet and allow their husbands to ignore the difficulties and create for themselves a more pleasant life away from everyday concerns with financial and family problems.

The cultural tension as experienced by young women in the south and the psychological reaction to culture change as mentioned by Ruggiero is in my opinion strongly influenced by the two factors I have mentioned, the Italian ideas of family and beauty.

The women's role in the traditional Italian family is not very appealing, the power differences with men in this context are striking, and the need to become emancipated, made attractive by the media as well as influenced by economic needs, are typical of the less affluent southern regions. But even if many young women from the south get acquainted with new lifestyles and new roles of women in Italian society through the media, or direct experiences, while studying for example at a northern university, the cultural background remains strongly influenced by the above mentioned sense of helplessness and the feeling that one's psychological and socio-economic well-being depends largely on the ability and power of others.

References

Banfield E (1958). *The moral basis of a backward society*. New York: Free Press.

Barzini L (1964). *The Italians*. London: Penguin.

Buzzi C (1994). *La salute del futuro*. Bologna: Il Mulino.

Cerroni U (1996). *L'identita' civile degli italiani*. Piero Manni.

Eurisko (1991). Eurobarometro. *Social Trends*, **54**, 14.

Gagliardi P, Barry T (1993) Aspects of Italian Management. In: *Management in Western Europe*, edited by Hickson D. de Gruyter.

Henning C (1996). *Überlegungen zum nationalen Habitus Italien*, SSIP.

Hofstede G (1980). *Culture's consequences: International differences in work related values*. Beverly Hills, CA: Sage.

Istat (Instituto Nazionale di Statistica) (2000). *Annuario Statistico Italiano 1998*. Rome: Istat.

Segall MH, Dase PR, Berry JW, Poortinga YH (1990) *Human Behavior in Global Perspective*. New York: Pergamon Press.

Wilton A, Bignamini I (1996). *Grand Tour, The Lure of Italy in the Eighteenth Century*. London: Tate Gallery.

Chapter 8

Argentina: The social body at risk

Oscar L. Meehan
Psychiatrist, Cordoba, Argentina
Melanie A. Katzman
Assistant Professor of Psychology, Weill Medical College,
Cornell University, New York, USA, and
Honorary Senior Lecturer, University of London, UK

> *Debate question:*
> *Psychologists should stay away from analysing information outside of the individual psyche as anything that could be gleaned from political and economic analyses will be too vague for clinical application.*

'We still sing, we still beg, we still dream, we still hope . . .
despite the blows that clever hatred struck on our lives . . .

For a different day, a day without worry, without fasting, a day without fear,
A day without tears'

Todavía Cantamos (We still Sing)
Victor Heredia

Caught in a culture clash, feeling confused, hungry for success but frustrated by false opportunities, the eating disordered woman turns to food for solace and relies on her appearance for approval. Her body becomes a potential receptacle for the marketers of perfection and promises of power.

In many ways the psychological profile of the eating disordered patient parallels the profile of Argentinean women in general and the sentiment expressed in the quote above in particular. While much has been written in the professional literature about the prevalence of eating disorders in North America and Europe, less attention has been given to what appears to be a serious and growing phenomenon in Argentina. The lack of widespread knowledge and specific data for this South American society may in itself encapsulate the struggle Argentineans endure to put themselves on the map – politically, socially, and in the world of mental health.

---

[1] Victor Heredia, a famous Argentinean folk singer, was forced into exile after the 1976 military coup. This song was written on his return to Argentina in 1986.

Eating disorders, an Argentinean epidemic?

Examining the evidence

Ask any Argentine if they think there is a problem with eating disorders in their country and many will respond that of course there is. Get off a plane at the Buenos Aires airport and be surrounded by women in purple mini skirts selling an array of goods and you too will believe this could be the case. However convinced people may be that eating issues are almost unavoidable in Argentina, careful epidemiological documentation is lacking. What does exist is a variety of behavioural and attitudinal indicators that a problem is brewing. For example, according to a recent study by the INDEC (Institut Nacional de Estadísticas y Censos – National Institute of Statistics and Census), 79% of Argentinean women consider slenderness a 'very important issue'. In a survey of 700 people aged 17–55 for the national newspaper 'La Nación' 60% of females were within normal weight limits, yet they considered themselves overweight. In the same study (Romer, 1996), 71% of women and 56% of men related doing 'something' to lose weight and 55% of teen girls, 45% of women and 37% of men agreed to the statement: 'You don't exist if you can't get people's attention by having a nice, perfect figure.'

Romer's (1996) research further revealed that Argentineans associate overweight with untidiness, laziness and illness while slenderness was associated with pleasing traits such as elegance, attractiveness, sensuality, beauty, personal security and youth. Using several questionnaires, Zukerfeld et al. (1998) found that in the capital city of Buenos Aires, in a study of 207 university freshmen girls, 10–30% reported dieting behaviours and 1.5–4% related bingeing behaviours.

As shown in Tables 8.1 and 8.2, Argentineans' dieting tendencies are also supported by a study on medication sales carried out by The Argentinean Chemist and Pharmaceutical Trust (Estudio de Auditoria del Mercado Pharmaceutics Argentina) which showed a sharp increase in both prescription and over-the-counter demand for slimming drugs (La Nación, 1996).

Although people appear quite involved in their caloric restriction, diets alone may not enable one to fit the Argentinean ideal and cosmetic surgery has become one of the most profitable medical specialities in Argentina, overtaking what used to be Argentina's national past time – psychoanalysis!

Table 8.1 Sales of prescribed slimming drugs in Argentina (1990–95)

Year	Units	Amount in US$
1990	900 000	5 000 000
1991	500 000	10 000 000
1992	1 600 000	15 000 000
1993	1 100 000	11 000 000
1994	840 000	9 500 000
1995	827 000	11 582 000

Table 8.2 Sales of over-the-counter slimming drugs in Argentina (1990–95)*

Year	Units	Amount in US$
1990	17 000	60 000
1991	140 000	2 000 000
1992	1 750 000	37 000 000
1993	900 000	15 000 000
1994	760 000	13 500 000
1995	465 000	7 900 000

*Source: The Argentinean Chemist and Pharmaceutical Trust, Nov 1996.

Romer (1996) reports that 45% of females and 19% of males would resort to cosmetic surgery to gain a better physical appearance. One of Argentina's current 'female heroines' is 'Cement Queen' Amalita Fortabat, a grandmother in her seventies who caused a stir when she had breast surgery. 'Now she has the tits of a 20-year-old', remarked a local journalist. A study done by '*Para Ti*', the Argentinean best-selling fashion magazine, reported that every year women in Argentina invest 90 million dollars in plastic surgery. Since 1992, the demand for plastic surgery in public hospitals has increased by 70% and the number of patients requesting cosmetic surgery has increased by 90%, of whom 10% are men (Revista '*Para Ti*', Semana 19–23 Marzo, 2000).

These diet and eating habits coincide with the curious data provided by The Fishing and Agricultural Department. In the last decade, beef consumption in Argentina fell by 16.5% while poultry consumption increased by 50%. The once world famous 'beef-eating' country has joined the 'light-food legion' (Fuente, 1996).

Initially eating disorders were only diagnosed in large urban areas (Chandler and Rovira, 1998) but eating disorders have now begun to appear in areas where you would least expect them, like north Patagonia (Neuquen) and in the west of the country. How does one make sense of such attitudinal and behaviour preocupations with weight and appearance?

The impact of national psychology on body pathology

Katzman (1998a) has argued that cross-cultural research provides a 'living laboratory' for expanding our understanding of social risk factors. In Argentina, with its emphasis on beauty, it would be easy to apply the liquid foundation of 'lazy' social theory and conclude that imported fashion pressures and marketing are to blame for the presumed increase in eating disorders. But that would be too simple.

Rather than merely reviewing the countless advertisements for slimming products and editorials declaring the need for body conformity, an appreciation of this country's susceptibility to superficial success requires a cultural biography informed by a political and economic history, not merely a fashion sensibility. In earlier works Katzman, (1998b) and Katzman and Lee (1997) have argued that eating disorders may be precipitated by problems with transition, dislocation and oppression that produce solutions in manipulations of weight, diet and food. The next section of this chapter will review the evidence that as a country Argentina is undergoing the very triad Katzman has identified. The data documenting the current obsession with shape will then be presented and, finally, available resources for care will be reviewed.

While the supposition that cultural forces provoke eating disorders cannot be proven with the available mental health methodologies, neither can these forces be ignored. Repeatedly in this book the effort to dismantle culture results in disabling realisations about the limits of our current tools. This chapter again struggles with how the outside forces get inside and produce an eating disorder. To do so requires venturing into disciplines beyond the familiar, with data that cannot as yet be deemed as causal. What follows is an attempt to stimulate new lines of investigation, to ask the questions without which there will be no future answers, interventions or suggested new paths of inquiry. It is by definition speculative.

Eating disorders in Argentina: The psycho-history of a nation

Transition and dislocation

Argentina is an 'untamed' place where societal constructs openly fight with natural forces, a country with a European imported history and an immensely wealthy past, prone to deny its geographical situation and its multi-racial ethnicity. The Argentinean writer, Jorge Luis Borges captured the Euro-Argentinean identity confusion saying, 'Argentineans are Italians who speak Spanish, dress like French and think they are English.'

Argentina is the second largest country in South Latin America, after Brazil, and occupies much of the southern part of the continent. The indigenous people were dark-skinned – Indians belonging to hunting tribes who were exterminated or driven away after fighting the conquistadors. Today, the approximately 35 million residents are of white European ancestry. There was a significant wave of European immigration in the mid-1800s from Spain and Italy and to a lesser degree France, Poland, Russia and Germany as well as Middle Easterners from Syria and Lebanon.

In 1869, the foreign-born residents made up 12% of the population. Between 1880 and 1916 there was an era of rapid population growth (largely from immigration) and Argentina's census grew from less than 2 000 000 in 1869 to nearly 8 000 000 in 1914 – a growth so significant that in large cities foreigners outnumbered natives by as much as two to one.

Big waves of further immigration took place at the end of the First World War, after the Spanish Civil War, and in the late 1930s, when during the peak of the Nazi oppression, thousands of Europeans fled to Argentina.

Unlike the United States, where the British went to 'build a new home and start a new life', the main interest of the earlier Europeans in South America was to make money and return home after 'making the most of America'. The various cultures of Argentina's immigrants were not motivated to achieve cultural homogeneity, and as a result home and one's culture remained elsewhere.

The Argentinean sociologist and philosopher Julio Mafud (1959) wrote that Argentina was born with what he called '*the Argentine defect*', or the 'uprooting' phenomenon. This prevailing sense of cultural fluidity and impermanence is a mood that persists today.

A recent national Gallup survey indicated that 21% of Argentineans would like to live in another country. Among young adults (18 to 24 years old) the percentage rises to 33%. Educational level and socio-economic background were correlated with the wish to emigrate. According to the INDEC, people with higher education have the greatest unemployment woes (*La Nación*, 15/7/00). The apparent search to be 'a part' of things results in at least two opposing behaviours, the search for something better and the assertion that perhaps better can be found at home as long as one is clearly 'different'.

'Different' in Argentina can be defined as different than one's South American continental neighbours, different than the native 'non-Europeans' or the difference between rural and urban dwellers. Urbanites tend to develop serious divisions between the rural interior and the urban coast. Many rural people resent the wealth, political power, and cultural affectations of the *porteños*, the 'people of the port' (the Buenos Aires region), while many *porteños* look upon residents of the interior as 'ignorant peasants'. These communities have found it difficult to understand each other, and despite having lived more or less side-by-side in this territory for over 200 years, mixing remains limited.

In addition, Argentina proudly boasts of its difference from other South American countries. Argentina, Uruguay and the south of Brazil (Rio Grande do Sul and Sao Paulo states) received a similar ethnic influence from Europe, which made them believe that they are somewhat distinct from the 'other' South America, the primitive one.

Modern-day Argentineans define their differences from their neighbours by reference to (among many other things) dialect, skin colour and education. For example, in contrast to most of South America, in Argentina today there are almost no Indians or Blacks (local Indians were systematically killed off, and Blacks were sold to bordering countries before slavery was abolished in 1812). The tango, the national dance, tells of the misery and despair of the lonely immigrant, the single mother or the betrayed lover. In Argentina, tango is played on European instruments, whereas the rest of South America sings of local beliefs using indigenous instruments.

Argentina also demonstrates its cultural distinction through her literacy rate, which is over 95%, compared to the 85% rate in Uruguay (the second best in South America). The fact that Argentina has produced five Nobel Prize winners (more than any of its neighbours), is yet another reflection of the country's high educational standard (Britannica, 1999).

Each of these qualities may serve to differentiate Argentineans from their South

American neighbours and prompt their over-identification with Europe as a way of confirming differences, affirming one's 'civility' and acculturating to an established society rather than creating a new one all ones own.

Davis and Katzman (1999), in their study of female Chinese immigrants in America, reported on perfectionism as a form of acculturation. The newly arrived Asian immigrant in the USA identified prevailing social styles and matched them to excess. An attempt to model oneself on the 'dominant' culture, even if the referred culture exists across the ocean, may prompt the Argentineans to behave as if they are 'acculturating' perfectly even if they never left home. In Argentina the clothing stores seem to have more French clothes than Paris!

And while women all over the world are trying to fit into clothes that are smaller than their natural body sizes, in Argentina the clothes available are the smallest they can possibly be and still have a market. This is particularly notable if one considers that the current fashion of being tall and lean is in direct contrast with the indigenous people's physique, which was short and round.

The ever-shrinking clothing sizes support not only a thin but also a childish image. The largest clothing size in Argentina is 44 (the equivalent of a size 8 in the US or 10 in the UK). It is almost impossible to get a 46 or larger. Thus even the visitor in an Argentinean shop can have an environmentally induced body image disturbance! The inevitable correlate of such restrictive clothing is pervasive dieting among women. Doctor Pedro Tessone, Senior Lecturer at the Department of Nutrition of the University of Buenos Aires, reports that 50% of patients have followed 'some form of a non-medical diet' (Revista *La Nación*, 1996).

Most recently, María del Carmen Banzas de Moreau, the President of the Buenos Aires province Radical Party Law Chamber, passed a ruling requiring the fashion industry to redesign clothing sizes according to 'normal' anthropometric measures and to produce clothes size 46 and over. This struggle to 'normalise' clothing options is similar to what has been reported in Barcelona, Spain. In Argentina, the reactions of the fashion industry have been extreme. Paula Cahen d'Anvers, a fashion designer, says, 'Our marketing experience tells us that clothes sizes larger than 40 will remain on the hangers week in and week out, they are almost impossible to sell'. Moni Rivas, of Chocolate Boutique, says, 'I don't think we should be obliged to make larger garments. Every fashion designer company has the right to choose their population target', and Pedro Szuchmacher, manager director of System Basic fashion shops chains, added, 'You cannot order companies to invest their money in something they don't believe. It would be the same as telling car factories or building companies to make special size cars, flats or TV models, actors and actresses to be fat . . . I don't think that Mrs. Banzas' law project is necessary'. (Revista '*Para Tí*', Mayo 2000).

Oppression

In addition to the identity confusion, cultural transition and attempted perfection, Argentina's political organisation demonstrates well the concept of oppression referred to in Katzman's model. After being ruled by Spain for nearly three hundred years, the country became independent in 1810. It attempted to adopt pure European liberal precepts, which theoretically allow an open social class stratification. However, Argentina also kept a socially and politically rigid colonial government system. In other words, this country attempted to achieve an ideal democratic model in an authoritarian fashion, which even though on the surface seemed to offer unlimited freedom of choices, the power to exercise them was restricted to a small number of influential people, who it so happened were almost exclusively men.

As the country continues to modernise, the experiences of the wild gaucho at the turn of the 20th century and the assimilated European at the start of the 21st century are similar in that both have had to deal with loss, disappointment and dislocation. Today, Argentina faces an undeniable psychological and economic frustration that affects nearly every inhabitant. For example, last year the unemployment rate was 12%, during 1999 car sales fell by 78% and food by 24%. Also in 1999 the National Growth rate grew by 1.2% instead of the 4% previously predicted, and salaries were curtailed by 30% (*La Nación,* July 2000).

At the same time that men are feeling dis-empowered, women are struggling to achieve parity in a doubly oppressive system with an economy that has failed for almost a century to match its potential.

In the early decades of the 20th century Argentina was referred to as 'the world's barn' since it was the world's leading exporter of corn, flax and meat. The First World War and the Great Depression of the 1930s curtailed prosperity. Successive governments over the next 40 years followed an import-substitution strategy designed to transform Argentina into a country self-sufficient in industry as well as agriculture. By 1960 manufacturing contributed more to the country's wealth than agriculture. Argentina had become largely self-sufficient in consumer goods, but also more dependent than ever on imported fuel and heavy machinery. In response, the government invested heavily in such basic industries as petroleum, natural gas, steel, petrochemicals and transport; it also invited investment by foreign companies. By the mid-1970s Argentina was producing most of its own oil, steel and automobiles and also was exporting a number of manufactured products. At the same time, the government waste of resources, large wage rises and inefficient production created a chronic inflation that rose until the 1980s.

When democracy returned so did hope. Alfonsin, the new president (1983–1989), declared 'Con la democracia se come, se cura y se educa' [With democracy, it is possible to eat, to cure and to educate] (Radical Party Presidential Rally Oct–Nov, 1983). But soon the citizens had to face the horrors hidden during the dictatorship. For example, thousands of people were murdered and countless 'disappeared'. The economy was in disastrous condition with all the resources depleted. The government collapsed under hyper-inflation.

The 1990s witnessed its own set of frustrations. Within a decade, borrowing from foreign creditors for many state and private-sector industrial schemes had quintupled Argentina's foreign deficit. Although the country had agricultural and industrial sectors similar to those of developed countries, they were considerably less efficient. As a result, the Argentineans enjoyed a high standard of living by South American standards but supported it with a foreign debt comparable to that of Third World countries.

Not surprisingly, the economic and political instability fertilised abuse, an abuse that has been endured by both men and women. In the 1940s university students were opposed to the Perón government because of its military origin and fascist style. Perón sided with the workers, the poor, and the 'ordinary people'. Intellectuals were discredited. After years of high educational standards, Argentina's education declined. Juan Perón's infamous phrase: 'Peasant boots in! Books out!' speaks for itself.

Thus a seed of superficial success may have been planted, contributing to the flowering obsession later in the century for Argentineans to adorn themselves physically and to model themselves on images that provoke disordered eating habits, for the sake of aesthetic appreciation. The beautification culture so vivid today may also be a reaction against the dark period of the 1970s, the last Perón government and the following military dictatorship. During that time, families and countrymen turned against each other and fratricide plagued the nation. Many Argentineans sought refuge in isolated communities, like North Patagonia, where political repression was less intense, while others were forced to live in exile. For many their communities and early attachments were lost, along with any sense of safety or predictability.

Connan, Katzman and Treasure (1999) have been working on a neuro-developmental model for anorexia nervosa that examines how a genetic predisposition combines with early attachment experiences and submission stress to produce changes in affect and appetite regulation that may lead an individual to anorexia nervosa. For some, food and emotional restriction become adaptive coping responses. Argentina, with its history of social and political constraints, and its more recent 'solutions' in appearance may provide the perfect case study of a nation at risk, particularly if one examines the dynamics at work in the 1970s.

Psychiatrist Jose Lumerman's (2000) description of his illegal detention depicts the atmosphere of those years:

'As usual, in a spring morning of 1974, when I was 19, I attended the Medical School, where I was the President of the Student's Union. On arrival I was told that our Union Centre had been destroyed by the secret military police – that they were trying to find out about our "political activities and connections". We were having an assembly when I was removed at gunpoint from the building. I still clearly remember gunshots and shouting, and then I was taken to a room where four heavily armed strong men were awaiting me. They beat me up and asked about people I did not know and about a weapon arsenal that did not exist. What followed was terrific: a mock execution where they described the way I would be killed, and sang songs about previously executed people. Finally I was blind folded and taken to an illegal "Prisoners

Camp" of the Federal Police where they kept me naked for two very long days and where I was interrogated by a 15-strong police squad, who, because of my Jewish condition, humiliated me. I was later set free with no charge. Many friends where not so lucky . . . they are in the "Missing" list (Desaparecidos), and I am a survivor of that generation.'

Women too were faced with different tortures. From the mid-1970s until the early 1980s, young mothers and pregnant women were reported to be killed and their babies were stolen and registered as being the natural children of military families who were expected to bring them up according to 'good traditional values'. (There are still families who are looking for these children, whose real identity has been disclosed through DNA tests.)

Could these abuses produce different impacts on men and women? The answer most likely is yes, but how does one even go about establishing causality? At least one thing seems clear, in a world where men who once experienced power were themselves restrained by an authoritarian government, the limitations on women are even greater and the achievement of economic and social power based on appearance would be more seductive.

In the past decades as people became poorer and poorer, the President and other politicians were showing their increasing wealth on magazine covers, mixing with models and spending Argentinean money on luxuries. For example, Menem bought an aircraft for official use that was more expensive than President Clinton's one, top international models were received with honours at the Pink House while relatives of victims of two major international terrorist attacks were never even invited in. Just as inequity has been on the rise, so has trivialisation – that is, superficial activities appear to be competing for government attention along with the suffering of people. Careers in medicine are poorly rewarded and government funds for scientific research teeter on bankruptcy while jobs in fashion and television are thriving. In fact, the head of the CONICET (Consejo Nacional de Investigación Científica y Técnica – National Council of Technical and Scientific Research) resigned in protest due to huge budget reductions (*La Nación*, July 25, 2000).

The struggle to get a decent education, voiced years ago by Silvina Ocampo, one of Argentina's great female writers, may still be true today: 'I was the victim of a patriarchal system to which I intensely rebelled against. I was a clever and curious adolescent, but I fell prisoner of the male segregation of the female gender. It felt as if women were not permitted to develop intellectually, and that the only thing that counts was our (female) physical attraction . . . and they (men) made me feel it every day of my life. Girls' education was intentionally incomplete and deficient. I remember my father laconically saying: Silvina, had you or one of your five sisters been born a boy you would have had a career . . . ' (Ocampo, 1982, p. 16)

Although today more women have university careers, they continue to work for less pay than men do. Domingo Sarmiento, Argentina's first educator and former president, stated that societal development can be measured by the social position and power reached by women, and warned that any state's future rests on the educational level achieved by its female population (Ocampo, 1982). Unfortunately, higher education in Argentina was seriously hampered by the censorship of the military government from 1976 to 1983 and further compromised by the reduction in funds to build new schools or pay teachers adequate wages during the 1990s. The lack of physical space was 'solved' by offering primary school students daily three-hour periods instead of keeping them at school the whole morning or afternoon. In addition, the low educator salaries created poor morale and decreasing quality. The ability to recoup any cultural appreciation lost during the fascist years has continued to be postponed.

Today's students not only have the overt pressures for bodily conformity but possibly the more subtle ones as well. In a recent study of smoking and eating behaviours of future nursery and pre-school teachers, Facchini and Rozensztejn (2000) found that one-third of the teachers in training had a lower than healthy body weight and yet most were not satisfied and wanted to weigh less. How this will impact students is not clear but certainly the culture of the classroom is likely to further body discomfort.

Numerous writers have pointed to the presence of eating disorders during times of frustrated ambition (see Nasser and Katzman, 1999). For Argentineans, both men and women have not been able to fully realise their potential. The complexities of promise gone wrong, abuse gone too far and education interrupted, are all familiar ones to the clinician seeing eating-disordered women. For Argentina, the possibility of controlling the size and appearance of one's body holds not only a psychic sense of mastery but potential economic gain as the current culture recruits and reinforces unreal physical characteristics. The legally displayed demands on appearance are no secret and are captured in the classified adds of 14 June 2000 (*La Voz del Interior*, Córdoba, Argentina).

> Important National Company wants ladies aged between 18/40. Minimum salary US$ 859 p.c.m. Requirements: Excellent figure, Complete High School studies, ample working hour availability, above average cultural and intellectual level, highly ambitious personality.

> We are looking for female students aiming to improve their incomes. Excellent figure is the only requirement.

> International Mobile Phone Company is looking for sale assistance ladies. Excellent figure. Send photograph and CV to Office.

Classified ads of 18 June 2000 (Employment Session *La Nacion*, Buenos Aires – Argentina)

> FORD Motor Co. Dealers, Marketing Dep. of Buenos Aires, Buenos Aires Province and La Plata will short list men and women. Requirements: Complete

High School studies, Good / nice physical appearance, previous experience not essential. Send CV.

Receptionist for general office work. Requirements: mobile phone and excellent physical appearance. Call. . . .

Important State Agency will short list a highly successful employee aged between 25/40. Requirements: very good physical appearance, own mobility and ample working hour availability. Send CV and up-to-date photograph to. . . .

As one can see, the weight discrimination, often disguised, illegal, or subverted in other nations is freely displayed and potentially augmenting the growing list of national risk factors for eating disorders.

Machismo men and small women

If men and women have shared pressures, why would women develop an eating disorder while men might not? In the absence of complete epidemiological data, it is difficult to know whether in Argentina there is a true gender difference in prevalence. While it is possible that equal numbers of men and women may ultimately be shown to have eating disturbances, it is likely that women endure additional risk factors. For example, the above mentioned limits on female education, the comodification of the body, women valued for their body and the need to be small for social and fashion reasons may all have an additive effect.

The renowned machismo culture of Latin America cannot be dismissed as mere stereotype. Pressures persist for men to assert their success and strength (to remain psychologically and physically large) despite social and economic factors hindering true accomplishments. While it may require a leap into the canyons of evolutionary theory, it is not unreasonable to consider that women may 'grow' smaller to not only physically assure that men can retain their 'largeness' but also their apparent 'largesse'. Especially now during a slumping economic period, women may be more willing than men to work out of necessity and for less pay. Although women may be slipping the food onto the table and accessing certain powers, their slight bodies may make them less threatening to men.

Can we say with confidence that there is an eating disorders epidemic in Argentina or that there will be in the future? Can we ascribe causality or even a mechanism? Certainly not yet; however, while one cannot prove the process, you can recount the risk. And as the next section suggests, you can also begin to address treatment.

The response

In Argentina there is a clear shortage of facilities for eating disorders (Meehan and Insua, 2000). Treatment for anorexia and bulimia is rarely paid for by any private health insurance and there are limits to the public services.

The first programmes for treating eating problems in the country were at Hospital Italiano (Cecile Herscovici, also Rubén Zukerfeld and Alberto Cormillot) and Aluba (Mabel Bello). The former Asociación de Lucha contra la Bulimia y la Anorexia (Association Against Bulimia and Anorexia) was an NGO organisation founded by Dr Mabel Bello in 1985. Today it has fourteen branches spread over the country, with two in Uruguay and one in Barcelona (Spain). The organisation claims a (controversially) high recovery rate for anorexia and bulimia (http://www.aluba.org).

Several more eating disorders treatment programmes have been created, based on Argentina's strong psychoanalytical tradition. Each of Argentina's two largest cities has university-based treatment centres. In Buenos Aires the country's largest University Hospital, the Hospital Nacional de Clínicas (University of Buenos Aires, UBA) opened an Eating Disorders Clinic in 1993. From January 1994 to November 1998 a total of 412 new patients have been assessed, out of which 53 were anorexic (12.8%) and 196 were bulimic (47.5%). Their treatment dropout rates are over 50% (Meehan, Chandler and Rovira, 1998)

The other university hospital, The Centre for Eating Disorder Treatment of the Hospital Nacional de Clínicas (University of Córdoba) opened in 1995. This centre has a treatment programme based on psychoanalysis and its treatment approach does not differ much from the University of Buenos Aires.

Overall in Buenos Aires there are eating disorder teams working at several of the city's hospitals, some of them having more than 15 years experience working with eating issues. Most of these teams have a psychoanalytical approach and provide mainly individual therapies; however, some of them include systemic family treatments and psychoeducational nutritional groups. Foundations such as Aigle provide day hospital and outpatients treatment with a cognitive orientation. ALCO/ABAN (Asociación Lucha contra la Obesidad/ Asistencia en Bulimia y Anorexia Nervosa) has offered support groups since the 1970s; while FUNDAIH and Centro Oro treat patients with psychoanalytical approaches. Fumtadip combines psychotherapeutic and psychoeducational treatments.

North Patagonia Instituto Austral de Salud Mental (IASaM), a community and psychiatric hospital servicing approximately a half million people in Neuquén City opened 12 years ago. The two psychiatrists working there saw just five bulimia nervosa cases in the first five years. This changed dramatically and in 1999 alone they were referred 15 cases of bulimia and five of anorexia nervosa.

Ruth Rozensztejn, from the Hospital Cosme Argerich in Buenos Aires, who in 1996 spent a sabbatical year at The Maudsley Hospital in London, has been practising MET (Motivational Enhancement Therapy) for eating-disordered adolescents with considerable success. She reports that an interdisciplinary treatment team has assessed 85 adolescents, of which 71 presented with an eating disorder, 37% restrictive EDNOS (Eating Disorders Not Otherwise Specified), 36% BN (Bulimia Nervosa), 18% ANR (Anorexia Nervosa, Restricting type), 6% ANP (Anorexia Nervosa, Purging type) and 3% BED (Binge Eating Disorder).

In Argentina anorexia nervosa and bulimia nervosa are usually treated as part of 'a package' that also includes obesity and weight reduction. In many cases, nutritionists and endocrinologists are in charge of the treatment, with little other input from psychologists and psychiatrists. The treatment approach and the development of multidisciplinary teams are slightly hampered by cultural and educational restraints. On cultural grounds, many Argentinean mental health workers are still too individualistic to consider seeking advice from other professionals. Often the assumption is that one has to be from a particular discipline to offer therapy. From an educational and training perspective, many workers are heavily influenced by the one-to-one psychoanalytical therapy structure. In some institutions, professionals practising psychology and psychiatry are not used to sharing and discussing patients or cases, misunderstanding teamwork for breach of confidentiality.

In spite of these differences, meetings such as the Eating Disorders International Meeting in Cordoba in March 2000 brought an audience of 600 professionals, and a community programme targeted at the general public, tackling issues of prevention and treatment, drew 300 participants.

During these meetings and with his private practice, Oscar Meehan has been introducing methods based on CBT (Cognitive Behavioural Therapy) and MET to mixed reactions. In Argentina some people think that CBT and MET therapies curtail patients' liberties with therapists becoming bossy and intrusive. This obviously clashes with traditional 'free association' techniques. As the Head of the Postgraduate Training Psychiatric Department of Córdoba's General Medical Council indicated: 'When watching American training CBT programmes on video, I was amazed at the therapists' and patients' attitudes during the interview, both marking on a sheet of paper and writing lots of notes (diaries) . . . what is this? A battle-ship game, for God's sake!!!' As MET and self-help programmes begin to show their potential and ground themselves in data, so does the Argentinean public demonstrate its interest. There is a huge need for developing programmes of all kinds and a growing interest to do so.

Unfortunately there is no law requiring the treatment of eating disorders, and only the wealthiest insurance systems provide coverage. It took legislation before Argentineans could receive help for HIV and AIDS viruses. Before that, persons who were discovered to have HIV were expelled from their health insurance. It is possible that it will take a law again to be sure that access to care for eating problems is made available for everyone.

Conclusion

The challenge for Argentina is a theoretical and practical one to understand how a society can incubate an illness and the many levels of change required to rid oneself of its harm. While we can discuss treatment options, less is known about prevention or prevention efforts. With cultural hazards so deep there is the persistent risk of blaming the individuals who develop the disorders. There is also a personal challenge for the people of Argentina to repair its past and to plan for the future, preserving its resources of agriculture, passion and people. Just as the eating-disordered patient must find a way to value her competencies and combine them to lead the fullest of lives, without attention to the evaluation of others, Argentina has been a nation with its back to the country and its eyes to the sea, it is time to turn back and see the body of the country and the fullness of possibilities.

Acknowledgements

The authors are indebted to Ruth Rozensztejn, clinical psychologist at Hospital Cosme Argerich in Buenos Aires, a careful observer of behaviour and manuscripts.

References

Agulla JC (1969). *Tiempos de Cambio: Testimonio de un Sociologo Argentino* (Changing Times: Testimony of an Argentinean Sociologist'). Editorial de Belgrano, Universidad de Belgrano. Buenos Aires, Argentina. Dic 271–278/ 289.

Biagini HE, Mafud J (1987). *Historia de las Ideas* (Argentina's Thoughts and Ideologies from 1950–59). Ideas en Ciencias Sociales (6). Universidad de Belgrano. Buenos Aires, Argentina.

Chandler E, Rovira A (1998). *Admission and Treatment Protocol: Eating Disorders Clinic*. Hospital Nacional de Clínicas 'José de San Martín', Buenos Aires, Argentina. **http://hc.fmed.uba.ar/**

Connan F, Katzman MA, Treasure J (1999). *A neurodevelopmental model for eating disorders*. Paper presented at the British Association for Behavioral and Cognitive Therapy Meeting, Bristol, England.

Davis C, Katzman MA (1999). Perfection as acculturation. *International Journal of Eating Disorders*, **25**, 65–70.

Encyclopaedia Britannica DVD 2000, MM Group, Springfield House, West Street, Bedminster, Bristol, BS3 3NX UK.

Estudio de Auditoria del Mercado Farmacéutico Argentino (1996). The Argentinean Chemist and Pharmaceutical Trust. *La Nacion*, 11 Oct 1996.

Facchini M, Rozensztejn R (under review). *Smoking Habit and Eating Behaviour in Pre-school Teachers Students in Buenos Aires*.

Fuente (1996). Ministerio de Agricultura y Ganadería – Argentina.

Heredia V (1986). *Todavía Cantamos* (We still Sing). Popular Argentinean folk song, 1986.

http://www.aluba.org (April 2000).

http://www.sevi.com.ar/Cormillot/web_corm/Alco.htm
http://www.psiconet.com/fumtadip

Katzman MA (1998a). *Cultural Curiosities: Questions for the next millennium*. Plenary Address given at the eight international conference on eating disorders. New York, NY, USA.

Katzman MA (1998b). Feminist approaches to eating disorders: Placing the issues in context. In: *Psychotherapeutic issues on eating disorders: Models, methods and results*, edited by De Risio S, Bria P, Ciocca A. Roma: Societa Editrice Universo, Italy.

Katzman MA, Lee S (1997). Beyond body image: The integration of Feminist and Transcultural theories in the understanding of self starvation. *International Journal of Eating Disorders*, **22**, 385–94.

La Nación (1996). Revista *La Nación*, Buenos Aires, Argentina, 11 Oct 1996.

La Nación (2000), Revista *La Nación*, Buenos Aires, Argentina, 15 July 2000.

Lariguet E (2000). *Discourse Analysis and Language Teaching*. English Literature and Stylistic Departments, Universidad Nacional de Córdoba, Argentina, May. Lecture to be given at VIII Congreso de la Sociedad Argentina de Lingüística, Mar del Plata, 20–23 Sep. 2000. Abstract on 'Discourse Analysis and Language Teaching'.

Lee S, Katzman MA (in preparation). Cross-cultural Perspectives on Eating Disorders. In: *Eating Disorders and Obesity: A Comprehensive Handbook*, edited by Fairburn C, Brownell, K. New York: Guilford Press.

Lumerman J (2000). *Instituto Austral de Salud Mental* (IASaM), Neuquén, Argentina, April. IASaM 2000 Internal Audit Report.

Mafud J (1959). *El Desarraigo Argentino*, (The Argentinean Unrootlessness). Americalee. Buenos Aires, Argentina.

Meehan O, Insua J (2000). '*Psychiatric Training in Argentina's Two Major Cities*', The Bulletin, BJPsych. In press.

Meehan O, Chandler E, Rovira (1998). The Hospital Nacional de Clinicas 'San Martin' Eating Disorders Clinic, *Audit 1994–1998*.

Ministerio de Agricultura y Ganedería (1996), Argentina.

Nasser M, Katzman MA (1999). Transcultural perspectives inform prevention. In: *Preventing Eating Disorders: A Handbook of Interventions and Special Challenges*, edited by Piran N, Levine, M, Steiner-Adair C. New York: Brunner Mazel, pp. 26–43.

Ocampo S (1982). '*El Imperio Insular*' – Autobiography II: The Insular Empire – Ediciones Revista Sur, 'Yesterday in Today's Language', Buenos Aires, Argentina, p. 16.

Revista, *Para Tí* Semana 19–23 Mayo 2000, Editorial Atlántida, Buenos Aires, Argentina.

Romer G *et al.* (1996). Para *La Nación* Oct 11.

Zukerfeld R, Zukerfeld R, Quiroga S (1998). Conducta alimentaria, peso corporal y psicopatología en mujeres jóvenes. *Rev. Argentina de Clínica Psicológica*; **VII**: 1–19.

Commmentary I

Niva Piran
Professor, Department of Adult Education and Counseling
Psychology, OISE/ University of Toronto, Toronto, Canada

The chapter entitled 'Argentina: The social body at risk' portrays a country undergoing acute political, social, and economic changes during the past century, including a 'dark period' of military dictatorship, during which personal safety was stolen from individuals at all levels of privilege. Further, the chapter suggests that Argentina had never developed its own identity and its own set of widely sanctioned cherished values as a country. It relied instead on a mixture of 'borrowed' values, an amalgam which could not provide a sense of continuity and a safety net to fall back on in the context of rapid transition.

A system of privilege, mainly accorded to urban white men connected with systems of power, is further described in the chapter, highlighting prejudices related to gender, dialect, urban status, racial and ethno-cultural heritage, and ancestry. In addition to the examples offered by the authors, many untold stories lie within the description of these societal structures and transitions, among them stories which offer clues to an understanding of the apparent increase in the incidence of eating disorders in Argentina. As a social action researcher and feminist scholar, I contend that professionals (either academics or practitioners) have a role in uncovering the complex social (and not only personal or familial) meaning of embodied practices such as eating disorders. In general, both the process of knowledge production and the social understandings that result from those processes either comply with and reinforce existing scientific, professional, and social structures, values, and mores, or challenge them to varying degrees.

From this vantage point, I contend that professional work at the intersection of the social and the personal spheres always contains political elements. I will aim to demonstrate this point through the ensuing discussion and to outline implications related to the understanding, treatment and prevention of eating disorders in Argentina.

The chapter eloquently describes the occurrence of multiple political and social changes in Argentina. One could wonder about the experience of diverse women living within these macro-level social transitions. It has been repeatedly documented, for example, that the violation of women's bodies, never a safe or respected territory in patriarchal structures, intensifies during the time of war and military occupations. Similarly, the backlash against women's participation in the public domain and well-paid occupations has been found to intensify during times of economic recession, often through targeting their bodies (Faludi, 1991; Wolf, 1991). In addition, during periods of social transformation, it is typically the advantaged who reap the benefit of such changes. Even wider access to education, which generally leads towards greater social equity, may not yield as many advantages to women and other minority group members, compared with opportunities it affords men who are members of the dominant group (Blakely and Harvey, 1988). Racial and ethno-cultural systems of prejudice, such as described in this chapter, also generally tend to support the exploitation of minority group women and their bodies (Buchanan, 1993).

I would suggest that in order to understand the increase in disordered eating practices among women in Argentina, we need to create a bridge between the broad social changes described in the chapter and the experiences of diverse women living within this complex system of social structures, transitions, and prejudices. There are a few glimpses in the chapter of the way in which macro-level social structures, such as patriarchy or dictatorship, could have affected the personal life of women. For example, the authors quote Silvina Ocampo's description of the objectifying sexualization of her body that co-existed with the provision of poor educational opportunities for girls. Her account challenges patriarchy, particularly its treatment of her body, and limitation of her social opportunities. Her eloquent description resembles accounts by women in the Victorian era, similarly trapped in a situation of inequity (Bordo, 1993), who developed 'hysteria'. Indeed, in a few North American studies, just such objectification and sexualization of women's bodies have been found to disrupt women's sense of power and instrumentality and to be associated with an increased incidence of eating disorders (cf. Piran, 2001a, 2001b).

The authors of the chapter further mention the stealing of babies from less privileged women during the time of military dictatorship. One can only imagine what horror is associated for these women (and their daughters) with their bodies in general, and experiences of fertility, pregnancy, birth, and motherhood in particular. It is likely that first-person accounts of these experiences, similar to that of Silvina Ocampo, are not widely available. Multiple social barriers, such as being the member of a minority group or low socio-economic status, render the experiences of less-advantaged members of society invisible.

How can we gain access to this embedded and 'embodied' knowledge? The authors of the chapter specifically mention that traditional paradigms of knowledge construction and research have not allowed for the systematic understanding of this important intersection of body and culture. Yet there are ways. Various approaches have been proposed as a means to incorporate a critical understanding of sociopolitical and other contextual factors when constructing the experience of individuals residing within varied social systems. For example, feminist approaches to therapy specifically require the social contextualization of individual symptomatology and thereby incorporate a critical examination of culture (Brown, 1994). Such an approach inevitably has political implications. Feminist counseling, for example, has had a constructive influence in putting sexual abuse and trauma on the social agenda (Herman, 1992). Similarly, the critical approach to research not only examines individuals' lives in context but also acknowledges and studies the researcher's own social location in terms of social privilege and biases.

Even though the body has been recognized by social critics as a most significant social domain (cf. Foucault, 1979), there has been a paucity of critical social research in the area of disordered eating. The few critical qualitative research studies conducted in this field have indeed led to introducing new critical concepts. Thompson (1994), for example, has introduced the relevance of poverty, classism and social mobility, heterosexism, and racism into the discourse of eating disorders. Piran (2001b) has described the 'Disembodiment through Inequity' theory of eating disorders, highlighting the role of disruption of ownership (including sexual harassment), body-targeted prejudices, and constraining social constructions of women and their bodies in understanding eating disorders. Larkin, Rice, and Russell (1999) examined the role of sexual harassment in negative body image. These studies are few and far between. Their paucity is likely related to widespread social and professional barriers, especially because such research challenges existing systems of privilege within the fields of psychiatry and psychology. Critical knowledge anchored in life experiences that emerges in qualitative inquiries may go beyond the expansion of existing theories or understandings. Such knowledge may lead to social transformations.

Feminist consciousness-raising groups in the 1970s, for example, relied on critical knowledge development in groups to guide transformations in women's lives, including larger scale social transformations. MacKinnon (1989) describes this process as follows: 'Consciousness raising socializes women's knowing and thus transforms it, creating a shared reality that clears a space in the world within which women can begin to move in a substantial, embodied way.' Similarly, particular approaches to qualitative research have been developed which emphasize the connection between the emergence of critical knowledge anchored in life experiences and community activism. Participatory Action Research (PAR) (Park *et al.*, 1993) comprises one such approach whose visionary leaders such as Paulo Freire, Augusto Boal, and Fals Borda resided in Latin America.

This approach emphasizes the political aspects of knowledge production. In this approach, expert knowledge is seen as located within members of the community studied. This knowledge develops through a process of shared reflection and dialog into critical consciousness and understanding of the forces that have shaped community members' social realities. A project following the PAR approach in one school setting in an urban center in North America has led to a critical understanding of disordered eating and to the transformation of the school setting (Piran, 2001).

How can the challenge of eating disorders be addressed in Argentina? Argentina's history is unique and includes social and political events, such as military dictatorship, far removed from the experience of most individuals residing in North America or Europe – where most information about eating disorders has been gathered to date. Applying social knowledge developed in North America or Europe about eating disorders to designing intervention strategies in Argentina may run the risk of both curtailing the development of grass-roots, critical knowledge by different groups of women and possibly curtailing the power embedded in social transformation that is anchored in such knowledge. Qualitative inquiries following critical methodologies could be central in problematizing women's diverse situations and the institutions that influence those situations (Eichler, 1986). This, in turn, can lead not only to theoretical advancements, but also to social action at the policy and at the grass roots levels in Argentina. Creating the space for women to discuss problematic experiences of the body is not only a scientific venture but it is also a political venture in that such inquiry leads to a critical examination of dominant societal institutions. The political component may be even more accentuated when including the knowledge and voices of groups that are multiply oppressed, such as members of ethno-cultural minority groups and of lower social classes.

To conclude, as a professional, I have great respect for the authors' analysis of multiple and complex historical and social processes that contextualize disordered eating practices among diverse women in Argentina. I further suggest that critical inquiry that relies on the embodied life experiences of diverse women living in Argentina will supplement this social analysis and hopefully lead to enhanced political consciousness and ultimately to meaningful social change.

References

Blakely J, Harvey E (1988). Market and non-market effects on male and female occupational status attainment. *Canadian Review of Sociology and Anthropology*, **25**, 23–40.

Bordo S (1993). *Unbearable weight: Feminism, Eastern culture, and the body*. Berkeley: University of California Press.

Brown LS (1994). *Subversive dialogues: Theory in feminist therapy*. New York: Basic Books.

Buchanan KS (1993). Creating beauty in blackness. In: *Consuming passions: Feminist approaches to weight preoccupation and eating disorders*, edited by Brown C, Jasper K. Toronto: Second Story Press, pp. 36–52.

Eichler M (1986). The relationship between sexist, nonsexist, woman-centered and feminist research. *Studies in Communication*, **3**, 37–74.

Faludi S (1991). *Backlash: The undeclared war against American women*. New York: Crown.

Foucault M (1979). *Discipline and punish: The birth of the prison*. New York: Vintage Books.

Herman JL (1992). *Trauma and recovery*. New York: Basic Books.

Kincheloe JL, McLaren PL (1994). Rethinking critical theory and qualitative research. In: *Handbook of qualitative research*, edited by Denzin NK, Lincoln YS. Thousand Oaks, CA: Sage Publications, pp. 138–157.

Larkin J, Rice C, Russell V (1999). Sexual harassment and the prevention of eating disorders: Educating young women. In *Preventing eating disorders: A handbook of interventions and special challenges* edited by Levine, Steiner-Adair C. Philadelphia: Brunner/Mazel, pp. 194–206.

MacKinnon CA (1989). *Towards a feminist theory of the state.* Cambridge MA: Harvard University Press.

Olesen V (1994). Feminism and models of qualitative research. In: *Handbook of qualitative research,* edited by Denzin NK, Lincoln YS. Thousand Oaks, CA: Sage Publications, pp. 158–74.

Park P, Brydon-Miller M, Hall B, Jackson T (1993). *Voices of change: Participatory research in the United States and Canada.* Toronto: OISE Press.

Piran N (2001). Re-inhabiting the body from the inside out: Girls transform their school environment. In: *From subject to subjectivities: A handbook of interpretive and participatory methods,* pp. 218–38, edited by Tolman DL, Brydon-Miller M. New York: New York University Press.

Piran N (2001, b). A gendered perspective on eating disorders and disordered eating. In: J. Worell (Ed.), *Encyclopedia of Gender,* pp. 369–378 edited by Worell J. San Diego, CA: Academic Press.

Reason P (1994). Three approaches to participative inquiry. In: *Handbook of qualitative research,* edited by Denzin NJ, Lincoln YS. Thousand Oaks, CA: Sage Publications, pp. 324–39.

Thompson B (1994). Food, bodies, and growing up female: Childhood lessons about culture, race, and class. In: *Feminist perspectives on eating disorders,* edited by Fallon F, Katzman, M, Wooley SC. New York: Guilford Press, pp. 355–78.

Wolf N (1991). *The beauty myth: How images of beauty are used against women.* New York: Morrow.

Commentary 2

Sneja Gunew
Professor of English and Women Studies,
University of British Columbia, Vancouver, Canada

As a post-colonial cultural feminist theorist (and no expert on Argentina) here are some of the questions I would raise in relation to the issues canvassed in this chapter.

There is a consistent argument being made that there is a link between 'cultural patterns' and 'the corporeal', and that women in particular are prone to internalizing culturally dominant values and representations. They respond by developing eating disorders as coping mechanisms in an unbalanced world. But in the course of the chapter the question constantly surfaces that both men and women are being subjected to these pressures and so what is the nature of the effect on women, more specifically, of the bewilderingly complex range of cultural elements?

If Argentina is a nation recovering from political trauma, anxious about its status in a globalized context, then how do the social problems of unemployment and so forth impact on men and women differently so that they manifest differing characteristics of corporeal pathologies? One of the questions I kept wondering about is whether men also displayed such corporeal excesses, but differently? Were they also under pressure to display the 'excellent figure' of the advertisements listed? Were they also resorting to plastic surgery in order to maintain a youthful demeanor?

From my own disciplinary training, to make the argument work that there is a continuum between problems with 'transition, dislocation and oppression' and eating disorders, one would need to be directed at more supporting material concerning the following issues.

(i) What are the major regulative discourses impacting on women and men? In what ways do the discourses of health and education impose certain norms regarding appropriate behavior, along gendered lines? For example, in the last few years prescriptive pronouncements concerning 'beauty' (for men and women) have tended to be coded in terms of 'health'. If we think of the boom in exercise regimes over the past decade we realize how much this is coupled with notions of a perfect/beautiful body. So the logic runs not so much that men and women are trying to achieve aesthetically pleasing bodies but that they are responsibly attempting to achieve optimum health in which the well-sculpted body is merely an outward manifestation of the fact that they are regulating their health regimes.

Diet thus becomes coded in terms of being healthy rather than as a narcissistic obsession to attain beauty.

(ii) What are the particular forms of cultural representation that impact on Argentine women? For example, rather than simply looking at advertisements demanding a 'very good physical appearance', what about the legacy of cultural codes provided by film, literature, theatre, music (popular as well as highbrow)? Does the example of Eva/Evita Perón, for example, hold particular lessons or insights regarding the construction of femininity, even as they have been reimported back via American popular culture?

Stuart Hall (1997) has been a theorist in the forefront of analyzing the effects of representation in terms of constructing both individual and larger national identities. Hall considers the nature of various kinds of languages or systems of representations that produce meaning which in turn leads to the production of knowledge as truths intimately tied to power. The logic (in its crude form) is that those who control the sociopolitical world also affect the ways in which legitimate or publicly endorsed signification is effected. Even if, as Meehan and Katzman argue, Argentina is a nation symbolically obsessed with European values, those values and codes comprising representational systems are not simply a template mapped onto the country but undergo a translation in their passage to the South American context. The nature of these changes in signification need to be unpacked. Systems of meaning production remain complex and (fortunately) contradictory and if we look, for example, at the work of the Argentine writer Luisa Valenzuela we find a radical destabilization of the regime of femininity so cogently summarized by Meehan and Katzman in the course of their chapter.

In a chilling short story called 'Symmetries,' which also names her recent collection, Valenzuela weaves together the voice of a male torturer and that of his victim: 'we make them wear the loveliest clothes. We put things inside them that are much more terrible than our things, because those things are also a prolongation of ourselves and because they are ours. The women I mean . . . "often they would bring hairdressers and beauticians to the detention centre and they would force us to put on long, embroidered dresses. As in other instances, we wanted to refuse, but we couldn't. We knew perfectly well where they had got the dresses from – covered in sequins and strapless as if to underline and emphasise our scars – we knew where they had got them from but not where they would take us when we put those dresses on. With our hair done, all made up and manicured and modified, with not the slightest chance of being ourselves"' (Valenzuela, 1998, p. 158). This places what appears to be a frivolous preoccupation with outward beauty into a much more convoluted psychic context which is organized around total control and the dehumanization of (one could argue) both participants.

Finally, as a feminist, I would want to know the degree to which there has been a women's movement in Argentina and what form this has taken in questioning received notions of representation as well as the full range of social practices. As early as Robin Morgan's exhilarating anthology 'Sisterhood is Global' (1984) we have Leonora Calvera's statements documenting this fledgling women's movement and mentioning the bizarre role models provided by both Eva and Isabel Perón. As Calvera somewhat sardonically put it: 'It is difficult – even for feminists – to do battle with a myth' (Calvera, 1984, p. 57). She also mentions the Mothers of the Plaza de Mayo whose strategic deployment of traditional attributes of femininity meant that they too had, in a sense, to be deconstructed in order for feminism to be able to reach for new forms and practices of cultural representation.

References

Calvera L (1984) '*Argentina: The Fire That Cannot Be Extinguished.*' Translated by Waldman GF, Gutiérrez ES In Morgan R *Sisterhood is Global: The International Women's Movement Anthology*. New York: Anchor/Doubleday Press.

Hall S (Ed) (1997). *Representation: Cultural Representation and Signifying Practices*. London: Open University/Sage Publications.

Valenzuela L (1998). *Symmetries*, Translated by Costa MJ. London: Serpent's Tail.

Chapter 9

Changing bodies, changing cultures: An intercultural dialogue on the body as the final frontier

Mervat Nasser
Consultant Psychiatrist/ Senior Lecturer, Leicester
University, Leicester, UK

Vincenzo Di Nicola
Consultant Psychiatrist, Eating Disorders Unit, Douglas
Hospital, Verdun, Quebec, Canada

Introduction

The interlocutors of this intercultural dialogue are two psychiatrists who share an interest in placing anorexia nervosa, or self-starvation, in cultural context. Mervat Nasser is a woman from Egypt who now works in England as a consultant psychiatrist and has written *Culture and Weight Consciousness* (1997). Vincenzo Di Nicola was born in Italy, educated in Canada and England as a psychologist and psychiatrist, and now works in Montreal as a consultant psychiatrist for an eating disorders unit; he has written on cultural and historical aspects of eating disorders (Di Nicola, 1990a, 1990b), child psychiatry (Di Nicola, 1992) and family therapy (Di Nicola, 1997). As well as anorexia nervosa, both psychiatrists share an interest in what they call, respectively, 'body regulation' (Nasser has studied the new veiling phenomenon among Moslem women, Nasser, 1999) and 'body modification' (Di Nicola has worked with self-mutilation among young people, Di Nicola and Epstein, 1998).

Nasser presents a range of clinical and cultural phenomena to propose some hypotheses for further investigation, coming to some provisional conclusions.

Di Nicola writes in the italicised postmodern voice of a cultural therapist, raising doubts, adding details, offering digressions and excursions, and above all, expressing irony about any likely conclusions.

> *Debate question:*
> *Does cultural transition impact on the definition of self and identity? In the following dialogue, we try to deal with this question in the light of current and conflicting transitional cultural changes. We speculate on the possible processes by which the transformation of the body into an identity or even a home, may become a method of coping with these prevailing cultural changes.*

1 Body as identity

In every epoch, bodies exist only in context. They form the felt equivalent of any age, in so far as that age can be experienced by a specific group.

Illich, 1992

Nasser: In the course of this volume the reader may have been puzzled at the way the different contributors have debated the nature of 'eating psychopathology' as potentially being susceptible to economic or political forces, and yet we know from history that 'neurosis' has a habit of taking different shapes and forms in response to changing societies. As eating disorders specialists, we know all too well that this peculiar psychopathology has barely anything to do with food or weight! If anything, the psychopathology seems to revolve instead around 'issues of identity', truly captured in Kim Chernin's (1986) eloquent statement: 'Eating disorders express our uncertainties, our buried anguish, our unconfessed confusion of identity . . . '

Di Nicola: *Yes, we live that paradox all the time as clinicians working with eating disorders. Our medical colleagues see us as 'mental gastroenterologists', whose job is to get people to eat. I partly agree. In establishing a working relationship with my patients, I try to balance a medical concern with what they put in their mouths with psychological questions about how they feed their minds! As a clinician working with the predicament of eating disorders, I work as a kind of 'psychological nutritionist'!*

Nasser: Let us, momentarily, go back to history and try to see how the 'body' managed to evolve into an 'identity' . . . could body history in some way mirror human history? Perhaps yes, for it seems that the body has in fact gone through phases and manifestations reflecting significant milestones in human history – from the fasting of the medieval female saints to the secularisation of the body into a commodity owned by the individual in our modern era. In the analysis of the anorexic phenomenon, the impact of the environment on the body can be traced back to early psychodynamic writings, where the dysfunctional family, representing the individual's microcosmic environment, was held responsible for the phenomenon. This was taken further by Hilde Bruch (1982) who viewed the anorexic pursuit of thinness as a defence against feelings of powerlessness within the family, suggesting therefore that the anorexic pathology could indeed be symptomatic of an identity deficit.

Di Nicola: *You've really set the stage for us to get beyond the clinic. Or more simply to think of lives lived rather than clinical outcomes ...*

Nasser: Well, the act of food refusal, according to Bruch (1982) is symbolic here of the striving towards autonomy and mastery over one's self as well as others. This obviously was more applied to women, the common sufferers of the anorexic syndrome, who were thought to be under considerable pressure derived from having to deal with conflicting social definitions of femininity. Hence, the feminist discourse framed the debate about the body as a progression of identity from the environment of the family, through gender, to the body as an environment in its own right, a 'corporeal government', where living is more *in* rather than *through* the body! (MacSween, 1993). An evolution, in other words, from the religious to the medical to the social. In the social construction of body regulation, the vulnerability of the body to control by existing social structures is clearly highlighted and its dependency on current social forces is crucially central (MacSween, 1993).

Di Nicola: *That's a breathtaking sweep of 'body history', as Ivan Illich (1992) calls this new interest in understanding how the body is experienced in different eras. While I do not want to glamourise the distress of people who suffer with predicaments such as anorexia nervosa, I agree that I sometimes see these women as being on the cutting edge of social change but that edge is not out there somewhere, but within themselves. I see them as intronauts of an inward journey, descending 'the spiral staircase of the self' in Montaigne's memorable phrase.*

And while women (and some men) are embarked on this psychological odyssey, there is a kind of guerilla war going on in the human sciences over the emaciated bodies of anorexic women. We are loading so much on the enfeebled, osteoporotic skeletons of these women that they are bound to collapse under the strain. What are the stakes in this guerrilla war? Nothing less than the imagining of contemporary embodiments of human distress in a larger project of the historical imagining of bodily experience.

However, I presume you are mostly referring here to Western European cultural history. It will be intriguing to consider Moslem societies in comparison. I have some reservations about invoking the medieval saints you refer to, the so-called 'holy anorexics' (Bell, 1985; Bynum, 1987). The heart of my concern is that while experiences from other eras and cultures are worthy of study in themselves and may suggest similarities with contemporary experiences, we should be cautious about glossing over key contextual features. Elaborating these differentiating features is what 'body history' would look like (for an example, see Barbara Duden's work, 1991). Even if the behaviour could be shown to be similar (which remains to be established), the relationships, the motivations, and above all, the meaning attached to these lives can easily be violated. Can we equate medieval expressions of piety such as fasting with the food restriction of an anorexic patient?

I live in a city that is almost 400 years old, whose co-foundress was a religious nurse, Jeanne Mance. And yet few people in today's Montreal can understand the motivation for fasting. Like New Orleans' Mardi Gras or Rio de Janeiro's Carnaval, such religious practices have become cultural events that verge on becoming empty rituals practised out of habit. Perhaps they persist because they generate new meanings. But are saintly fasts and anorexic restrictions the same behaviour with different meanings? And what about the context of these behaviours?

Nasser: In his analysis of ascetic starvation, Bell (1985) regarded the pursuit of body control to achieve autonomy as 'timeless' even if its shape or colouring changes across time. Let me now borrow your concept of 'anorexia multiforme' (Di Nicola, 1990a, 1990b) to explain this. You managed to utilise the model of social predicament by Taylor (1985) to show the complex nature of the relationship between the diverse forms of expression of bodily control across both time and culture. You said that it is through the interaction of the stable universal need for autonomy and definition with the unstable and constantly changing cultural variables that differing forms or styles of bodily control are created. Under these circumstances the body becomes the target of unstable social situations, called 'predicaments' which are morally charged and vary in their import in time and place (Taylor, 1985). At certain times, however, a collision between history and culture will inevitably take place, ultimately producing forms that may appear distant from the familiar presentation of anorexia nervosa and yet share with it the same sociocultural substrate.

Di Nicola: *Yes, at that time, I was using a set of phenomena (anorexia nervosa, medieval piety and other notions) to elaborate a specific hypothesis (anorexia multiforme) as a probe in search of a guiding theory. I now see, ten years later, what was missing in my account was body history. Placing the experience of the body in history and contextualising it culturally is the bridge.*

2 Self-production and self-evasion

Nasser: In a paper entitled, 'The new veiling phenomenon, is it an anorexic equivalent?' I polemically drew an analogy between the new veiling phenomenon and the Western anorexic position. I argued that new veiling could possibly be a cultural variant of anorexia nervosa, in other words a new form of body regulation in a different cultural setting, achieved through the wardrobe and not the mouth!

In my argument, I was greatly assisted by MacLeod's elegant analysis of the new veiling phenomenon in Egypt. The veiling of Moslem women in Egypt or elsewhere may appear at its face value as completely different, if not alien from the stance of the Western anorexic. However, in order to see its complex meaning, there is a need to go beyond the traditional 'orientalist' definition and perception of the veil and to depart from the static Western vision of women of the 'orient'. We have to remember that the adoption of the veil here clearly goes beyond the apparent Islamic revival or the simple reactivation of tradition. It is a voluntary gesture adopted by young educated and working Moslem women and I have to say that it is no longer restricted to the Middle East, as young Moslem women of various national backgrounds all over the world appear nowadays to be equally enthusiastic about this style of dress.

Di Nicola: *Your use of the term 'orientalist' is worth unpacking a little for our readers. Edward Said, the Palestinian polymath, wrote a fascinating polemic,* Orientalism *(1979) about the East looking at the West looking at the East. We could have fun with that – what with you coming from Egypt and my having lived in Israel with a Jewish family of Arabic origin! Talk about layers of identity! But that's for another dialogue! I was struck in* Orientalism *with Said's questioning of how 'other places' and 'otherness' is imagined. And he turns this notion, orientalism, this turning East (which was a decisive moment in European modernity, by the way, because it brought another time and place into its defined present) into a metaphor for how we reduce each other into form-fit moulds.*

The trouble with such revisioning exercises is that they create tremendous irony among the cognoscenti but are used as bullets by more concrete souls. And I'm not sure if Said is part of the problem or part of the solution. I would like Said to write the other half of the book – how the East looks at the West. Said brought an Eastern sensibility in his critique of the West's discourse on the East. Could he apply a Western sensibility in examining how the East looks at the West? A salutary companion piece, I think, to Said's Orientalism*, is his autobiography,* Out of Place *(1999) which is in no small part a meditation on identity of someone* from over there who lives over here *and of both the pain and the richness that such dislocations enculture.*

Nasser: Edward Said has given us invaluable insights into the elusive nature of culture and he was inspirational to me in my previous book. However, I like to use here the German writer, Friedrich Schiller's concept of culture which is taken from his book on *The Aesthetic Education of Man*, and cited in Terry Eagleton's recent book, *The Idea of Culture* (incidentally dedicated to Edward Said). For Schiller, culture would seem at once to be the source of action and the negation of it. There is a tension between what makes our practice creative, and the very earth-bound fact of practice itself. 'In both cases, there would seem to be some constitutive gap between culture and its fleshly incarnation, as the many-sidedness of the aesthetic inspires us to actions which contradict it in their very determinateness' (Eagleton, 2000).

In my discussion of the new veiling phenomenon as a possible anorexic equivalent, I was struck by what appeared to me as an act of reproducing one's self through hiding or evasion. Reproducing one's self through evasion or negation is integral to the self-starvation phenomenon which seems to render the body invisible, for it appears to disappear! A process referred to by Lawrence (1979) as an 'anorexic shell', and Orbach (1986) even called this anorexic outcome an 'invisibility' that screams out. The ever-diminishing body is clearly disappearing while remaining firmly visible and ironically more noticeable, imparting a clear message through its apparent invisibility.

Undoubtedly, covering one's self is part and parcel of the act of veiling that denies external femaleness. In a traditional sense, the veil is nothing but a mobile curtain that automatically removes reminders of gender (even if ironically it still meant gender distinction). In both self-starvation and veiling, the dialectic is clearly between the visible and the invisible, where the outer look serves as a stand-in for the invisible and acts as a form of communication between the wearer and the viewer. Both veiling and the anorexic look are attempts by women to define limits and set boundaries around themselves. Being very thin, according to Lawrence, seems to say to the world, 'I have sharp contours, I am not soft. I do not merge with you' (Lawrence, 1979). It is, as in the case of anorexia nervosa, a quest for self-redefinition in relation to the needs of others.

There is also another striving here, aimed towards moral elevation and purity, similar to the familiar moral crusade of the anorexic woman. Each woman pursues her externally different but psychologically analogous and culturally approved objective with fanatical and compulsive devotion. Both are symbolic of woman's self-denial and self-control as well as her search for self-validation. The moral elevation and the sense of superiority the anorexic feels about her position are also echoed in the privileged motif of the veil which sets its wearer above the other non-wearers and demonstrates her capacity for self-discipline.

Di Nicola: *That's an astute reading about the boundaries of the self and the body as a final frontier, which is worth pursuing here. On the other hand, anorexic women and their therapists offer many other readings of their distress . . .*

Nasser: Yes, Vincenzo, you are right, but perhaps what connects these experiences is a psychodynamic interpretation that underpins both phenomena. In both cases there is a kind of 'veiled' resistance, pushing visibility through invisibility – what I called 'rebellion through conformity' (Nasser, 1997) and what MacLeod (1991) referred to as an 'accommodating protest'. MacLeod argued that the reversion to the veil was not simply a reactionary gesture, but indeed a new form of social action. If we consider again the feminist analysis of anorexia nervosa, we will see perhaps that both gestures are responsive to conflicting gender roles against a backdrop of erosion of power.

Di Nicola: *Now, let's talk about power. I had a long and enriching dialogue with the Milanese family therapist Mara Selvini Palazzoli (who was my mentor) about anorexia nervosa, the family, and the question of power. Over time, I became very doubtful, or – as Richard Rorty (1989) would say – ironic, about the notion of power. I see power in human affairs as an illusion. 'Power may be an illusion,' Selvini Palazzoli replied, 'but the struggle for power is a fact!' (Selvini Palazzoli, personal communication).*

I am struck, however, by this notion of 'veiled resistance' – I find it a richly layered reference that serves as a metaphor for what we are calling 'self-evasion'. But here's a prickly question: can it be both voluntary and an evasion of oneself? Can you hide from yourself? Of course, say the psychoanalysts, that's what defence mechanisms are. But they are largely unconscious or, in your metaphor, 'veiled' from subjective view. So here's the rub: who, or what, selects what is veiled and how?

I kept re-reading your words, 'voluntarily', 'adoption' and 'choices', about the state of mind of the women in coming to their supposed choices. I am ironic about these descriptions in the same sense that I am ironic about descriptions of patients' symptom choices in some of the psychoanalytic literature. I sort-of understand that this conveys the notion of symptomatic expression in a passive sense, but I don't understand how something can be both an unconscious process and a choice. Sometimes I think the psychoanalytic project (which is nothing if not Jewish in its Talmudic dissection of hermeneutic interpretations) got mixed up with the Protestant preoccupation with guilt. Either you imagine an autonomous, responsible actor who makes choices (and suffers for it) with all the complex moral resonances that implies (a little like the notion of predicament that we have both invoked in our work) or you imagine someone immersed in the cacophony of the inner dialogue in the labyrinth of the self that has to be decoded and translated in order to determine which of many such voices will be the authentic and governing self.

But beyond this issue is the larger and more important one, in my view, of anchoring this discussion in something beyond merely personal choices or fads or contemporary concerns. And I think that Illich's notion of body history gives us just this anchor. With this historical approach, we can understand 'the body as the primary locus of experience' (Illich, 1992) and 'the Western body as a progressive embodiment of the self' (Illich, 1992). With body history, we may develop the perspectives needed to make sense of the experience of the body in a given time, and whether medieval saints were experiencing similar states of mind and bodily experiences as the anorexic of today or whether body regulation/modification in the form of veiling or self-mutilation are contemporary analogues of self-starvation in some important way.

3 The fictional and the real self: Image civilisation

Nasser: So far in our dialogue I have been tempted to focus so much on the dialectic between the visible and the invisible, and this forces me to make yet another sweeping statement about the culture we live in, that 'appears' to be celebrating the fictional and dealing with it almost as synonymous with the real, the so called 'image civilisation'.

Di Nicola: Yes, you are placing these phenomena within a vast panorama. Help me understand how this impacts on identity?

Nasser: Identities are normally constituted within a social system and require the reciprocal recognition of others, what we call group affiliation. It is a way of placing one's life in a larger context (Rorty, 1985). For instance, the bearers of either the anorexic look or the veil convey referential messages through their chosen form of body expression or image. Both forms are clearly conspicuous in any group setting. The image difference between the wearers of a particular look and the spectators is thought to generate among the spectators (that is, the non-image sharers) a sense of anxiety resulting from non-recognition ('I don't fit in') which is often translated into identification ('I want to be like that') motivated by a need for attention and more importantly group affiliation (Becker and Hamburg, 1996). This results from the strong need to reclaim or re-imagine a sense of referential identity. This desire for a referential and contextualised solidarity eventually leads to the composition of an image and of imagined small communities based on forms of bodily expressions.

In today's life, where the boundaries between national and audio-visual geographies overlap and technological mediation turns the individual into a switching centre for all its networks of influence, the estrangement from the real is inevitable. A civilisation of images is born, in which reality becomes a mere reflection of an image (Kearney, 1988). The possibility now exists for the fictional discourse to induce effects of truth (Foucault, 1980) whereby the psychic world becomes as colonised as the physical world by the whole image industry. This issue is discussed in some detail in Günther Rathner's chapter in this book (chapter 5).

Di Nicola: Yes! To respond to your image civilisation, I think of two wonderful cartoons. In the first, children are watching their father change a flat tyre in the rain. And the father says, Don't you understand, this is reality, we can't change the channel! The second has a bride sitting bored on the edge of the bed while the groom excitedly watches television! In a world of virtual relationships, I wonder how many people lie in bed alone while their partners are looking for solace in cyberspace?

All I can add here to the discussion are a few reference points which I have found useful so far. The work of two women at MIT is very informative. Janet Murray's (1997) work on narrative in cyberspace seems very relevant here, as is Sherry Turkle's (1995) work on identity and the Internet. Montrealer Naomi Klein's (2000) polemic against the colonisation of identity by brand name products, and especially the advertising culture created to promote this redefinition of the self, takes a more caustic look at this image civilisation.

Nasser: I would also like highlight here *Spaces of Identity, Global Media, Electronic Landscapes and Cultural Boundaries* (Morley and Robins, 1997), a book that I recently read and found it to be an excellent source. Many pertinent questions are raised in this lovely book, for instance, what range of possible new identities are now available for the individual within the boundaries of this image culture?

I agree with their contention that identities within the context of image need to continue to be symbolic of national space but reconcilable with our cognitive existence in hyperspace. Identities that succeed in bridging the gap between the virtual space of electronic networks and our bodily existence in localised space. This form of abstract universalism with its denial of the particular location of human lives/bodies in place and time begs for the new identity to be both global/local and cosmopolitan/nomadic. The new image identity will therefore need to be constructed to incorporate historical pastiches and assume an aura of false tribal/ethnic authenticity. This reminds me of the drive towards 'Africanisation within the global Western project' that has been discussed in connection to eating psychopathology among black women in South Africa (Szabo and Le Grange in this book, chapter 2)

4 Identity: Between the modern, the pure and the diasporic

Di Nicola: Image civilisation is perhaps one of several by-products of an enormous culture change. A decade ago I put forward the idea that self-starvation could be reactive to cultures undergoing transformation (Di Nicola, 1990a, 1990b), what you also referred to rather provocatively as 'culture chaos syndrome' (Nasser, 1997). This highlights the importance of the cultural imperatives in shaping the final expression of body control.

I do think, however, that we need to qualify this a bit. What do we actually mean by culture change? In the last decade, it has been come to mean 'globalisation', another term that engenders irony . . .

Nasser: I also dislike the term now, although I was initially enthusiastic about it, perhaps because it is now so over-used that it has become almost void or meaningless, very much like the other dated concept 'Westernisation'!

Di Nicola: We share the same sensibilities. Can I digress a little more? I discovered a delightful book in the British tradition of Swift and Orwell by a German linguist Uwe Porksen (1995) called Plastic Words. *He has the lively and disturbing idea that some of these rather vague words like 'development' and 'globalisation' are consciously constructed for their malleability and uncanny adaptability for every circumstance. There is a parallel notion in jurisprudence of writing laws with enough 'fuzziness' in them to adapt to future, and sometimes unforeseeable, circumstances. The British educator Raymond Williams (1983) provided a kind of dictionary of such terms with well-researched essays on the 'keywords' of cultural transformation.*

Nasser: What I really meant by 'culture chaos syndrome' was an attempt on my part to support Turner's hypothesis (1984) that pathological body regulation is simply a metaphor for social crisis. However, I will try to be more specific. I think we need to discuss modernity and how identities are formulated or reformulated in cultures undergoing modernisation and I am particularly referring here to the type of culture I came from.

In theory, modernisation creates modern environments (whatever this is, including urbanisation and industrialisation). According to Berman (1983) these modern environments are said to cut across all boundaries of geography and ethnicity, of class and nationality, of religion and ideology, and, in this sense, modernity can in essence unite all humanity. However, this unity is paradoxical since a parallel process of cultural decentralisation and a contradictory process of revival of place-bound traditions is going hand in hand with modernisation. As a result, a new form of regionalism is working against forces of homogenisation and uniformity.

Now we can return to the veiling issue which MacLeod (1991) referred to as a deliberate act of choice that makes a personal statement in response to conflicting pressures and competing cultural values. She described those women as being caught between a drive towards modernity, ambitious economic goals and traditional female identity. This has clear parallels to Western women expressing their identity conflicts through self-starvation.

Di Nicola: *Modernity was a European idea meant to define a moment and a place. In modernity, the moment is always 'now' and every place is 'here'. Modernity has a radical demand. To be modern, of this time and of this place, means a radical rupture with the past. It is creative and synthetic insofar as it invites us to refashion this time and place. I try to avoid using that word in any language now, preferring words like 'contemporary' or 'at this time'. It wasn't meant to unite human experiences but to define them in relation to some centre. I see it as a centripetal cultural force, drawing things to its own defined centre. Sometimes, I invoke the notion of modernity to induce a sense of what the Portuguese call 'saudade' – a kind of wistful yearning for a lost, perhaps mythical time. Saudade is to the past what modernity was to the present: not the precise, digital time that flashes from LED indicators everywhere in the technopoly we live in (Postman, 1992) but the past imperfect of saudade or the stylised present of modernity. To put it in a Madison Avenue style slogan, Nothing ages faster than the modern. It's yesterday's news, disposable, stale, irrelevant.*

Nasser: This is very interesting and echoes some of the thoughts that crossed my mind on visiting the New York Museum of Modern Art during the New York Conference on Eating Disorders (May 2000). I was struck by this section of the museum that calls itself, 'Modern art despite modernism'. It clearly provokes a debate on the difference between modern and modernism, that is, the mere living in a modern time/place and modernist directions, which aims to examine the aesthetic systems over and above art's traditional goals of depicting the world. This tension between the modern and the modernist created a new form of art that is anti-modernist, the so-called New Classicist, responding to aesthetic nostalgia! This is sometimes called 'anti-avant-garde' or 'return to order', I may call it here, perhaps for the purpose of this discussion, anti-progress, inability to embrace progress or even refusal of progress. Giovanni Ruggiero in his analysis of the 'two Italies' touches on an issue that is relevant here, modernity without development or consumerism without production (refer to Ruggiero's chapter in this book, chapter 7).

I do find, however, Chernin's (1986) idea of a collective refusal of development particularly tempting here. I also think that there are inherent contradictions with both anorexia nervosa and veiling. These women appear on the surface very modern (including the veiled ones who are in many instances highly educated young women). They have been understood to be a manifestation of women's alleged inability to cope with their own progress, that is, liberation or equality, where their supposed increased freedom is paradoxically experienced as a hardship. In the end, this fosters the reproduction of traditional social structures, despite surrounding noises of modernity. Relevant here perhaps is the discussion about the position of women in post-communist Europe in relation to body regulation, where there is an apparent oscillation between development and regression (refer to Catina and Joja's chapter in this book, chapter 6).

Di Nicola: *I'm with you, Mervat. There's another one of those plastic words again, development. And I certainly don't know how to listen to post-communist societies (which intrigue me enormously) because their cultural vocabulary has been degraded and discarded so rapidly (Porksen is eloquent on this, as are many other German writers, notably Christa Wolf, 1997, who got caught in the ideological shift from being a critical artist in the former East Germany adored in the West to defending herself in the new, united Germany against charges of having collaborated with the communist regime). To return to culture change, there are still many particular ways of living and each one is encountering change in its own peculiar and fascinating way. Finally, many people are still somehow locating the centre for identity in universals, what George Steiner (1974) called 'nostalgia for the absolute', or reducing the whole question of identity to a linguistic construction (Baumeister, 1986).*

Transcultural psychiatry has been characterised as torn between two ideological approaches, the comparative universalist (etic approach) and the culture-specific (emic approach) (see Di Nicola, 1997). You have nicely shown how we need to interweave both approaches for the phenomena in question. And I think you are absolutely on the right track that for a significant group of people, identity centres on their idiosyncratic bodily experiences. In this sense, torn between the attractions of modernity and the demands of tradition, I understand your use of the term 'solution' to grasp the predicaments of Western women who starve themselves and Moslem women who don the veil.

Nasser: I see what you mean, but we are in a way trying to synthesise an analysis for what is commonly regarded as a modern phenomenon in modern times. What we are saying is that the issue of body control does not stop at self-starvation, there are possible other equivalents (even if debatable), all these forms of body regulation/modification reflect the need to redefine identity. The individual's identity has become now 'placeless' in a 'culture of paradoxes', post-feminist, post-racist and post-national that still have their cultural 'insiders' and 'outsiders', the 'pure' and the 'diasporic'. The individual is therefore torn between two contradictory forces, globalism and localism. How, then, would the body cope with the paradox?

Through solutions of body control, perhaps . . . forms of body regulation that are equally contradictory in nature, where the messages conveyed through the body impart irreconcilable values reflecting what is fundamentally at stake in the culture itself. In search of identity through body regulation, the body could convey conflicting messages of protest through apparent obedience, rejection of indulgence through self-obsession and the creation of the racially pure within the realm of racial diversity. A kind of authentic identity that filters out threats in social experience and attempts to reconcile the 'national' with the 'nationalist' (Morley and Robins, 1997).

Di Nicola: I have often used the terms 'insiders' and 'outsiders', which to the best of my knowledge were given their cardinal expression in social science by sociologist Robert Merton (1973). In my book on cultural family therapy, I offer them as fertile and useful notions that can be used as clinical tools in working with people across cultures (Di Nicola, 1997). Your notions of the 'pure' and the 'diasporic' are new to me. They resonate with the terms of the debate on identity here in Quebec, les québecois de suche, de pure laine (old-stock Quebeckers, of pure virgin wool), versus the rest of us, les ethniques (the ethnics), lumped together as 'anglos' (from 'anglophones', English-speakers) or sometimes as 'allophones' (speaking other languages). Those of us who are outsiders here were insiders somewhere else. We are diasporic to some perceived homeland, where we were presumably pure. In a world where we have all left the garden, where we are all diasporic, how do we purify ourselves again? Recall English poet John Milton's 'Paradise Lost, Paradise Regained'. These are old themes in the Western tradition, founded on religious motifs from the Middle East.

Nasser: Well, this is exactly the problem with studying culture; however, the notions of the 'pure' and 'diasporic' are not mine. I borrowed them from the book, *Spaces of Identity* (Morley and Robins, 1997) to which I referred earlier.

Di Nicola: *I am continually struck by the necessary plasticity of our dialogue and one of the metaphors I use most in my therapeutic work is of space and perspective. Mervat, I'm thinking that our readers will want to know how we see the relevance of all this in responding to the predicament of someone struggling with their body and their identity. I wonder if we could sketch out a therapeutic stance informed by our dialogue?*

Nasser: I agree that some of our dialogue sounds as though we are flirting with abstract philosophical notions that have little to do with suffering or predicaments. At the recent New York Eating Disorders Conference (May 2000), I was impressed by a workshop delivered by Kelly Vitousek on 'transforming the meaning of anorexic behaviour through an emphasis on personal values'. She talked about how abstract values are native to the symptom or behaviour package of the anorexic which becomes a reason for living like religion and philosophy, hence the philosophical framework of the patient needs to inform therapy. In our dialogue, we are looking at the wider picture of how values of identity are translated into the vocabulary of the body, not only through weight regulation but also through veiling and perhaps other forms of body modification.

Di Nicola: *My work on self-mutilation with young people often strikes me as having all the characteristics that make eating disorders so complex (see Di Nicola and Epstein, 1998). As with anorexia nervosa, the clinical phenomena require careful distinctions, while the cultural readings are extremely varied, suggesting everything from the sadomasochistic subculture to anthropological trance rituals and religious stigmata.*

People who cut themselves, for example, sometimes do it because they are numb and want to feel something, sometimes because they feel too much and want to force their own attention and others' onto their bodies. Its a voluntary choice and an impulsive act. It's an outlet for interpersonal conflict and a mental anguish. It's a mental dissociation and 'the body speaking it's mind'. It's a way of living in itself (sometimes connected to youth and sexual subcultures) and associated with many psychiatric problems. And while it's easily mistaken for suicide, the sufferers often make a plea for living on their own terms. In other words, as in eating disorders, we see people crossing frontiers and borders and we can read their bodies like passports, bearing the imprints of their travels and travails.

Nasser: How do you work with them? I think in our work now we need to break away from the notion of body pathology and focus more on issues of identity and the longing to belong!

Di Nicola: *This is what I call the 'cultural reading of the clinical'. I consider that half of the task . . . collaborating with patients on a description of their reality. This helps us give a voice to their suffering. In this aspect of the work, which is where we build the working relationship, the patient is speaking to us.*

    But people do suffer and talking about it is not enough (that's the old behaviour therapist in me!) and we need to answer the patient. We need to create the conditions for change. Now, you can change yourself, you can change the world, or you can change how you look at and live with the world around you. Changing the world is social action, changing the self is traditional therapy and changing the way we look is where I would place a postmodern therapy (see Di Nicola, 1993).

Nasser: Isn't that cognitive therapy?

Di Nicola: *I would use elements of cognitive therapy, yes. But the history of psychological therapies is about the claims of each approach to represent the 'real' problem, which is to say, each therapy privileges one aspect of the problem. Cognitive therapy privileges an examination of ways of thinking which is very appealing to people like us who are verbal and abstract. Elsewhere I have criticised this as 'elitist cognitivism' (Di Nicola, 1990b) where explanations are privileged over other human experiences. For the sake of analysis, we can imagine levels of experience, such as bodily, behavioural, cognitive, interpersonal and ontological (to do with the meaning of being).*

    We have heard the bemoaning of brainlessness versus mindlessness in psychiatry, suggesting that psychiatry should be informed by both biology and psychology. Let me add that if we do not want to practise a profession that risks being heartless and soulless, we need to help people find a voice for their suffering in order for them to make sense of their predicaments.

    Let's look at Simone Weil, for instance, a woman who breaks free of traditional notions of identity (a French woman from a Jewish family who is read as a Christian mystic). After being forced to flee her native France with her Jewish family, she was stricken with tuberculosis in England and voluntarily restricted herself to the rations that her fellow French citizens were allowed during the Second World War as an act of solidarity, an act of meaning. I see this act of self-denial as an embodiment, if I may put it that way, of soul. She had an evident hunger for human solidarity while 'waiting on God' and I should never wish it to be said that she was anorexic.

Nasser: Vincenzo, this statement is somewhat resonant with Melanie Katzman's and Sing Lee's work on the meaning of self-starvation in Hong Kong, both saw it as representing a lost voice in an oppressive world and in this way could be a metaphorical bridge for our sense of cultural disconnection and discontinuity (refer to the chapter by Sing Lee in this book, chapter 3).

Di Nicola: *There is the echo of another China, another time here too. At the Sorbonne, Simone Weil was the classmate of the feminist writer Simone de*

Beauvoir. In her book, Memoirs of a Dutiful Daughter, *Simone de Beauvoir (1974) wrote of Weil:*

She intrigued me because of her great reputation for intelligence . . . A great famine had broken out in China, and I was told that when she heard the news she had wept: these tears compelled my respect much more than her gifts as a philosopher. I envied her having a heart that could beat right across the world. I managed to get near her one day. I don't know how the conversation got started; she declared in no uncertain tones that only one thing mattered in the world: the revolution which would feed all the starving people of the earth. I retorted, no less peremptorily, that the problem was not to make men happy, but to find the reason for their existence. She looked me up and down: 'It's easy to see you've never been hungry,' she snapped!..

References

Baumeister RF (1986). *Identity: cultural change and the struggle for self.* Oxford: Oxford University Press.

Becker A, Hamburg P (1996). Culture, the media and eating disorders. *Harvard Review of Psychiatry,* **4**, 163–7.

Bell RM (1985). *Holy anorexia.* Chicago: The University of Chicago Press.

Berman M (1983). *All that is solid melts into air: the experience of modernity.* London: Verso.

Bruch H (1982). Anorexia nervosa: therapy and theory. *American Journal of Psychiatry,* **139**, 12.

Bynum CW (1987). *Holy feast and holy fast: the religious significance of food to medieval women.* Berkeley: University of California Press.

Chernin K (1986). *Women, eating and identity.* London: Virago.

De Beauvoir S (1974). *Memoirs of a dutiful daughter* (translated by Kirkup). New York: HarperCollins.

Di Nicola V (1990a). Anorexia multiforme: self-starvation in historical and cultural context. Part I: Self-starvation as a historical chameleon. *Transcultural Psychiatric Research Review,* **27**, 165–96.

Di Nicola V (1990b). Anorexia multiforme: self-starvation in historical and cultural context. Part II: Anorexia nervosa as a culture-reactive syndrome. *Transcultural Psychiatric Research Review,* **27**, 245–86.

Di Nicola V (1992). De l'enfant sauvage à l'enfant fou: a prospectus for transcultural child psychiatry. In: *Transcultural issues in child psychiatry,* edited by Grizenko N, Sayegh L, Migneult P. Montreal: Editions Douglas, pp. 5–53.

Di Nicola V (1997). *A stranger in the family: culture, families, and therapy.* New York: W.W. Norton & Co.

Di Nicola V and Epstein I (1998). Self-mutilation in adolescents. *Parkhurst Exchange.* October 1998, 75–80.

Duden B (1991). *The woman beneath the skin: a doctor's patients in eighteenth-century Germany.* Cambridge, Mass: Harvard University Press.

Eagleton T (2000). *The idea of culture.* Oxford: Blackwell.

Foucault M (1980). *Power/Knowledge: selected interviews and other writings, 1972–1977*. Brighton: Harvester.

Illich I (1992). Twelve years after Medical Nemesis: a plea for body history. In: *In the mirror of the past: lectures and addresses 1978–1990*. London: Marion Boyars, pp. 211–17.

Kearney R (1988). *The wake of imagination*. London: Hutchinson.

Klein N (2000). *No logo: taking aim at the brand bullies*. Toronto: Knopf Canada.

Lawrence M (1979). Anorexia nervosa: the control paradox. *Women's Studies International Quarterly*, **2**, 93–101.

Lawrence M (1984). *The anorexic experience*. London: Women's Press.

Lewis I M (1971). *Ecstatic religion*. Baltimore: Penguin Books.

MacLeod A (1991). *Accommodating protest: working women, the new veiling and change in Cairo*. New York: Columbia University Press.

MacSween M (1993). *Anorexic bodies, a feminist and sociological perspective on anorexia nervosa*. London: Routledge.

Merton RK (1973). The perspectives of insiders and outsiders. In: The sociology of science: theoretical and empirical investigations, edited by Storer NW. Chicago: University of Chicago Press, pp. 99–136.

Morley D and Robins K (1997). *Spaces of identity, global media, electronic landscapes and cultural boundaries*. London: Routledge.

Murray JH (1997). *Hamlet on the holodeck: the future of narrative in cyberspace*. New York: Free Press.

Nasser M (1997). *Culture and weight consciousness*. London: Routledge.

Nasser M (1999). The new veiling phenomenon – is it an anorexic equivalent? A polemic. *Journal of Community and Applied Social Psychology*, **9**, 407–12.

Orbach S (1986). *Hunger strike: the anorexic's struggle as a metaphor for our age*. New York: W.W. Norton & Co.

Porksen U (1995). *Plastic words: the tyranny of a modular language* (trans. by J Mason and D Cayley). University Park, PA: Pennsylvania State University Press.

Postman N (1992). *Technopoly: the surrender of culture to technology*. New York: Vintage Books.

Rorty R (1985). Solidarity or objectivity? In: *Post-Analytic Philosophy*, edited by Rajchman J, West C. New York: Columbia University Press.

Rorty R (1989). *Contingency, irony, and solidarity*. Cambridge: Cambridge University Press.

Said EW (1979). *Orientalism*. New York: Random House.

Said EW (1999). *Out of place: a memoir*. New York: Knopf.

Selvini-Palazzoli M (1974). *Self starvation: from the individual to family therapy in the treatment of anorexia nervosa* (trans.by A. Pomerans), second edition. New York: Jason Aronson.

Steiner G (1974). *Nostalgia for the absolute*. Montreal. CBC Enterprises.

Taylor D (1985). The sick child's predicament. *Australian and New Zealand Journal of Psychiatry*, **19**, 130–7.

Turkle S (1995). *Life on the screen: identity in the age of the internet*. New York: Simon & Schuster.

Turner B (1984). *The body and society*. Oxford.

Vitousek KB (2000). *Transforming the meaning of anorexic behaviour through an emphasis on personal values*. A workshop delivered at the 9th International Conference on Eating Disorders. May. New York.

Williams R (1983). *Keywords: a vocabulary of culture and society*. London: Fontana.

Wolf C (1997). *Parting from phantoms: selected writings, 1990–1994* (trans. by J Van Heurck). Chicago: University of Chicago Press.

Commentary 1

Arlene Elowe MacLeod
Political Science Department, Bates College, Lewiston,
Maine, USA

I would like to thank the authors for their invitation to enter this discussion, which involves such interesting and complicated questions, questions of how body, identity, and cultural change intersect. I'm especially excited to see my work on women and the new veiling in Egypt used to think about another, and possibly related, issue – eating disorders.

I am a political theorist, intrigued by questions of power and resistance, and interested in times of cultural transitions. The questions raised here bridge the gap between the philosophical and the concrete, dealing with problems of politics and identity. I think of politics as the various ways we answer certain questions: Who are we? Who do we want to be? What do we think we should be? How can we get from here to there? These questions push the boundaries of politics well beyond governments to the basic moral questions of self, other, and change. Most recently, they have pushed me in the direction of focusing on issues of imagination, or rather, the politics of imagination.

I think of actions such as the new veiling in Cairo as imaginative political projects. While many Westerners see women's choice to wear veiled dress as a sign of reactionary delusion, I think it is more useful to think of this dress as a form of imaginative resistance to a set of conditions, economic and ideological, which constrain women. Inventing a new form of dress is a creative way to evade the box women have been assigned to; instead of agreeing to a damaging set of choices – be a proper woman and stay in the home as a wife, or be an indiscreet woman and venture outside the home to work – women have invented a new way to leave the home and still be proper wives and mothers.

The new veiling shows that imagination, contrary to our expectations, is not always a matter of the mind, but also of the body. Changes in dress, in the codes regulating the body, can become signals of a new identity, both highly personal and ultimately also highly social and political.

I am intrigued by the possibility that eating disorders can be seen as a similar resistance tactic through body regulation, a 'rebellion through conformity', as Mervat Nasser suggests. But I also wonder if the differences between wearing veiled dress and not eating loom too large. Veiling is often viewed in the West as a terrible infringement on women's ability to be human, to participate in a public world. And it is true that such gestures of resistance, cast in the language of the old ways, have tremendous potential to be misunderstood and used by those with power to control those with less resources. But, in point of fact, veils are simply clothes, symbolic clothes to be sure, but clothes nonetheless. Eating disorders signal a different degree, or even different kind, of decision. I wonder if the difference in degree is too important to ignore? I do agree that a focus on identity may lie at the heart of eating disorders as well as veiling decisions, and countless other actions, from the choice of hairstyle to body piercing to restrictive clothes, whether veils or short skirts, to our uses of body language. Certainly this refocuses our understanding of such suffering and problems from the 'sickness' of the individual, to the issues at stake for a society. Casting these issues as political seems a most useful realization.

Acts of the body can signal, and perhaps even precede, acts of the mind. Gramsci (1971) talked about such intriguing discrepancies as signs of contradictory consciousness, the gap between behavior and consciousness, which he saw as ruptures in the constant hegemony of those in power. Such openings are powerful potential sites for change.

These forms of resistance, particularly veiling (the area that I could comment on with confidence) clearly focus on identity issues. They suggest that we need, desperately need, new images of the self, new ways to be, in our contemporary world. Many have bemoaned the power of commercial images in the service of commercialism to structure our consciousness and invade our very capacity to be a self. The ideological power of such images is unprecedented, and the need for something that reaches outside the 'labyrinth of mirrors' as Kearney (1998) puts it, is urgent. Yet where are these new versions of the self to come from? Can we just think them up?

Following Nietzsche, Kearney suggests that through tracing the genealogy of imagination, we may find new images and insights that may lead us out of the labyrinth of looking glasses and toward a political future in which encounters with the self and others are truly possible.

It is easy to get lost in the pessimisms of post-modernist visions of a constrained world, shaped only by the repetition of images, but women, in creating new forms of constraint, appear to paradoxically manage to get out of this constraint!

Berman (1988), for example, traces the 'politics of the streets' in his account of pre-Revolutionary Russia, detailing the story of a clerk, bemused and unhappy, who finally has the audacity to conceive the idea of confronting an officer in the street. He manages to bump the man, who does not even acknowledge him, but it is a beginning of consciousness and a momentum of change. Perhaps sometimes the language of the body must come first?

Jean-Jacques Rousseau (1964) influenced by de Montaigne, sought a new understanding of the self, a self that could be at home in the whirl of modern life, the whirling power to self-create. In all his writings, he bemoaned the difficulty of trying to articulate what he meant in the language available to him; he argued that the lack of words to talk about a new kind of self and a new kind of politics meant he would be misunderstood, and viewed as contradictory and flawed. But perhaps such contractions are the most exciting areas for change, and perhaps Rousseau, writing at the beginning of the modern age, is still timely when considering the complexities of being ourselves now.

Solutions of body control may not be the fundamental answer to the predicaments of modernity, but they do show what is at stake, and they do offer some imaginative possibilities albeit occasionally morbid – for transformations.

References

Berman M (1988). *All that is Solid Melts into Air*. Penguin.

Gramsci A (1971). *Selections from the Prison Notebooks*. International Publishers.

Kearney R (1998). *The Wake of Imagination*. Routledge.

Rousseau J-J (1964). *The first and second discourses*. New York: St. Martin's Press.

Commentary 2

David Bardwell Mumford
Reader in Cross-Cultural Psychiatry, Division of Psychiatry,
University of Bristol, UK

I greatly enjoyed the wide-ranging dialogue between Mervat Nasser and Vincenzo Di Nicola. They are at their most stimulating where they disagree – or at least where their language 'engenders irony'! It is Mervat Nasser particularly who engages in the boldest flights of speculation.

Take the discussion about the 'equivalence' of the new veiling phenomenon and anorexia nervosa. Arlene MacLeod argues persuasively that veiling is a positive, creative choice by young women in Islamic societies to allow them to steer their own path between traditionalism and modernity. It is a sign of health and vigour, politically and emotionally. In contrast, would anyone seriously suggest that anorexia nervosa is a healthy or life-enhancing way out of a human predicament? Is the woman with anorexia nervosa really exercising free choice or is she, rather, constrained by her own compulsive drives?

Not all self-starvation is anorexia nervosa. Di Nicola's example of Simone Weil is apposite: a modern ascetic whose chose to restrict her diet during wartime exile in Britain as an act of solidarity with her compatriots in occupied France. Her example should also act as a bridge to help us understand the mind-set of medieval ascetics for whom fasting was a way of life. To identify all of them as anorexic (in the modern sense) seems to me altogether unhistorical.

We are faced again and again in cross-cultural psychiatry with issues around the classification of human behaviour. There are three aspects to every human being: those shared with all humanity, those shared with some others but not all, and those which are unique to that person. The value of any classification depends on the size of the second of these categories relative to the other two (Kendell, 1983). When we try to classify or diagnose different kinds of fasting behaviour, for example, it is surely helpful to distinguish the syndrome of anorexia nervosa (because in the Western world it is a relatively distinct and coherent phenomenon) from fasting to death as a political protest.

To place discussion of eating disorders (and indeed all somatoform disorders) within a historical account of the social construction of the body and body control has to be illuminating. If our age has thrown up unique pathologies, it certainly makes sense to explore them as a window on its underlying social processes.

Perhaps the decline of conversion hysteria in the Western world and the rise of anorexia nervosa may have similar roots.

As a contribution to 'body history', the nature and frequency of somatic symptoms, psychological expressions, and constructs of emotional distress have been explored in the Hebrew Bible (Mumford, 1992) and the Iliad of Homer (Mumford, 1996). In neither of these ancient cultures do concepts of the body seem conducive to the development of eating disorders, but in both literatures emotional distress is certainly expressed in vivid somatic terms.

Making interesting links between different phenomena is a long way from establishing that they are in some sense 'equivalent'. (Do we need some operational criteria of 'equivalence' in cross-cultural psychiatry?) Before I came into medicine and psychiatry, I was a student of Christian theology and subsequently spent two years in India studying Hinduism. The Hindu–Christian dialogue throws up very many points of contact in all areas of religious belief and practice. Yet I found, time and again, that concepts which superficially seemed similar (for example, the Christian belief in the incarnation of God in Christ and the Hindu belief in the avatars of Vishnu) turned out to be quite fundamentally different; whilst concepts and practices that initially seemed far apart (for example, animal sacrifices and ascetic practices) sometimes converged in interesting ways. However 'equivalence' is not easy to establish or even define in cross-cultural studies.

I admire the broad sweep of the authors' dialogue about how body, identity and cultural change intersect. Nevertheless, as someone wedded to 'evidence-based psychiatry' and empirical methods, I feel bound to ask – where is the evidence for these challenging speculations? Or more to the point, where might the evidence be found? If an idea or theory is somewhat diffuse, what would it predict? We need to transform imaginative speculation into specific hypotheses which can be tested by an appropriate research methodology.

The first place to look for evidence is the thoughts and expressions of women with anorexia nervosa themselves. We should not be too quick to put interpretations on them, but let their words speak for themselves: not reading a meaning into the text, but reading the meaning from it (exegesis). Here, for example, are the ipsissima verba of a young British south Asian woman with anorexia nervosa: 'I don't really like women's bodies, and I don't like that word "woman". It sounds funny, but I just think of a woman as a fat earth-mother – and I don't want to be that. I don't like children or anything maternal. I just wish I was a boy, or just a person – just nothing – have no sex – asexual.' Certainly issues of cultural and sexual identity are central here: but this young anorexic woman is not seeking to put on a performance – rather the opposite, she shrinks from any public display, she wants to be inconspicuous.

The second type of evidence is epidemiological, that is to say, studies of populations at risk for eating disorders, comparing one group with another in order to tease out associated (and perhaps causative) factors. For example, what is the relative risk of developing anorexia nervosa as a south Asian schoolgirl in Bradford compared with schoolgirls in Lahore or in rural Pakistan, and how does this relate to dissatisfaction with their body shape (Mumford *et al.* 1991, 1992; Choudry and Mumford 1992)? What are the links between body dissatisfaction and eating attitudes among attenders of slimming and fitness gyms in London and Lahore (Choudry and Mumford 1999; Mumford and Choudry, 2000)?

Because there are so many ways in which ethnic groups differ from one another, it is always difficult to draw definitive conclusions from cross-cultural studies. What are the aetiological factors among so many possibilities – individual, familial and social? The challenge is to design studies so as to focus in on particular putative risk factors. The study of eating disorders is like a giant jigsaw. Many more pieces need to be assembled from studies around the globe, in different cultures and in contrasting social groups (especially those undergoing 'modernisation'), before a fuller picture can emerge.

References

Choudry IY, Mumford DB (1992). A pilot study of eating disorders in Mirpur (Pakistan) using an Urdu version of the Eating Attitudes Test. *International Journal of Eating Disorders*, **11**, 243–51.

Choudry IY, Mumford DB (1999) Eating behaviour and body dissatisfaction in slimming and fitness gyms in Lahore. *Journal of the College of Physicians and Surgeons, Pakistan*, **9**, 28–31.

Kendell RE (1983). Diagnosis and classification. In: *Companion to psychiatric studies*, third edition, edited by Kendel RE, Zealley AK. Edinburgh: Churchill Livingstone, p. 207.

Mumford DB (1992). Emotional distress in the Hebrew Bible: somatic or psychological? *British Journal of Psychiatry*, **160**, 92–7.

Mumford DB (1996). Somatic symptoms and psychological distress in the Iliad of Homer. *Journal of Psychosomatic Research*, **42**, 139–48

Mumford DB, Whitehouse AM, Platts M (1991). Socio-cultural correlates of eating disorders among Asian schoolgirls in Bradford. *British Journal of Psychiatry*, **158**, 222–8.

Mumford DB, Whitehouse AM, Choudry IY (1992). A survey of eating disorders in English-medium schools in Lahore (Pakistan). *International Journal of Eating Disorders*, **11**, 173–84.

Mumford DB, Choudry IY (2000). Body dissatisfaction and eating attitudes in slimming and fitness gyms in London and Lahore: a cross-cultural study. *European Eating Disorders Review*, in press.

Author index

Subject index